PRAISE FOR

Left Adrift

"If the Trump Era were a television series like *Game of Thrones*, *Left Adrift* would be the fascinating prequel. Timothy Shenk has written a riveting portrait of the moment when the subterranean plates of American politics began to shift. By focusing on two of the key players in the internal struggles of the Democratic Party, he brings a vividness and emotion that makes *Left Adrift* much more than a political science treatise. I'd urge anyone who finds the politics of today perplexing—and don't we all?—to read *Left Adrift*. No one else has told this story and it's compelling, entertaining, and important."

STUART STEVENS,
political consultant and author of *It Was All a Lie: How the Republican Party Became Donald Trump*

"*Left Adrift* may be the wisest, most original book to explain the dilemmas of class and culture that bedevil the electoral left in the US and its counterparts around the world. It's also a delight to read. In zestfully narrating the parallel careers of two master consultants who despise one another, Timothy Shenk reveals how liberals got into this mess and what they must do to escape it."

MICHAEL KAZIN,
author of *What It Took to Win: A History of the Democratic Party*

Left Adrift
What Happened to Liberal Politics

COLUMBIA GLOBAL REPORTS
NEW YORK

Left Adrift
What Happened to Liberal Politics

Timothy Shenk

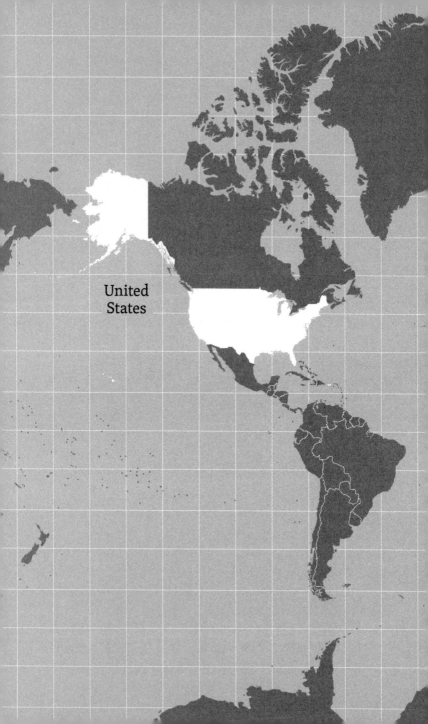

United
States

Published by Columbia Global Reports
91 Claremont Avenue, Suite 515
New York, NY 10027
globalreports.columbia.edu
facebook.com/columbiaglobalreports
@columbiaGR

Library of Congress Cataloging-in-Publication Data
Names: Shenk, Timothy, 1985- author.
Title: Left adrift : what happened to liberal politics / Timothy Shenk.
Description: New York, NY : Columbia Global Reports, 2024. | Includes
    bibliographical references.
Identifiers: LCCN 2024007211 (print) | LCCN 2024007212 (ebook) | ISBN
    9798987053669 (paperback) | ISBN 9798987053676 (ebook)
Subjects: LCSH: Political culture--United States. | Political
    consultants--United States. | Liberalism--United States. | Politics and
    government--United States.
Classification: LCC JA75.7 .S48 2024 (print) | LCC JA75.7 (ebook) | DDC
    320.510973--dc23/eng/20240328
LC record available at https://lccn.loc.gov/2024007211
LC ebook record available at https://lccn.loc.gov/2024007212

Cover design by Kelly Winton
Interior design by Strick&Williams
Map design by Jeffrey L. Ward
Author photograph by Renu Regunathan-Shenk

Printed in the United States of America

For Nikhil, who points the way

"The perverse and unorthodox argument of this little book is that voters are not fools."

—V. O. Key Jr.

CONTENTS

14
A Note on Language

16
Introduction

33
Chapter One
The Emerging Democratic Minority

65
Chapter Two
U-Turn

99
Chapter Three
A Classless Quality

136
Chapter Four
How to Break the Left

169
Chapter Five
A Better Life for All

198
Conclusion

215
Further Reading

226
Acknowledgments

228
Notes

A Note on Language

Political terminology is a thorny subject. When pollsters ask Americans to classify themselves politically, the spectrum usually runs from "very conservative" on the far right to "very liberal" on the far left. Outside the United States, liberalism often stands for what Americans call libertarianism, or what political theorists refer to as "classical liberalism"—a politics of open markets and individual rights that's more Milton Friedman than Elizabeth Warren. "Liberalism was a dirty word to us," recalled Haim Oron, former head of the leftwing Israeli party Meretz. What Americans know as liberalism is more likely to go under the name of "social democracy": in favor of a generous welfare state and strict economic regulations but reconciled to the need for market competition. Even a grudging acceptance of the market sets social democrats apart from orthodox socialists who hold open the possibility for transcending capitalism—at least in theory. But the most prominent socialist in the United States, Bernie Sanders, has defined socialism as the attempt to complete the unfinished business of Franklin Roosevelt's New Deal.

Back in the 1930s, socialists were not so friendly. "Roosevelt did not carry out the socialist platform," groused Norman Thomas, six-time presidential nominee of the Socialist Party of America, "unless he carried it out on a stretcher." FDR, for his part, thought of himself as a liberal.

In other words, the whole thing is a mess. And that's before you try to pin down the meaning of contested concepts like "neo-liberalism" and "progressivism," or parse the difference between a merely center-left party and an authentically left alternative. More than a few leftists would insist that none of the major parties described in this book—Democrats in the US, Labour/Labor in the UK and Israel, the African National Congress in South Africa—are part of the real left. But I would bet that there are at least as many conservatives who would say otherwise.

The bad news is that the only way to settle these debates over terminology is to ignore context and impose retrospective definitions on a muddled history. The good news is that the stakes of this argument are low. How liberalism or socialism have been defined at different places and times are subjects worth investigating, and if you want more on those kinds of questions, then you've come to the right place. But the fact that American liberalism would elsewhere be known as social democracy matters about as much as the nonexistent difference between what I grew up calling soccer and what the rest of the world calls football. Consider the use of "liberal politics" in this book's subtitle as a reference to the broader left, and keep your eyes on this target in the story to come.

Introduction

Politics has never been easy, but the rules used to be simple: Republicans for business, Democrats for labor. Blue-collar voters consistently backed the party of FDR, and the GOP dominated with the country club set. Although there were plenty of exceptions, the guiding principles were clear.

The battle lines have become a lot messier these days. Democrats now often do better with the highest fifth of the income distribution than the bottom fifth, and it's no longer a surprise if Republicans carry a majority of voters without a college degree. Partisans on both sides like to say that Democrats and Republicans are farther apart than ever. Judged strictly by income, however, the two coalitions look awfully similar.

It's going too far to say that the GOP has turned into the party of the working stiff, or that Democrats have been taken over by the billionaire class. Most poor people still go blue, and the top 1 percent of income earners are usually a toss-up. But the erosion of class-based voting is real, and it has transformed

both parties. Political scientists call the initial part of this process dealignment, meaning a period when voters have shed old
loyalties without settling on a lasting replacement. The question
today is whether dealignment has given way to realignment, with
culturally polarized electorates replacing the economic divisions
of the New Deal years.

The case for realignment looks strong when you compare
these two snapshots of the Democratic Party. The first is from
1948, when FDR's coalition rallied behind Harry Truman. The
second is from 2016, when Hillary Clinton was on the top of the
ticket. Voters are divided by levels of education, which is a crude
but useful proxy for class.

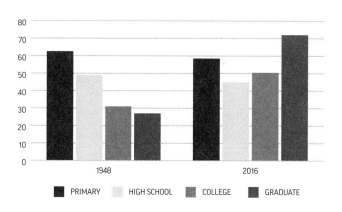

In 1948, the more education—and, not coincidentally, the
more money—you had, the less likely you were to cast a ballot for Democrats. The rules had changed by the time Hillary
Clinton ran for president. Democrats retained their firm base

18 of support with voters who hadn't graduated from high school, although by now this was a much smaller percentage of the electorate. (Just 9 percent in 2016, compared to 63 percent in 1948.) But Clinton's best numbers came from the most highly educated slice of the country, the kind of people who put up "Stronger Together" signs in front of their stately colonials in Scarsdale.

Between Truman and Clinton, the shape of the Democratic coalition changed. In 1948, it was a diagonal line. By 2016, it looked more like a U: starting high, moving down, then surging back up again. A downward sloping line had turned into a fishhook—and American politics still has not recovered.

This book is about that transformation, and the world it made. It explains that change by following two political consultants who played a unique role in this history, first as academics trying to understand dealignment, and then as architects of campaigns to reverse it.

Their names are Stanley Greenberg and Douglas Schoen. Don't feel bad if you haven't heard of them. I didn't know much about either of them until I started researching this book, and I write about this stuff for a living. But following these two characters quickly led me in surprising directions. Before long, I wasn't just rethinking my views on the making of the modern Democratic Party. I had a different perspective on the transformation of the left across much of the world.

Some context is helpful. When Truman was running for president eighty years ago, the United States was just one of many countries where the coalitions for the left and right broke down along economic lines. It's also one of many countries where those divisions have come apart, allowing educated professionals to find a home on the left and providing rightwing populists an opportunity to make deep inroads with workers.

This is often described as a move from class politics to culture war, but the reality is more complicated. From today's fractured landscape, it's clear how much the older left depended on baseline levels of social cohesion. It was easier to hear the clash of economic interests when the volume was turned down on other conflicts, and politicians on the left made sure to step carefully around cultural issues that could split their base. When Franklin Roosevelt sold the New Deal, he draped it in the American flag and bundled it with quotations from scripture.

If earlier parties on the left were more attuned to culture than is usually recognized, it's also fair to point out that politics has not left class behind. Yes, some of today's most heated controversies are straightforward battles over identity, including almost every debate over what gets taught in public schools. But the most polarizing topics—abortion, crime, immigration—almost always mix cultural and material concerns, and the canniest rightwing populists rarely forget about pocketbook issues. Think of Donald Trump promising to bring back manufacturing, protect Social Security, and make sure everyone had access to "beautiful health care." At the same time, even in countries where white-collar workers have turned away from the right, parties on the left often post their best numbers with the lowest-income voters.

Instead of saying that culture has replaced class, it's better to think of a shift in how both the left and right are defined, a change that expresses itself in how people vote. The left was once a bottom-up coalition where organizations representing workers set the tone for politicians who styled themselves as champions.

20   Today, it owes more to universities than to unions, and its coa-
      lition looks like an alliance between professionals and the poor,
      where the virtues of diversity are obvious but solidarity is harder
      to come by, especially with the middle of the electorate.

          Greenberg and Schoen were part of a small group of political
      consultants with global reputations who saw this transformation
      firsthand. This could have given them a lot to talk about, except
      for the fact that they couldn't stand each other. Their feud was
      stoked by petty grievances and personal jealousies accumulated
      over decades competing for the same clients. (More on all of that
      to come.) But there was a deeper cause, too—a fundamental dis-
      agreement over how politics worked in the era of dealignment.

          The pages ahead tell the story of that argument, starting
      with its intellectual origins in debates following the crackup of
      the New Deal coalition, then following Greenberg and Schoen's
      rival theories as they were tested on the campaign trail. A dispute
      that started in the US quickly spilled outside the country's bor-
      ders. In addition to the US, this book will focus on three coun-
      tries that deserve special attention in this larger history: Great
      Britain, Israel, and South Africa. (A lot more on what makes those
      three stand out is coming, too.)

          Greenberg and Schoen had a knack for appearing at cru-
      cial moments in unlikely places, witnessing history being made.
      They were not puppet masters pulling the strings while politi-
      cians danced. But the history they saw—and, in small but sig-
      nificant ways, influenced—happens to be crucial to grasping the
      decisive political story of our time.

To understand how these two campaign operatives fit into a global political revolution, it helps to go over the most popular accounts of why dealignment took hold in the United States.

Among Democrats, the answer usually starts with white backlash to Lyndon Johnson's embrace of civil rights in the 1960s. As the South moved into the Republican column, Democrats tried to replace lost voters with a rising cohort of young, affluent, and well-educated baby boomers who leaned to the left on cultural issues and to the right on economics. Ambitious reformers, sometimes calling themselves neoliberals, bid farewell to the hard-hat politics of the industrial age. Under Bill Clinton's watch, Democrats took to praising the genius of markets and celebrating the end to big government. After 2008, the one-two punch of a catastrophic financial crisis and the election of the first Black president made for a toxic combination of racial grievance and economic frustration. And then Donald Trump decided that a presidential campaign would be good for his brand.

This account isn't wrong, exactly, but it doesn't explain as much as Democrats would like. Blue-collar voters began turning away from Democrats well before the 1970s, when histories of the neoliberal shift normally get going. Well-to-do suburbanites didn't complete their exodus from Republicans until the 2010s, long after Democrats pivoted to the center. Between these two phases of dealignment—first, the losses at the bottom, then the gains at the top—Bill Clinton's endorsements of free trade and financial regulation didn't stop him from putting together a coalition grounded in the working class. (He was the last Democratic presidential candidate to do better in

22 West Virginia, the second-poorest state in the country, than in California.)

If chronology is a problem for a strictly economic interpretation, then geography is a major stumbling block for the white backlash narrative. The American version of dealignment was undoubtedly shaped by the legacies of slavery and Jim Crow. But a unique American experience can't explain an international shift. The change has been especially pronounced in Europe, where educated professionals have found a welcoming home on the left.

Here, for instance, is how the left's coalition has evolved in France, once again divided by education.

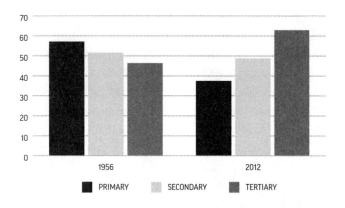

Support for Leftwing Parties by Education, France

Which is a lot like what has occurred in Italy:

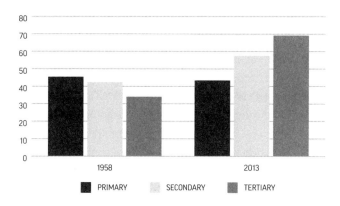

Support for Leftwing Parties by Education, Italy

Or Denmark, which is often called a bastion of social democracy:

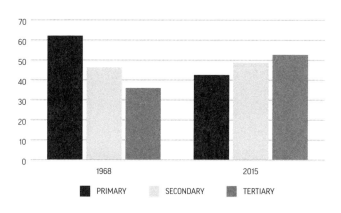

Support for Leftwing Parties by Education, Denmark

24   Although the process usually isn't so clean-cut outside of Europe, similar transformations have taken place in nations as different as Brazil, India, and the Philippines.

The scale of the transformation has been so great that it might lead you to conclude that class polarization was always living on borrowed time. Political scientist Ronald Inglehart made a version of this argument almost fifty years ago. According to Inglehart, baby boomers who had come of age during the long postwar expansion were set to lead a "silent revolution." Younger people were accustomed to prosperity, and they were drawn to a new set of "postmaterialist issues," ranging from human rights to environmentalism. As national incomes rose, it only made sense that class warfare would lose its bite.

But the record hasn't quite borne out Inglehart's prophecy either. Some wealthy nations, including Canada and Japan, have never gone through periods of intense economic polarization. Others, like Ireland, only experienced it in the last decade—proof that class politics can still pack a wallop under the right circumstances, even when voters are comparatively well off. And materialism isn't a guaranteed winner in impoverished countries either. Class divisions are virtually absent with voters in many of the poorest parts of the world, where charismatic leadership, ethnic factionalism, religious beliefs, and political patronage count for more than abstract disputes over policy.

Casting a glance over global politics reveals exceptions to every supposedly universal truth, and it drives home one crucial lesson: the overwhelming importance of *choice*. Voters are always going to be separated from each other—by class, yes, but also by race, gender, region, age, education, religion, and countless other potential fault lines. The key question is which differences get pushed to the center of the debate, and which ones are shoved to the side. Social divisions are constant. Which ones get politicized, and how, is up for grabs. In a democracy, no choice is more important.

Class, then, is just another way of slicing up the electorate, and not usually the most important. But even though economics can't explain everything, class politics has a distinctive, and important, history. It's hard to imagine the achievements of the twentieth-century left—robust welfare states, falling economic inequality—without the electoral muscle supplied by parties accountable to the working class. And it seems like more than a coincidence that economic inequality began its upward climb not long after polarization shifted into high gear.

Going back to the comparison between the Democratic coalitions of 1948 and 2016 underlines the stakes of this question. By the standards of our time, the American electorate that voted Truman into the White House seems like it should have been prime Republican territory. The United States was a much whiter country, and in the most racially diverse states—the Jim Crow South—African Americans were disenfranchised. Only 6 percent of voters had a bachelor's degree or higher. The gender gap between the parties was smaller, and women actually leaned toward Republicans. On the full sweep of social issues that distinguish the parties today, the country was vastly more conservative. It was also much more Christian.

But that same country had spent the previous decade giving Democrats some of the most resounding victories in American history. In 1948 the New Deal coalition came through once again,

26   reelecting Truman and giving Democrats control of Congress by comfortable margins.

Polarization broke that majority. Today, it is the reason that Republicans are still competitive at the national level. Anyone hoping that demographics will sink rightwing populists in the years to come should keep this history in mind.

Even if Democrats take power, it's an open question whether today's more upscale left can sustain the battle for economic fairness at the heart of the New Deal. On the one hand, there's no denying that Democrats have taken a progressive turn across the board since Bill Clinton was in the White House, including on economic issues, even though the party has lost ground with blue-collar voters. But it's also true that some of the states with the highest income gaps in the country are the most reliably blue, including New York, California, Illinois, and Massachusetts—not the most comforting sign if you think rising economic inequality has contributed to the populist revolts of the last decade.

The future of democracy, then, is bound up with the fate of class politics. But even though the stakes feel urgent today, arguments about dealignment have been going on for decades. The outlines of the debate were already familiar to political scientists more than fifty years ago, and the question was never simply academic.

As the New Deal coalition was coming unglued in the 1960s, a new political actor was emerging—the professional consultant using polls and focus groups to unravel the secrets of public opinion. The shrewdest of these operatives recognized that the future of both parties would come down to whether cultural polarization had killed off class politics. The struggle over this question eventually sparked a civil war inside the Democratic political class. Overlooked in the moment, and still misunder-stood today, this debate provided the framework for a decisive battle over the future of the Democratic coalition—and, later, for parties on the left around the globe.

Which brings the story back to Stan Greenberg and Doug Schoen. Even if you don't recognize their names, there's a decent chance that you know about their business partners. In Greenberg's case, it's James Carville, who has been a staple of cable news punditry so long it's easy to forget that he made his reputation as one of the lead strategists in Bill Clinton's 1992 presidential run. For Schoen, it's Mark Penn, best remembered today as the maestro behind Hillary Clinton's failed 2008 race.

Backgrounds like this might not inspire confidence in either Greenberg or Schoen. They're fully paid-up members of a consultant class that has earned its shady reputation. Critics blame them for draining the purpose out of politics, replacing substantive debate over issues with tired sound bites and empty spectacle. Skeptics say the industry is a multibillion-dollar racket that plays off the fears of candidates with money to burn and not enough sense to realize that elections are determined by forces outside their influence, most notably the partisan breakdown of the electorate and the state of the economy. Political scientists have shown, in detail, how tactics that consultants have sold as surefire winners—from old-fashioned yard signs to cutting-edge microtargeting—fail to move votes. Activists are fond of pointing out that public opinion is fluid, which means that a campaign fixated on polls runs the risk of missing an opportunity to reshape the electorate. And it doesn't help that high-profile consultants often wind up as talking heads on cable

28   news, a quick and easy path toward becoming a caricature of
      yourself.

      The best summary of the case against consultants was
delivered by a member of the guild. "If Donald Trump becomes
president of the United States, *then* you can tell me we don't
need political consultants anymore," said Whit Ayres, veteran
Republican pollster. It was April 2016.

      So there's reason to be suspicious. But after digging into this
subject, I've come away with a respect for parts—let me emphasize: *parts*—of the consultant's trade, and for Greenberg and
Schoen in particular.

      It started when I read their first books. Each was adapted
from a doctoral dissertation, Schoen's from Oxford, Greenberg's
from Harvard. To my surprise, the books were . . . good. Really
good. Schoen's was a perceptive study of rightwing populism
that taught me more about the subject than almost anything
I'd come across during the Trump era. Greenberg's provided
an extended look at the politics of poor people—Appalachian
whites; Mexican Americans in San Jose; African Americans in
Atlanta, Detroit, and Philadelphia—asking why shared economic struggles failed to produce a common class consciousness. The analysis was compelling, and it bore the telltale
marks of an aspiring Marx-ish academic—not a starting point
I expected for one of the guiding hands behind Bill Clinton's rise
to the White House.

      More than just impressive pieces of scholarship, the books
revealed something important about their authors. It wouldn't
be fair to say that Greenberg and Schoen were the brains behind
their respective operations. But, unlike their better-known
partners, each entered politics with a theory of how the system

worked. These ideas went on to shape campaigns in the United States and across the globe.

Democracy, to both of them, meant a system for translating the views of ordinary people into government policy. They believed that public opinion was a real force, and that it could be discovered through extensive research. Most people weren't versed in the details of policy debates, but they were sophisticated judges of the issues that mattered in their daily lives. Their views deserved respect, especially if you wanted to get their vote.

Good strategists were the opposite of the talking heads filibustering around the clock on cable news. They learned how to put their own views to the side and listen—really listen—to what voters were saying.

Over decades spent working in campaigns around the world, Greenberg and Schoen kept running into the same pattern. Most people most of the time focused on a similar handful of issues: jobs, education, housing, health care. But those subjects were rarely at the top of the agenda for the political class—not donors, not activists, and not even politicians. Greenberg and Schoen considered themselves voices for the people, in part because it paid well, but also because elites were out of touch, and democracy couldn't survive unless the government represented public opinion.

This, to me, was interesting. So was the fact that, despite having so much in common, Greenberg and Schoen loathed each other with the intensity that comes when personal and political grievances are so intermixed that it's impossible to draw a line between the two.

For Greenberg, winning a campaign was never good enough. He believed that elections should be part of a larger political

30 project, and his was bringing the New Deal coalition back to life. By mixing a dose of class warfare with concessions to the cultural anxieties of blue-collar voters, he thought Democrats could once again split the electorate along economic lines, forging a bottom-up multiracial majority that could tilt the balance of power in favor of working people. He approached this project with a missionary zeal, and he had no time for unbelievers.

Including Schoen. Greenberg wanted to change the world. Schoen was happy to take it on its own terms. Politics didn't have to be an agonizing clash between good and evil. It was a game that you could win if you understood the rules better than the other side, and that you ought to have fun playing.

Schoen's reading of the electorate told him that cultural polarization had permanently skewed the playing field toward Republicans. If Democrats wanted to survive, they had to follow voters rightward, tacking to the center on both economic and social issues in a desperate bid to fight a winning battle on hostile terrain. Schoen didn't want to write off blue-collar America, but he thought class politics wouldn't get their votes. Where Greenberg's clients traded in a soft populism, Schoen's talked about finding unity. Greenberg hoped for a realignment that would restore the New Deal order. Schoen told Democrats it would take an all-out war just to stop polarization from blasting their coalition to pieces.

In person, neither cut an imposing figure. Even when Greenberg was advising presidents and prime ministers, he was every bit the recovering academic—bespectacled, soft-spoken, and quite a bit shorter than his most famous clients. Schoen was a nattier dresser, and he cultivated a reputation as a man about town, but in meetings he was just as professorial, advancing methodically through the items on his agenda. "Ponderous" was the term his ex-friend Dick Morris used after the two had a falling-out.

But they weren't paid for style. They made their living as strategists, and their careers were defined by the recurring clash between their rival visions. By the 1990s, consultants at the top of a winning presidential campaign in the United States had become hot commodities in a global marketplace. Greenberg and Schoen belonged to a short list of figures that some of the planet's most ambitious politicians wanted to have in their corner. Where they traveled, variations of their debate trailed close behind.

Many of their clients have become staples in histories of neoliberalism's rise. Those accounts typically focus on policy— taxes, trade barriers, government regulations. But neoliberalism was never just a policy agenda. It came wrapped up with a political strategy that was forged in the debate between Greenberg and Schoen. Ask a Democratic operative how they think about politics, and you'll probably hear echoes of it today. Elements of it have also become essential to the populist right. Bill Clinton and Tony Blair might talk about globalization in a different way than Donald Trump and Boris Johnson, but their politics revolved around a similar set of figures: clueless elites, an alienated public, and politicians who could exploit the gap between the two.

The hidden thread connecting neoliberal reformers to populist crusaders illustrates another crucial feature of the argument between Greenberg and Schoen. This was a war that both sides lost. Neither of their plans for remaking the Democrats, or any other party, came to fruition. Today, the differences between

32 them seem less significant than one point where they agreed. Both spent their careers fighting against cultural polarization. And the polarizers won.

This means the pages to come are a story about failure, but not for the reasons you might think, or in the ways you would expect. It's worth telling this story not because it supplies a playbook that can be applied directly to the present, but because we've missed a crucial part of the history that's made our world, and you can't learn from a history that you don't know.

In this case, it's the history of a battle against dealignment stretching back decades and reaching around the world. The failure of that battle was a precondition for the transformation of the left and right that defines politics as we know it—and led directly to today's crisis of democracy.

Here is how it happened.

The Emerging Democratic Minority

The years between the dropping of the atomic bomb and Neil Armstrong's moon landing were a golden age for men in crisp lab coats looking for problems to solve. Experts peddling their version of the next Manhattan Project found a receptive audience, and deep pockets, inside government agencies and private foundations. Casting a jealous eye at the physics and chemistry departments, political science moved to recast the major questions of their discipline in exquisitely empirical terms. One puzzle loomed over the rest: What makes people vote the way they do?

Academics marched to their target like ants to a Snickers bar. Large-scale polling was a recent innovation, and it gave fresh scientific credibility to surveys of public opinion. But as the studies became more complex, the subject of these sophisticated inquiries started to look rather less impressive. The professors seemed brilliant; the American electorate not so much. The numbers said that voters were blind to their prejudices, uninformed about public affairs, and prone to changes of heart based on quirks of personality—all in all, a shaky basis for democracy.

34   V. O. Key Jr. was not persuaded. Genial skepticism had been an essential part of Key's rise to the top of his field, taking him from a childhood in West Texas to a professorship at Harvard. In the final project of his career, left unfinished when he died at the age of fifty-five, he wanted to provide a more sympathetic perspective on the public mind. "The perverse and unorthodox argument of this little book," he wrote in the slim volume that emerged from this study, published posthumously in 1966 under the title *The Responsible Electorate*, "is that voters are not fools."

Yes, individuals sometimes behaved foolishly. But, Key believed, elections were normally decided by serious policy differences. Ordinary Americans might not master the intricacies of party platforms, but they were more than capable of figuring out the driving issues in a campaign, and of choosing candidates whose views matched their own.

Key made his case by pointing to a political revolution that Americans had just lived through. In 1932, Franklin Roosevelt had swept into power on the strength of not being Herbert Hoover. Four years later, he was reelected by an even greater margin—but, this time, with a crucial shift in the Democratic coalition. New Deal politics looked to much of the country like a battle between the rich and the poor. In 1936, the struggle carried over to the polls, where low-income voters rushed toward Democrats, and the well-to-do shifted back toward Republicans. The birth of FDR's new majority became, in Key's telling, a case study in more or less rational voters acting like the reasonable fellows they usually were. More than just a triumph for Roosevelt, it was a victory for democracy.

But not, for Democrats, a permanent one. As Key's book was rolling off the presses, the New Deal coalition went into free fall.

The responsible electorate that had bestowed Lyndon Johnson with the largest mandate in modern American history watched as Americans flailed in Vietnam, cities burned, and campuses melted down, and then in 1968 it punished Democrats by giving Richard Nixon and George Wallace a combined 57 percent of the vote.

Key was dead, and it looked like the New Deal coalition would soon join him. But his theory of reasonable voters and a rational-enough electorate had life in it yet. Although most partisan operatives didn't spend their time perusing academic monographs, Stanley Greenberg and Douglas Schoen did, and *The Responsible Electorate* arrived at a formative moment for them both. Key provided a framework they used to explain the breakdown of the old Democratic majority, and to start planning the next one. Greenberg and Schoen learned from Key that the right message could win a campaign. But they suspected it could do a lot more than that. Each of them would bet their careers—and the future of the Democratic Party—on it.

The Test

Stanley Greenberg always had a plan. It was how he found himself enrolled as a graduate student in Harvard's government department—the university's term for what everyone else called political science—not long after Key's death.

Like Key, Greenberg had followed a circuitous path to Cambridge. Born in 1945, he grew up in a family teetering on the border between working and middle class. Although neither of his parents had a college education, his father was a self-taught engineer with a steady job at American Instrument Company. He was raised for part of his childhood in one of Washington DC's largely African American neighborhoods during the last stages

36   of Jim Crow. "I was very much in a racial culture," he recalled, friendly with Black kids in the neighborhood, but attending white schools, until the city established integrated education in 1955. Shortly after, the family moved to lily-white suburbia, where the teenaged Greenberg came to politics through the Civil Rights Movement. At a summer job before heading to college in 1963, he saw the mostly white workforce—Black employees were kept in a separate part of the factory—shout down activists headed to the March on Washington.

In the Greenberg household, religion came before politics. Social life revolved around the local synagogue, where both his mother and father served terms as president. Party loyalties were decided ahead of time. "Everybody was Democrats," Greenberg remembered. "I didn't know any Republicans." And he was not allowed to know any radicals. American Instrument Company handled government contracts, and his father needed to keep his security clearance. With the Cold War at its height, his parents cut off ties with family members who they suspected of being Communists.

Life opened up for Greenberg after he started college. A mostly indifferent student in high school, he wound up at Miami University of Ohio. He thrived in the classroom, where he blended readings in political theory and history with quantitative research, including his first poll, a student survey for his senior thesis. In the summer of 1964, he interned on Capitol Hill and worked for the Democratic National Committee. After supporting the White House's Vietnam policy in the early going, he turned against the war by 1965.

By the time he arrived at Harvard, Greenberg was moving rapidly toward the left. In graduate school, he immersed himself

in the Marxist canon, where he was particularly struck by the
writings of Antonio Gramsci.

The affinity for Gramsci was an important sign of the kind of
radical Greenberg aspired to be. Gramsci was part of the first generation of Marxists to grapple with the twinned shocks of World
War I—when the proletariat had chosen national loyalty over
class solidarity—and the rise of fascism. With history veering
off the course that orthodox Marxists had written for it, Gramsci
focused on the problem of hegemony, his term for the ways that
capitalists secured the consent of the working class. Instead of
treating politics as a mechanical reflection of economic interests, Gramsci emphasized the importance of ideas, especially
the everyday notions that we call "common sense." Socialism,
Gramsci argued, wasn't destined to rise like the morning sun.
Workers would have to make their own revolution, forging a collective class consciousness out of the disparate cultural materials that were available to them. Common economic oppression
provided the starting point for a socialist movement, but revolutions also required cultural change and deft political strategizing.

To a leftwing thinker of Greenberg's generation, this was
an intoxicating mix. Gramsci supplied a model of ideological
commitment and intellectual dexterity, proving that you could
embrace radical politics while facing up to the complexities of the
real world. With Richard Nixon in the White House and George
Wallace barnstorming the country, capitalist hegemony and popular fascism seemed like more than strictly academic concerns.

But radical politics alone weren't going to make a scholarly career. For his doctoral supervisor, Greenberg chose
James Q. Wilson, a giant in the field of urban politics with
safely Democratic loyalties. (At the time. Wilson later went on

38   a political journey of his own, moving to the right and ending up as a key figure at the American Enterprise Institute, the first major conservative think tank.) Building on the student polls he conducted as an undergraduate, Greenberg signed up to run a hundred-city survey for the federal government assessing the outcomes of the War on Poverty. He spun off part of this research into a dissertation on the politics of the urban poor, landing a position as an assistant professor at Yale before he finished his PhD.

Greenberg synthesized these influences in *Politics and Poverty*, the book that resulted from this dissertation. It begins with a gesture at two competing perspectives on its topic, staging a kind of dialogue between "radical political man" and "liberal political man"—two sides of Greenberg's divided political mind. Radicals looked beyond conventional politics, from sit-ins and marches all the way to violent revolution. Liberals had more modest aspirations, convinced that the path to progress ran through building coalitions and winning elections.

The great achievement of the pages that follow is to show that neither perspective fits the evidence. Drawing on a survey of over 1,000 residents in five poor neighborhoods scattered across the country, Greenberg took pride in the sophistication of his research. "We coded and counted the responses of the poor," he remembered. "We scaled, correlated, and tested them for significance." He also showed off his graduate school reading, making *Politics and Poverty* the rare book to combine regression analysis with references to Camus and Hegel (along with, inevitably, V. O. Key).

Greenberg delivered his argument with a tone of unsparing realism. "In none of these communities," he wrote, "is there a simple or consistent script where the poor hate the rich and labor challenges capital." He found grinding material deprivation, along with an acute awareness that life was easier for the wealthy. But that didn't translate into consistent support for income redistribution among the poor, let alone a robust sense of class consciousness.

The American dream might be a fantasy, but it commanded significant public support. Workers might clash with management, but they also felt bound together with their employers. They might also view other groups at the bottom as a threat, especially if they had a different skin color.

Yet with class solidarity hard to come by, a strong sense of racial identity was often the quickest route toward a political awakening that could eventually transcend group loyalty. "Identity and politics," he maintained, "are inseparable." In the constricted circumstances both liberals and radicals faced—or, as Greenberg put it, given the "limited range of political opportunities reflected in the reality of American politics"—the road toward class polarization might have to run through race.

This was not a purely theoretical question for Greenberg. A few months before starting his dissertation research, he joined three other Harvard graduate students to put together a study for Robert Kennedy's 1968 presidential race. The campaign wanted a detailed analysis of the coalition that RFK was putting together in the primaries so that it could figure out which candidate appearances would turn out the most votes.

The investigation became the central event of Greenberg's political life, leading to a brief report that set the terms of Greenberg's thinking for the rest of his career. After running the numbers on the Indiana primary, where Kennedy had taken on

40   Eugene McCarthy, darling of the young antiwar left, Greenberg
       concluded that the Democratic electorate was splitting into
       two distinct groups. McCarthy's coalition was, for a Democrat
       of the time, quite unusual: young, well-educated, and skewed
       toward middle-income suburbanites. Kennedy's, by contrast,
       was a throwback to the New Deal, a multiracial coalition that
       ran strongest with the poor and working class, including Blacks
       and blue-collar Catholics.

       McCarthy was the heavy favorite with Greenberg's peers
       at Harvard, the gallant hero who had been willing to challenge
       Lyndon Johnson when Kennedy was still refusing to get into the
       race. Already there was talk of a new Democratic majority assem-
       bled out of young people, racial minorities, and the upper-middle
       class, with just enough blue-collar whites to push Democrats
       over the top.

       Greenberg was not persuaded. He dismissed McCarthy's
       bid as a way for college kids to reach a truce with their white-
       collar parents while turning their backs on the poor and the
       working class. His research convinced him that Kennedy was
       the path forward. Sifting through the precinct data, Greenberg
       saw a different way to unite the past and future of the Democratic
       Party—the politics of the 1930s and the 1960s, machine bosses
       and student protesters, class politics and racial justice. RFK's
       campaign was the site where a Gramscian bid for leftwing hege-
       mony could start, the place where liberal and radical political
       man should clasp hands.

       The Harvard team submitted its findings on May 14. Kennedy
       was assassinated three weeks later, but the lessons from the
       campaign stayed with Greenberg. "For my generation," he wrote
       decades later, "the choice between Eugene McCarthy and Robert

Kennedy revealed your political heart." Greenberg saw the campaign as a test—political, intellectual, even moral—and he wasn't prepared to grade on a curve.

A Piece of the Pie

Douglas Schoen broke Greenberg's theory. He supported RFK during the primary but moved easily to Hubert Humphrey after Kennedy's murder. The campaign wasn't a moral reckoning in Schoen's view. It was just politics.

Which was revealing in its own way. Greenberg wanted the Democratic Party to enlist in the class struggle on behalf of the have-nots. Schoen saw it as a place where disparate interest groups could find common ground before heading out to win some elections. Both looked backward to the New Deal consensus, but for Greenberg the key part of the phrase was "New Deal," and for Schoen it was "consensus." Greenberg wanted to change the world. Schoen was happy to take history on its own terms, provided he could get a bit of the action for himself.

He was raised to expect nothing less. The son of a corporate lawyer, Schoen grew up on Manhattan's Upper East Side and attended the tony Horace Mann School, where he met his future business partner Mark Penn. Although Penn's quantitative skills were already apparent—he put together a survey of the faculty's views on civil rights demonstrating that teachers leaned to the left—Schoen was the more complete political animal. His uncle was a New York State senator, and the young Schoen watched with fascination as he was called away from family dinners to take phone calls with local eminences. He learned that politics was the path to power, and that he had a taste for both.

42   By the age of sixteen, he was already spending much of his time on local campaigns. The antiwar movement was surging, and teenagers around the country were discovering the counter-culture. Rather than heading to Woodstock, Schoen joined a clique of young politicos calling themselves the West Side Kids, headed by Dick Morris, at the time a recent Columbia graduate. Not lacking for ambition, the group saw itself as the incubator for a new Tammany Hall. Where earlier city bosses gained influence through patronage, the West Side Kids planned to build an empire around information. After extensive canvassing, they split up voters by apartment building, came up with rough profiles of each micro-electorate, and tailored messages to fit their targets.

It was a formative experience for Schoen. "Understanding public opinion," he came to believe, "was the true currency of political power."

Old-fashioned graft helped, too. In the first campaign Schoen worked on, a race for New York State Assembly, Morris sealed the deal for their candidate by striking a bargain with a machine politician from the old guard. Morris then set up Schoen with a sweetheart gig at the Board of Water Supply for a summer job. "To this day, I'm somewhat unclear on what exactly we were supposed to be doing," he later admitted, but he remembered getting paid three hundred dollars a week to do it.

With plenty of free hours in his day, he signed up for a city campaign where the candidate happened to be a fundraiser for Harvard—and who promised to reward Schoen by making a call on his behalf to the right folks in Cambridge. His candidate won in a squeaker, and Schoen's acceptance letter arrived in due course. "This," he decided, "was the way politics really worked."

But as campaigns took him outside Manhattan, Schoen realized that he was seeing more than just politics as usual. Traipsing through working-class neighborhoods in Brooklyn, he noticed that the voters who had turned the city into a New Deal bastion were simmering with resentment toward racial minorities and the liberal establishment. They didn't know if the government was still on their side, and they doubted that Democrats in City Hall—or Washington, DC—cared. White ethnics in the outer boroughs hadn't transformed into Goldwater Republicans, but they weren't sure if they belonged with the Democrats either.

At Harvard, Schoen looked for mentors with a grasp on the high and low sides of politics. Daniel Patrick Moynihan, a one-time staffer for both LBJ and Richard Nixon, and a future New York senator, warned him between sips of sherry that Democrats were drifting away from the center. Bill Schneider, a young professor in the government department working to bring reliable but timely polling into both campaigning and journalism, put him on a team that produced an instant exit poll of Jewish voters in the 1973 mayoral primary for *New York* magazine. They delivered results in twenty-four hours that normally took six weeks. (The poll got Schoen a summer job with the campaign for Abe Beame, winner of the Democratic primary.)

Perhaps the most important lesson came from Martin Kilson, a specialist in comparative politics and the first African American to receive tenure at Harvard. "Everyone is fighting for power," Kilson taught him. "What we're going to talk about is how you get your fair piece of the pie. That's what this is ultimately about. Never forget it."

Kilson was firmly on the left, and his emphasis on the material underpinnings of politics had deep roots in that tradition.

44   (Stan Greenberg thought about the world in much the same way.)
Schoen was more comfortable in the middle of the road, wherever that happened to be. But Kilson's leftwing brand of materialism overlapped with Schoen's more ideologically modest realism.
It also pushed them away from seeing politics as a site of moral
struggle, whether the moral viewpoint in question came from
the center or the radical left. Schoen did not expect voters to be
righteous, or even all that rational. "People are often unreason-
able," he later wrote. "They act in their own self-interest, and you
should not trust what they say until you figure out what their
self-interest is."

Outside the classroom, Schoen devoured Kevin Phillips's *The
Emerging Republican Majority*. He recognized the strength
of Phillips's argument that backlash to the upheavals of the
1960s—starting with but not limited to the civil rights revolution—
gave the right an opportunity to tear apart the New Deal coalition. The formula was simple: combine Richard Nixon's and
George Wallace's votes in 1968, and you had the numbers to
reshape American politics. Polarization along cultural lines
would cost Republicans support with the silk-stocking crowd
who viewed the party as their natural home, along with African
Americans still loyal to the party of Lincoln, but the GOP
would more than compensate for those losses by winning over
working-class whites.

Schoen also had a front row seat to what polarization could
do to the left. If George Wallace offered a preview of the next
Republican Party, John Lindsay did the same for Democrats. A
patrician Yankee who grew up on Park Avenue and rowed crew
at Yale, Lindsay was both a Republican by birth and the inspiration for the term "limousine liberal." In Congress, where he

represented the country's wealthiest district, Lindsay backed all of the major pieces of Lyndon Johnson's Great Society. Running for mayor of New York in 1969 against a machine Democrat, Lindsay squeaked out a victory by ramping up the margins with his wealthy white base—the people with "Princeton and Radcliffe etched in their Scott Fitzgerald faces," wrote one journalist—and winning over Black and Puerto Rican voters. Blue-collar whites were not impressed. "What the hell does Lindsay care about me," complained an ironworker in Brooklyn. "None of these politicians give a good goddamn. All they worry about is the niggers."

George Wallace and John Lindsay, the populist redneck and the limousine liberal. According to Phillips, this was the future of American politics, and it spelled electoral disaster for Democrats.

Schoen wasn't entirely persuaded. He took Phillips seriously, but he was even more influenced by *The Real Majority*, a mostly forgotten Democratic rejoinder to Phillips written by Richard Scammon and Ben Wattenberg, two veterans of the Johnson administration. They began by emphasizing an important lesson for a rising politico from Schoen's gilded background. The typical voter, they said, was someone like "a forty-seven-year-old housewife from the outskirts of Dayton, Ohio, whose husband is a machinist." This kind of person:

> Likely has a somewhat different view of life and politics from that of a twenty-four-year-old instructor of political science at Yale. Now the young man from Yale may feel that he *knows* more about politics than the machinist's wife from suburban Dayton, and of course, in one sense he does. But he does not know much about politics . . . unless he understands what is bothering that lady in Dayton.

46   The twenty-year-old student of political science at Harvard took the lesson to heart.

By 1968, Dayton housewives weren't happy with the Democratic Party, and their frustrations were shaking the New Deal coalition. Support for Democrats fell across income groups that year, but the declines were steepest with voters in the bottom half of the electorate—the heart of what had been FDR's majority.

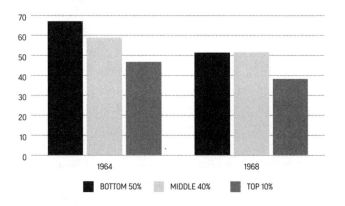

The numbers were clear; their meaning wasn't. Where Phillips said that demographic shifts made a realignment almost inevitable, Scammon and Wattenberg insisted that Democrats could win back power by finding the middle ground in divisive cultural debates. (They also dismissed the budding cult of RFK, warning against the temptation to draw sweeping conclusions from a race where Kennedy and McCarthy agreed on the most important issues, and neither had to compete with Hubert Humphrey, let alone Nixon and Wallace.)

"That the electorate is unyoung, unpoor, and unblack," 47
Scammon and Wattenberg wrote, "does *not* mean they are anti-young, antipoor, or antiblack." The space between "un" and "anti" was the site where majorities were made—and the place where Schoen planned to stake his career.

Rivers of Blood

But first, he had a little more studying to do. Time and again on the campaign trail he had seen how politicians could ride to victory by tapping into voter frustrations. After Schneider helped secure him a fellowship to Oxford, he set out to research this phenomenon in detail with a dissertation analyzing the George Wallace of the United Kingdom.

Enoch Powell spent most of his first two decades in politics shrouded in the comparative obscurity of a backbench Tory member of parliament. If he was known for anything, it was for his gifts as a classicist. (He had graduated from Cambridge with a first-class degree in the subject.) Then, in 1968, he turned himself into one of the most famous, and polarizing, figures in politics with a single speech.

Powell's subject was immigration, and his views were incendiary. He began by recounting a conversation with a constituent who told him, "In this country in fifteen or twenty years' time the black man will have the whip hand over the white man."

Without explicitly endorsing racial prejudice, Powell said that his constituent—"a middle-aged, quite ordinary working man"—was right to be afraid. Immigrants were filling up hospitals, crowding schools, lowering wages, raising the crime rate, and changing the character of the country. After beginning the speech with a voice from the public, Powell ended it by reaching into his

48   bag of classical allusions, with a reference to the poet Virgil. "As I look ahead, I am filled with foreboding," Powell declared. "Like the Roman, I seem to see 'the River Tiber foaming with much blood.'"

Leaders in both the Conservative and Labour Parties were outraged, and so was the British press. The "Rivers of Blood" speech was an outrageous violation of a consensus inside the British establishment. It cost Powell his position in the Tory leadership, which should have been the prelude to being excommunicated from political life—except that Powell's views were quite popular in the rest of the country. After Powell was driven out of Conservative leadership, a thousand dockworkers in London marched to the House of Commons with signs saying "Back Britain, not Black Britain."

Virtually overnight, Powell had shaken the British political system to its core. Schoen used his dissertation to explain why. Poring over public surveys and election returns, he produced a comprehensive study of Powell's supporters. He was gripped by the project, and his excitement drew in his doctoral supervisor, R. W. Johnson. "My family got quite used to the notion that dinner-time conversation would involve Schoen and me working out new ways to run the findings," Johnson said. "Even when my small son went to hospital, Schoen came along and spread out the data on the ward floor and we worked on them as the somewhat bemused little boy looked on."

The findings, Johnson recalled, "were startling beyond anything we had at first imagined." Schoen began by establishing that a majority of the country shared Powell's hostility to immigration. The "Powellite" coalition was national in scope and cut through lines of age, income, and party. And, astonishingly, the evidence suggested that it had determined the outcome of two

elections. In 1970, Powell had drawn millions of voters toward
the Conservatives, even though the party leadership took pains
to keep him at a distance. Then Powell's supporters followed
his lead when he endorsed Labour in 1974, costing Tories the
election.

Although Powell was too incendiary a figure to lead a party,
he had redirected the course of British politics. The short-lived
influx of working-class voters into the Conservatives rattled the
foundations of a political system built around economic divisions. Between 1966 and 1970, support for Conservatives among
the top 10 percent of income earners actually fell by 6 percentage
points. But the Tories more than compensated for those losses
by boosting their performance with the bottom half of the electorate by 7 points.

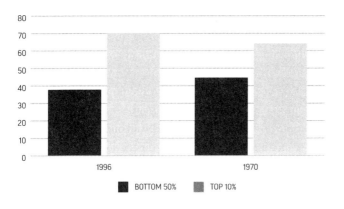

Support for Conservative Party by Income

Even when economic polarization was at its strongest, the
right kind of conservative could perform well with the working

50 class. About 40 percent of union members cast a ballot for Dwight Eisenhower's reelection in 1956. In France at around the same time, Charles de Gaulle forged a new majority with a nationalist conservatism that proved compelling to large numbers of blue-collar workers, including some 5 percent of the electorate that had regularly voted for the Communist Party.

But Enoch Powell wasn't a military hero like Eisenhower or de Gaulle, and voters in Britain had been even more economically stratified than in the US or France. By charging headlong into the immigration debate, Powell transformed his reputation. After scrutinizing the results, Schoen saw the makings of an electoral revolution.

Powell's rise provided Schoen with a template for thinking about public opinion that stayed with him for the rest of his career. Like Key before him, but with much more impressive statistical backing, Schoen rejected interpretations that attributed political decisions to social forces or psychological drives. Instead, he took voters at their word. Britons liked Powell because he spoke with passion on a subject they cared about, a point that was consistently reflected in the polls. His appeal was magnified because he challenged an elite consensus. It was this distinctive combination—putting himself on the side of the majority *and* bucking the establishment—that fueled Powell's ascent. Voters were looking for someone to listen. Eventually, they found him.

Studying Powell's followers did not make Schoen into one, although he was accused of that when his results were published, first in an article co-authored with Johnson, then in a book. In fact, he was a Labour supporter who did polling for a campaign to bring the UK into the European Common Market—anathema to Powell.

But Schoen believed the merits of Powell's views were irrelevant. Drawing on Key once again, Schoen argued that the ultimate judge in a democracy had to be public opinion. Before Powell came along, a growing percentage of the British public had given up on politics. Government looked like a private club where membership was handed out to elites who already agreed on the most important issues. That skepticism was fatal in a democracy, a tumor silently growing in a body that looked healthy on the surface. Popular views could not be ignored over the long run without eating away at the legitimacy of the entire system. A politician who did not remember this basic truth would sooner or later be replaced by someone who did.

With his dissertation complete, Schoen headed back to the United States. He had been accepted to Harvard Law School, but he couldn't stay away from politics for long. His understanding of the new rightwing populism was a marketable skill. He intended to find out just how much it was worth.

The Class Project

Greenberg had begun working on some theories of his own. The project started pressing on him as he researched his second book, a study on the formation of "racial orders"—that is, societies built around formalized and pervasive racial hierarchies. Published in 1980, *Race and State in Capitalist Development* was even more ambitious than its predecessor, sprawling to almost five hundred pages, and shaped around a comparative analysis of South Africa, Alabama, Israel, and Northern Ireland. Greenberg depicted a world where industrial workers, farmers, and businessmen might each find advantages in white supremacy—or, when interests shifted, turn against it. A searching examination

52   of how the relationship between class and race can evolve with
time, the book was an exemplary case of what Greenberg, still the
academic radical, called "Marxian political economy."

It also marked a departure for Greenberg in a few important respects. The first had to do with method. His argument in
Politics and Poverty had come out of polling. For this book, he
turned to interviews, dozens of them, with representatives for
business and labor groups.

Out of those interviews came a change in focus. Where
his earlier research centered on the experience of racial
minorities—the Black and Mexican American subjects who
took up most of the space in *Politics and Poverty*—he was now
drawn toward understanding the position of white trade union-
ists. "These people were social democrats, sometimes spirited
socialists, yet they were dividing their societies along ethnic or
racial lines," he said. "Many were clearly racist, but even the racists within their world were working to lift up and secure something for their members."

Greenberg tried to put aside moral judgments during his
interviews. He mostly saw working people struggling to keep up
in a system they knew was tilted against them. They might be
prejudiced, but they also had a clear sense of self-interest that
could lead toward a more egalitarian politics. "White steelworkers
in Alabama and the white mine workers in South Africa, whatever their awful role in excluding blacks," he concluded, "were
not without social democratic impulses."

Coaxing those buried sentiments to the surface required the
right message, which prompted Greenberg to revisit another of
his early views. *Politics and Poverty* had described a strong sense
of group identity as a potential route toward class mobilization

for the poor. With the examples of South Africa and Alabama
fresh on his mind, Greenberg now saw this kind of racial politics
as poison for multiracial coalition building, the project that he
still believed was the great unfinished task for the left.

Those questions became urgent for him when he was denied
tenure at Yale. The decision did not come as a complete surprise
to Greenberg, who knew that his activism—meetings for a local
New Haven union took place in his house, and he was a vocal
supporter of Yale divesting from South Africa—put him on the
wrong side of the university administration. Although Greenberg
remained an adjunct professor at the university until 1987, the
prospect of life in the academic precariat drove him onto an alternative career path.

He found it in the rapidly growing industry of political consulting. Politics had remained a sideline for Greenberg at Yale.
He met his future wife (and congressperson), Rosa DeLauro,
on a New Haven mayoral campaign. In 1980, with his academic
career barreling toward a dead end, he took over polling for Chris
Dodd's Senate campaign, which, as it happened, was being managed by DeLauro. Dodd won the race, leading to more clients for
Greenberg—and, eventually, a new career as a pollster and messaging guru.

His big break came in 1984. It was a tough year for Democrats
swamped by Reagan's landslide reelection, and a golden opportunity for Greenberg, who was commissioned by the Michigan
Democratic Party and the United Auto Workers to write an
autopsy explaining where the party had gone astray.

Greenberg focused his attention on white middle- and
working-class voters, once loyal Democrats, who had voted overwhelmingly for Reagan. In a series of focus groups with residents

54 of Macomb County, a heavily unionized Detroit suburb, he encountered sentiments with more than a passing resemblance to what he heard in South Africa. "White Democratic defectors express a profound distaste for blacks," he wrote, "a sentiment that pervades almost everything they thought about government and politics." After hearing a defense of the nation's historic obligations to African Americans, attributed to Robert Kennedy, one focus group member replied, "That's bullshit." Another said, "No wonder they killed him."

Yet Greenberg did not believe that racism was the only factor at play in Macomb's transformation. The people he spoke with saw themselves as part of a middle class that carried the rest of the country on its back. Their hard work made Wall Street rich, and their taxes paid for a welfare system they despised. Resentment of immigrants was already a hot-button issue, and it mixed together with fears about globalization. "We are losing money, and they're importing all these people from Vietnam, Mexico, from everywhere," one person said. "Here's a bunch of people that can't even speak English, are half illiterate, came out of an adobe hut, and they are going to compete with us for our jobs? And we don't have them."

Even workers with salaries well above the national average were terrified about what would happen to their children. Those anxieties crystallized around the issue of higher education. In theory, it was a ticket to the good life for the next generation. But they worried that rising tuition costs and cutbacks in student loans would put college out of reach for their kids. "What happens is you're creating an elite, those families that can afford to put their children through college," one person said. "They're going to run the country."

Politics in Macomb was anything but simple. Even union
members were ambivalent about the role that organized labor
played in politics. They believed that unions were essential for
protecting worker rights, but they worried about pushing wages so
high that it would drive factories to Mexico. And they hated being
told who to vote for (not that surprising in a group where everyone voted for Reagan). The men could be skeptical about women
in public office, but they believed sexism was a real problem in the
workplace, and they wanted equal treatment for women on the job,
especially now that two-income households had become the norm
for families trying to stay afloat. They drew a sharp distinction
between national Democrats (hopeless) and Michigan Democrats
(not bad). And they supported Reagan despite knowing full well
that he did not always agree with their positions on the issues.

Although citations to *Capital* weren't exactly welcome in
his new line of work, Greenberg retained enough of his Marxist
instincts to put class at the center of his story. "Even though
I was writing about people who were racist," he said, "I wrote
about what decisions they made as rational decisions that drew
on their lives, their history, their needs, interests." These one-
time Democrats were driven to the GOP by a mixture of cultural
anxiety, economic grievance, and wide-ranging frustration with
the political establishment, especially with a Democratic Party
they felt had betrayed them.

Which, paradoxically, was the good news. If Macomb had
been pushed away by Democratic mistakes, then it wasn't lost for
good. Just like his subjects in South Africa and Alabama, these
voters harbored latent egalitarian impulses that Democrats could
speak to. These people weren't monsters. They were "Reagan
Democrats"—a term Greenberg popularized—who had not yet

56   found a secure home with the Republicans and might once again become part of a multiracial majority, if Democrats exorcised what Greenberg later called "the demons of the 1960s."

The Democratic National Committee did not share Greenberg's sunny assessment. With memories of Jesse Jackson's unexpectedly strong performance in the 1984 primaries still fresh, DNC Chair Paul Kirk was not looking to kick-start a debate over racial politics. "I found the conclusion inflammatory," Kirk said, "that what Democrats have to do is pay less attention to minorities."

Greenberg had a much friendlier reception at the Democratic Leadership Council. Like Greenberg's Macomb study, the DLC came out of Reagan's reelection. Established in 1985, the DLC saw its mission as bringing Democrats back to the center, with "center" defined as market-friendly economics, hawkish foreign policy, and caution on the culture war. It was an elite organization dominated by elected politicians with no pretenses of building a grassroots movement. The early members were disproportionately southern, and overwhelmingly white and male. Jesse Jackson said a more accurate label would be "Democrats for the Leisure Class," and just the threat of its founding led the AFL-CIO to threaten cutbacks in their campaign donations. The renowned liberal historian Arthur Schlesinger Jr.—himself no stranger to elite organizations run by white men—called it a "quasi-Reaganite formation" bowing down "at the shrine of the free market."

To Greenberg, it was a lifeline. He polled regularly for the group for the better part of a decade, helping ease his transition out of academia—he quit for good in 1987—as he set up his own firm in Washington.

He recognized that it wasn't the most natural partnership. It is safe to assume that Greenberg was the rare DLC affiliate who started off the Reagan years contemplating the finer points of Lenin's writings on nationalism. And, in an abstract sense, his goals were the same as Jesse Jackson's—a rainbow coalition uniting working Americans of all races.

Except Greenberg believed there was no way that Macomb County would support a party led by Jesse Jackson. Although his patrons at the DLC might have different political visions, they shared a common set of enemies: liberal activists blind to the electoral damage they caused; a Democratic establishment unwilling to pick necessary fights; and, ultimately, the Republican Party. They also wanted to reach out to the same voters, including white ethnics, Southerners, men, and a broadly defined middle class. Greenberg was friendlier to the labor movement, but even he believed that trade unions were no longer reliable spokesmen for the views of blue-collar America. "If you want to know what working people think, you can't turn to these organizations," he said. That's what polls and focus groups—especially those interpreted by Stan Greenberg—were for.

Greenberg's politics had changed less than it might seem. He made that clear in a 1991 essay for the left-leaning *American Prospect* that laid out a strategy for rebuilding the Democratic majority. According to Greenberg, that goal could only be accomplished by making "a new class politics."

His plan started with an ambitious economic program oriented around universal policies. "A party that can speak expansively of broad, cross-class issues, such as full employment, tax

58   relief, and health care" could forge "a mass party, encompassing the needs of the have-nots and working Americans."

But material interests alone wouldn't get the job done. Disillusioned white voters would not listen to what Democrats had to say about economics until the party showed respect for their values. A shift to the center on polarizing social issues was the price of admission for resurrecting the New Deal coalition. He had seen time and again in his work that class wasn't just a matter of economics. It was an identity, and a fragile one at that. Getting voters to hear its call required turning down the volume in the culture wars.

Greenberg's eclectic Marxism had evolved into a class-forward liberalism committed to shifting the balance of power (and resources) away from the top, backed up by a Democratic majority drawing support from working people of all races. He dubbed it the "class project," often describing it as an attempt to complete Robert Kennedy's unfinished work. Occasionally, he lapsed back into the language of his academic days and called it an assault on "conservative hegemony."

For Greenberg, references to RFK and Gramsci were two ways of making the same point. An electoral realignment driven by the resurrection of class politics might not be the full expression of leftwing hegemony, but it was an essential first step. In a profession that has never been known for its idealism, Greenberg was a believer.

Reagan Country

Schoen thought Greenberg told a nice story, but not a terribly persuasive one. And as a partner in one of the most important

consulting firms in Democratic politics, he had a platform for
making his views known.

The business had its roots in Schoen's relationship with
Mark Penn. Although the two had known each other since
their days at Horace Mann, they only began working together
in 1974, after Schoen had graduated from college, and picked
up a contract to do polling for Hugh Carey, Democratic candidate for New York governor. Schoen needed help managing the
workload, and he reached out to Penn, who, despite being two
years behind him, had a track record of polling for the *Harvard
Crimson*.

They picked up their connection a few years later, after
Schoen finished his dissertation at Oxford. Although both were
still in law school—Schoen at Harvard, Penn at Columbia—they
came under the mentorship of David Garth, recently dubbed "the
nation's most sought-after campaign strategist" by *Time*. Garth
brought them onto Ed Koch's New York mayoral campaign. The
pair were cheap and technically savvy. Using a home building
kit, Penn assembled a computer that allowed them to produce
daily tracking polls.

Garth used those polls to shape a campaign designed to turn
Koch, a Greenwich Village reformer whose last mayoral campaign
had folded after seven weeks, into a champion of outer borough
white ethnics. A self-described "liberal with sanity," Koch ran as
a tough-on-crime fiscal conservative. The performance caught
the eye of Rupert Murdoch, who had recently purchased the *New
York Post*. After some backroom dealing with Garth, Murdoch
arranged for the *Post* to endorse Koch. The *New York Times,* meanwhile, supported liberal favorite Mario Cuomo.

60   Following Koch's victory, word spread in Democratic circles of the whiz kids from Harvard dragging politics into the computer age. In 1979, they formed Penn & Schoen Associates. A profile the following year in the *Washington Post* described the "kid pollsters"—at the time, both were twenty-six—as rising stars in the field, adding that Schoen, "the smoother operator of these partners," had "transformed himself after college from an overweight and rather slovenly undergraduate into a trim, well-dressed man about town." Their list of successful clients stretched from Philadelphia to Venezuela, where Penn helped elect Luis Herrera as president. Schoen was also trying to build a reputation as a man of letters, publishing his second book—a glowing biography of his old professor Daniel Patrick Moynihan—in 1979.

Home-built computers and instant polls set Penn & Schoen Associates apart from its competitors, but the technical innovations only mattered because they fit inside a larger political framework—the interpretation of democracy that Schoen borrowed from Key and used to explain Powellism. Treating voter preferences as stable, at least for the duration of a campaign, Penn and Schoen promised to weave real-time estimates of public opinion into a coherent message that put candidates at the center of the electorate, where campaigns could still be won.

The formula didn't always work, as Schoen saw firsthand when he blew around $250,000 of his own money (almost $800,000 today) on a long-shot bid for Congress. After losing the Democratic nomination, he fabricated a third party and came up with 16 percent of the vote.

He had better luck when another candidate was on the ballot. Penn and Schoen helped win campaigns for Democrats from New Jersey and New York to Alabama and West Virginia. Teddy

Kennedy used their polls early in his 1980 presidential campaign, and Donald Trump brought them on when he was contemplating a White House run in 1988. They were even more ideologically flexible when they worked abroad, where their clients included Menachem Begin in Israel and parties across the left and right in Latin America. At home, they had a knack for helping wealthy candidates transition from business into politics, not always the easiest career switch.

Their corporate-friendly reputation eventually led to consulting in the private sector, where the firm's clients included Texaco, Eli Lilly, and AT&T. "As we moved deeper into the business world," Schoen later observed, "we were increasingly struck by the similarities between campaigns and corporate marketing." Without knowing it, they had been practicing brand management all along. One technique they developed for AT&T—recruiting focus group members from shoppers at the mall—became a staple of their political work.

Although their specific recommendations varied from campaign to campaign, Penn and Schoen regularly came back to a handful of guiding principles. They began from the premise that Democrats were living in Reagan country. Polarization around hot-button social issues had killed off the FDR coalition, and no viable successor had emerged to replace it. In a 1986 op-ed for the *New York Times*, they announced that "an anti-New Deal consensus" had become the dominant force in American politics. Populist broadsides against Wall Street no longer moved the electorate. The only hope for Democrats was to "demonstrat[e] that they shared the Republicans' basic positions on fiscal issues" and then pivot to "local issues and personality differences." Diligent constituent service and running on policies that cut across the usual partisan

62   divide—cleaning up nuclear waste in Nevada, for instance—could be a winning strategy, but only if voters believed that a candidate wasn't just another tax-and-spend liberal.

In states trending toward the GOP, running on "local issues" might require moving well to the right of the national Democratic Party. When the *Wall Street Journal* said that one of their clients, Indiana's Evan Bayh, "often sounds more Republican than his Republican opponent," Schoen and Penn took it as a compliment.

Looking at the nation as a whole, Schoen and Penn believed they had outlined a blueprint for making the next Democratic majority—a coalition that would only come into being if the party gave up on both class politics and the culture war.

The best example of their approach came in Louisiana, where they were brought on to help plan the campaign against David Duke, the former Ku Klux Klan grand wizard who in 1991 was running for governor as a Republican. Although Duke's initial polling was anemic, Schoen predicted—correctly, as it turned out—that his numbers would rise.

The point wasn't that Louisianans were thirsting to elect a white supremacist. In their polls, only 3 percent said that they were more likely to vote for Duke because of his KKK membership. But most white voters accepted Duke when he distanced himself from the Klan, and they liked what he said on issues where African Americans were seen to benefit at the expense of whites, including welfare and affirmative action. With the economy heading into a recession, they were looking to punish the establishment, and nobody in politics was more outside the system than Duke. It was the replay of a routine Schoen had witnessed with Enoch

Powell. A protest that began with race turned into a larger revolt
against the status quo, without ever giving up on its racial core.

Schoen's solution was to make Duke seem like any other politician. Point out that his 1988 presidential campaign was managed by a former commander in the American Nazi Party, and white voters could shrug it off. Say that he was a tax cheat who lied about serving in the military, and they might start to pay attention.

Schoen's campaigns had a guiding vision that could be hard to see underneath all the bobbing and weaving. In an electorate where polarization benefited Republicans, Democrats had to embrace consensus. Although division was always going to be a winner for the right, Democrats who moved to the center could claim one of the country's most popular values for themselves—unity. They could be the voice for voters who didn't want politics to take over their lives and believed that a country filled with reasonable people could find a way for everyone to get along, or at least stop screaming at each other.

Yes, it was a strategy for winning elections. But was that such a bad thing? Schoen was telling Democrats to give the public what his polls said most Americans wanted. And he didn't see anything wrong with that.

The alternatives were clear. Conflict versus consensus. Division versus unity. Reviving the FDR coalition versus accepting Reagan's America. Focus groups in Macomb County funded by the UAW versus sessions at the mall paid for by AT&T. Or, as the choice would eventually be known within the insular world of Democratic operatives, Greenberg versus Penn and Schoen.

64   Outside those narrow circles, the differences didn't look quite so significant. It was easy to assume that the stakes couldn't be that high in a fight where everyone was an Ivy-educated white guy born in the decade after World War II who based their arguments on polls and focus groups.

The similarities were more than a matter of demographics and tactics. Both sides shared an underlying vision of politics. They thought taking a moral stance was easy. Finding out what voters believed was hard. Persuading a majority to take your side was harder—and, in a democracy, essential.

This worldview gave them a shared set of enemies. Liberal activists were at the top of this list. They were natural antagonists for Democratic consultants, just as movement conservatives were for their Republican counterparts. Interest groups existed to promote a cause, strategists to win elections. One side claimed to speak for the grassroots, the other for public opinion. One said that the road to victory started with bottom-up organizing, the other with campaigns run from the top down.

But the strategists had a common weakness, and they knew it. Greenberg and Schoen were consultants who did their best work behind the scenes; they were not candidates who could take their case to voters. Each one had a message they believed could kick-start a political revolution. They didn't have a messenger.

Soon they both found one. It just happened to be the same person.

U-Turn

Bill Clinton had a gift for making himself at home in the world. He was the good old boy with a Rhodes Scholarship who could spin out folksy sayings on the campaign trail ("If you see a turtle sitting on top of a fence post, it didn't get there by accident") and hold forth on the global economy at Davos. Get him into the pulpit on a Sunday morning, and he would get the crowd roaring. Take him to a conference on Wall Street, and the boys at JPMorgan would open up their checkbooks. Put him in a meeting with his political team, and he might just seem like the future of the Democratic Party.

That future was up for grabs when Clinton entered the 1992 presidential race. Clinton said he was a New Democrat, but "new" was open to interpretation. "The change we must make isn't liberal or conservative," he declared in the speech that launched his campaign. "It's both, and it's different." The promise was ambiguous, and his advisers tended to fill in the blanks for him. Greenberg, who helped draft that first speech, saw Clinton as a

66 partner in the grand project of resurrecting FDR's majority. Four
    years later, Penn and Schoen thought he would finally persuade
    Democrats to give up on turning the clock back to 1936.

    The Clinton years did indeed transform the Democrats, but
    in ways that none of the people at the top saw coming. Clinton
    left behind a party committed to making diversity a national
    strength, making important inroads with what would later be
    called the coalition of the ascendant—young people, racial
    minorities, and the college-educated. He built a bridge to the
    twenty-first-century Democratic Party: more educated, more
    affluent, more liberal on cultural issues across the board, and
    (eventually) more progressive on economic matters, too. This was
    the party that Hillary Clinton won over in 2016 with a strategy
    built around the assumption that the next Democratic major-
    ity had arrived.

    Which it had, at least in the popular vote. But the result came
    as a shock to Democrats, and not just because Republicans came
    out of the election with unified control of government. In 2016,
    Democrats carried the top 1 percent of income earners *and* did
    worse with self-identified members of the working class than
    with the electorate as a whole, both for the first time in the statis-
    tical record. Comparing the economic makeup of the Democratic
    coalition under Hillary Clinton with the party that reelected Bill
    Clinton brings the transformation into focus.

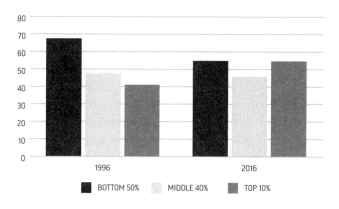

Support for Democratic Party by Income

In 1996, support for Bill Clinton declined as incomes rose, just as it had for Democrats in almost every election since the New Deal. By 2016, the future that Kevin Phillips predicted in *The Emerging Republican Majority* had come to pass, with Trump as a twenty-first-century synthesis of Richard Nixon and George Wallace, and Hillary Clinton as a latter-day John Lindsay. The Democratic coalition had completed its U-turn, leaving the party strong at the top and the bottom, and weaker in the middle.

There has been no shortage of explanations for where this coalition came from. One of the most popular describes it as a pyrrhic victory for Democratic elites who, according to this story, have believed since the 1970s that upwardly mobile college graduates held the keys to a new majority. The 1990s are the turning point in this story, the moment when Democrats leaned into making a neoliberal coalition for a neoliberal party.

68   But that's not how the people in charge of winning elections for Bill Clinton saw things. None of them believed that city dwellers and affluent suburbanites could build a national majority, and each of them considered blue-collar voters an essential part of a Democratic majority. Greenberg insisted that Democrats could pull off a realignment that brought back the New Deal coalition. Penn and Schoen urged them to manage dealignment as best they could. All three spent their careers fighting against the forces pushing to polarize the electorate along cultural lines. They lost that battle thanks in good measure to two candidates—Bill and Hillary Clinton—they helped elect.

Democrats are still, to a considerable degree, the party that both Clintons helped to make. But to understand this party, we need a much better sense of what it was supposed to be. And the story of this party—the real New Democrats—begins with a campaign to save Democrats from themselves.

This Is a Crusade

When Stan Greenberg looked at Bill Clinton, he saw the answer to his prayers. A fellow Bobby Kennedy supporter, Clinton spoke movingly about returning the Democratic Party to its roots as the natural home for the powerless. Running for Congress in 1974, the twenty-eight-year-old Clinton cast himself as a classic southern populist. In a close defeat, he did best in the poorest parts of the district, carrying multiple counties that had gone for George Wallace in the Democratic presidential primary. He made his reputation in the state by taking on utility monopolies, and he sharpened his political skills with a punishing electoral calendar—Arkansas governors served two-year terms until 1986—that kept him on the road.

Greenberg and Clinton first worked together in 1990, during Clinton's last gubernatorial race. The two already knew each other by reputation. Clinton was the great hope of the DLC, where he served as chairman starting in March 1991, while Greenberg was their best pollster. After Clinton won an easy reelection in Arkansas, Greenberg joined the team of handlers pushing him to run for president, not that Clinton needed much persuading.

More so than is usually remembered today, Clinton defined himself as a populist. "This is not just a campaign," he said in a major early speech. "This is a crusade to restore the forgotten middle class, give economic power back to ordinary people, and recapture the American Dream." In private, a red-faced Clinton ended a meeting with his campaign staff by saying, "Bush has never used the bully pulpit to attack the wealthy for screwing the workers."

In the ever-expanding network of Clinton staffers, friends, and assorted hangers-on, Greenberg was the keeper of the populist flame. He provided the rhetorical framing and statistical justification for the strategy, using polls and focus groups to build a consensus for the approach inside Clinton's political team.

Clinton's project wasn't just rhetorical. Although the DLC had staked out a reputation for market-friendly policies and extensive corporate fundraising, Clinton's platform had a distinct populist edge. He promised to turn the page on the Reagan era, cutting taxes for the middle class and raising them for the wealthy. He supported free trade but called for a crackdown on companies moving jobs overseas. He wanted to slash the federal bureaucracy and tackle the deficit while spending more on education and establishing national health insurance. When in doubt, he went back to the guiding principle of the campaign—"It's

70   the economy, stupid"—and hammered Bush for abandoning the middle class.

But Clinton and Greenberg agreed that economics alone wouldn't bring back blue-collar whites. A shift to the middle on social and cultural issues was the price of the ticket for restoring class politics, and he was happy to pay it. Clinton wove both sides of the strategy together with a pledge to "honor the values and promote the interests" of ordinary Americans. He would overhaul welfare and demand that absentee fathers pay up for child support, crack down on drugs and put 100,000 cops on the street. Even when the policies were standard for Democrats, he calibrated the language with the center in mind. "I am not pro-abortion," he said. "I am pro-choice, strongly."

Clinton was not always the happiest of populist warriors. He hated the criticism his strategy received from journalists and the toll it took with college-educated voters in the Democratic primary. "They were the jury of his peers," an adviser said, and he wanted to please them. He was also more sensitive than Greenberg to the importance of keeping the donor class happy, although watching Clinton schmooze with investment bankers at Goldman Sachs provided Greenberg with what he called "some appreciation for the conflicting pressures on the candidate."

Greenberg shouldered the burden of keeping Clinton on task during his not-infrequent struggles with cold feet. The pollster was part cold-eyed operative pointing to the numbers, part disciplinarian keeping a wayward student in line. "The little motherfucker had balls," James Carville said after watching Greenberg once again play bad cop with Clinton.

Even Clinton's sometimes reluctant populism stood out in the Democratic field. There were no major liberals in the race,

and the other candidates were sprinting even farther to the
right. Clinton's leading opponent, Massachusetts senator Paul
Tsongas, said he would be "the best friend Wall Street ever had."
Former California governor Jerry Brown made a regressive flat
tax into the centerpiece of his campaign. When reporters pointed
out that the plan would quadruple taxes on the bottom fifth of
earners while reducing the bill for the top 1 percent by half, Brown
cited libertarian hero Milton Friedman in his defense.

Clinton stuck with the populist attack because it delivered
on Greenberg's promises. While the other candidates targeted the
white-collar set, he cleaned up with the working class. Clinton
wasn't just a different kind of Democrat. He was a different kind
of New Democrat trying to build a majority from the bottom up.
Other reformers came straight out of the Eugene McCarthy tradition, each one promising to build a coalition of conscience.
Clinton was reaching back to RFK, at least in Greenberg's mind,
and sometimes in Clinton's own.

Black voters were crucial to the strategy. During the last two
Democratic primaries, they had backed Jesse Jackson in overwhelming numbers. In 1984, Gary Hart was the favorite of reform
Democrats, coming in a close second to Walter Mondale with
36 percent of the primary vote. But his performance with African
Americans was disastrous, averaging just 3 percent overall. In
1992, with Jackson out of the race, Black voters delivered crushing majorities for Clinton: 78 percent in Mississippi, 82 percent
in Tennessee, 86 percent in Alabama.

The news wasn't all good. Turnout in the primary was down
from four years earlier, and the slump was especially pronounced
with African Americans. But the size of Clinton's margin—he won
52 percent of the total vote—eased a lot of doubts. An editorial

72   in the *New York Times* described the results as a potential turn-
      ing point for American politics, saying that Clinton's victory
      marked "the first time since Robert Kennedy's Indiana primary
      campaign in 1968, that it is politically possible to bring poor
      blacks and blue-collar white voters together."

      Greenberg could have written the line himself, and the
      reports from his focus groups were even sweeter. Years later,
      he remembered crying over results from a session that showed
      Clinton's message resonating with African Americans in Georgia
      and South Carolina. "The people who gathered around the table
      in the focus groups were a test of my life's work," he said. And
      the campaign passed with flying colors.

      A secure base of support with African Americans enabled
      Clinton to ramp up his courtship of Reagan Democrats. He could
      afford to pick fights with Jesse Jackson because he trusted that
      Black voters would stick with him, even after he embarrassed
      Jackson by chastising the reverend for associating with the
      controversial rapper Sister Souljah, turning "Sister Souljah
      moment" into shorthand for picking fights with the base to
      establish credibility with moderates.

      How much any of this mattered in the general election was
      tricky to say. The parade of scandals that followed in Clinton's
      wake—cheating on his wife, dodging the draft, smoking but not
      inhaling—made it difficult to focus on policy, and a lifelong pol-
      itician wasn't the most natural choice to play the role of pop-
      ulist outsider who would shake up Washington. Americans in
      a sour mood with both parties expressed their frustration by
      voting for Ross Perot. Although Clinton won a landslide in the
      Electoral College, the big stories were Bush's collapse (down
      almost 10 million votes from 1988) and the 18.9 percent of the

electorate that supported Perot, the best performance for a third
party since Teddy Roosevelt's 1912 campaign.

The verdict on Clinton's populist strategy was mixed. In line with the primary results, Clinton's vote had a clear economic basis: highest at the bottom, falling as incomes rose. Elsewhere, however, the Clinton coalition looked more like George McGovern's than Harry Truman's. He was strongest in the Northeast and the West Coast, weakest in the South and Great Plains. Core Democratic constituencies—liberals, racial minorities, the poor—still made up the base of his support. He was also the favorite among voters with post-graduate degrees, and he performed better with voters in the top third of the income distribution than any Democrat since Lyndon Johnson. In total, the results were a good sign for Democrats who just wanted a win, but a warning that rebuilding the New Deal coalition would be even harder than Greenberg imagined.

Whether Democrats could turn a revolt against the status quo into a lasting realignment depended on Perot's nearly 20 million voters. They came from a familiar type: white, blue-collar, disproportionately male, most without a college degree—the latest version of the Reagan Democrat. Clinton had not done terribly with this demographic. For the first time since Jimmy Carter's 1976 campaign, non-college-educated whites had supported a Democrat in significantly greater numbers than whites with a four-year degree. But a reluctant vote for Clinton after a longing look at Perot was more a rejection of the GOP than an affirmation of whatever Democrats represented.

To Greenberg, the story could be told through Macomb County. Although Clinton didn't carry Macomb, his narrow defeat marked an improvement over Michael Dukakis's

74   twenty-point rout in 1988. When Macomb reentered the
Democratic fold, the party would have its new majority. The
incoming president's favorite pollster intended to be there when it
happened.

Trending Right

Meetings at the White House soon became a regular part of
Greenberg's routine. The most important were his weekly fifteen minutes with Clinton. In rigorous and eventually agonizing
detail, Greenberg summarized the results of his latest polls and
focus groups as the president's approval rating fell from a high of
58 percent at the start of his term down to 41 percent in October
1994, just before Republicans trounced Democrats in the mid-
term elections, regaining control of the House and Senate for the
first time since the Eisenhower years.

Greenberg had a simple explanation for the debacle. "The
administration's silence on populist themes," he told the president, "was the single biggest error." The middle-class tax cut was
nixed after Federal Reserve Chair Alan Greenspan insisted that
shrinking the deficit come first, with the promise of lower interest rates as the carrot, and the threat of monetary tightening as
the stick. Universal health care went down in flames, but NAFTA
survived a tough fight in Congress. And the president's closest economic adviser, former Goldman Sachs chairman Robert
Rubin, kept insisting that even a hint of class warfare could tank
business confidence.

Not that Greenberg objected to all of Rubinomics. He was a
free trade supporter, and he came around to the White House's
tougher line on deficits. Nor did he object to borrowing Rubin's
private jet for a quick flight back home to New Haven. On a host

of issues the difference between the two was negligible, including the importance of fighting poverty.

But Greenberg still thought the divide between him and Rubin was fundamental. "He just did not want the president to talk about taxing the rich," Greenberg explained. "I wanted to shake Bob because this kind of 'liberalism'"—culturally progressive and concerned with the plight of the poor but deaf to middle America—"is exactly the politics that ... blocked Democrats from creating a real majority."

It was also the politics that came to define Clinton's first two years in the White House. As the administration shifted to the right on economics, a series of early steps pushed it to the left in the culture war, alienating the Perot voters that Democrats needed to build their majority. "Bill Clinton," Greenberg wrote in a dyspeptic memo, "was not sent to Washington to put gays in the military, open our borders to all HIV positive immigrants, create abortion on demand and cut the deficit by taxing the middle class."

Clinton thought Greenberg's diagnosis missed one crucial point: the White House pollster hadn't saved Democrats from an electoral massacre. After the midterms, Greenberg's weekly meetings with Clinton were dropped from the presidential calendar, and, without being formally terminated, he was eased out of the administration's inner circle. Clinton needed a scapegoat. Greenberg's reputation as one of the administration's chief liberal voices—he had urged the White House to go big on universal health care—made him a convenient sacrifice.

At first, Dick Morris stepped into Greenberg's place. He had known Clinton for almost twenty years, first meeting him in 1977, not that long after recruiting Schoen for the West Side Kids. Morris was an ambitious young political consultant, and Clinton

76   was his first out-of-state client. Clinton called him "my alter ego," but the two had an on-and-off relationship, and Morris's record for advising candidates on both sides of the aisle—including hardline conservatives like Jesse Helms—made hiring him for the 1992 race a nonstarter.

Now that Clinton was in trouble, Morris was summoned back into the arena. But he needed help to run a national campaign, and he called on his old friend Doug Schoen, who brought Penn in with him.

Tensions inside the group ran high. Morris and Penn couldn't stand each other, and all three were regarded as ideologically suspect by a good portion of the White House staff—Morris because of his work with Republicans, Penn and Schoen because they conducted early polling for Perot in 1992.

Despite the internal strife and the external hostility, the trio quickly settled on a plan. "The perception across America was that Clinton was a liberal," Schoen later observed. "Our first task would be to change that."

They began, as usual, by sounding out the public. Penn and Schoen drew on the full repertoire of techniques they had developed in their political and corporate work, mixing conventional surveys with a modified version of a Myers-Briggs test they dubbed a "neuro-personality poll."

After slicing the electorate into eight distinct categories, they zeroed in on two key demographics, labeling them "Swing 1" and "Swing 2." Swing 1 voters leaned to the right on economics and to the left on culture. Often well-educated women in dual-income families, they fell squarely into the middle and upper-middle class but worried about keeping what they had.

Swing 2 was more blue-collar and male, hostile to Washington
and uncomfortable with social change.

These were rebranded versions of political types that were already familiar characters in punditry on the campaign—soccer moms in the first case, Perot voters in the second. Both of those categories were slight updates of two standbys in debates over the future of the Democratic coalition, educated suburbanites and the white working class.

According to Schoen and Penn, the main challenge facing Democrats was that Clinton couldn't afford to choose between the two. They gave a slight preference to Swing 1 voters, who polls showed were more gettable, but warned that a blowout with Swing 2 would be fatal. There wasn't one "center" to the electorate, but two, and Democrats had to contest both fronts.

So the Clinton team set out to draw both groups into the coalition. On culture, the campaign depicted Clinton as the moderate alternative to a reactionary GOP that would drag the country back to the 1950s; on economics, an advocate for sensible government who would protect Social Security and Medicare without busting the budget. The president signed welfare reform legislation that prominent Democrats, including Schoen's old mentor Daniel Patrick Moynihan, viewed as draconian. At Schoen and Penn's urging, Clinton supplemented this central message with programs aimed at their target audiences—initiatives against teen smoking for Swing 1, tough talk on trade for Swing 2; stronger environmental regulations for one, strict border controls for the other.

Many of the policies could have fit into Clinton's 1992 platform, but the campaign's overarching message marked a clear break from Clinton's earlier populism. "When you divide rich

78 and poor," Schoen insisted, "the middle class sides with the rich." Too much talk about conflict risked distracting attention from a more important theme. "It's not about economics," Penn told Clinton. "It's about values." The president should be a healer rising above the partisan scrum, the one looking for common ground, not ginning up conflict.

Clinton won a clear victory on election day, making him the first Democrat to win a second term since Franklin Roosevelt. But the win came with asterisks. Republicans held on to the House while adding two seats to their majority in the Senate. Ross Perot had run again, and he drew enough votes to keep the president under 50 percent of the popular vote. After soaring in 1992, turnout crashed to the lowest level since the 1920s.

Critics from the left pounced, including Greenberg. "Rather than ushering in a new progressive era the current period seems to reflect the exhaustion of political forces that have battled to an inconclusive and ugly draw," he declared. According to Greenberg, Clinton won by persuading middle- and working-class voters that he would protect Medicare and Social Security. A conventional Democratic message had turned out a conventional Democratic coalition, resulting in an "incomplete victory."

But to the brains behind this incomplete victory, Clinton's slender margin proved that they had made the right choice. "Downscale voters are *not* the center of the electoral universe," Penn sniped in a debate with Greenberg. Clinton had improved on his 1992 performance across the board, and even his gains at the bottom, Penn argued, had more to do with culture than class. Young people, for example, had below-average incomes, but they responded more to the generational appeal of Clinton running against septuagenarian Bob Dole.

Schoen went even further. "Democrats must face a hard truth," he said. "We do not have the natural majority coalition in American politics." Schoen thought Dick Morris's preferred term for Clinton's strategy, "triangulation," was sugarcoating the issue. Voters didn't want an activist government, and populist appeals weren't resonating with the electorate. "The country," in short, "was trending to the Right."

To back up his argument, Schoen only had to point to the polls. According to Gallup, about two-thirds of the country believed that taxes, crime, and immigration rates were too high. Sixty-two percent had a favorable opinion of corporations. Only 49 percent said the same for labor unions, whose membership had plunged to just 11 percent of the private sector workforce. Forty-one percent of the country identified as moderate, 38 percent as conservative, and 17 percent as liberal. There was room to maneuver within these constraints—plenty of self-described "conservatives" loved Social Security and Medicare—but the limits were real.

Which left Democrats with few options. "Wishing for a mass conversion is not a political strategy. Neither is rallying the base," Schoen said. Comprehensive polls and microtargeted policies were just ways of navigating around these unpalatable facts, tools for making it through a hostile environment with a bare majority of the vote. (Or, in Clinton's case, an even-less-impressive plurality.) "For Democrats to win elections," Schoen concluded, "they must come up with a compelling broad-based vision that ... must be moderate—even conservative—in tone."

Progressives might grumble about what could have been, but Clinton was satisfied with the results. Penn took over weekly meetings with the president. (Morris had been dropped from

80   the campaign after reporters discovered that he had been seeing a prostitute, and articles began appearing with lurid details
about the consultant's kinks.) "In a White House where polling is virtually a religion," the *Washington Post* observed, "Penn
is the high priest." The remaining heretics in the administration had another name for their perennially disheveled oracle:
"Schlumbo."

Penn supplied the kind of detailed advice on policy that
Greenberg had shied away from, regularly meeting with key
policy advisers and testing their proposals in his polls. He and
Schoen also replaced Greenberg as the DLC's go-to pollsters,
a transition that was eased by the fact that many of the DLC's
funders were already their clients, and that they were much more
sympathetic to favorite DLC policies like entitlement reform.
And they began advising Al Gore during the run-up to his presidential campaign in 2000.

Their influence was all the more impressive because neither
Penn nor Schoen was a full-time member of the administration.
They were private consultants, with an office half a block from
the White House, and a list of clients that included Microsoft,
AOL, and Citibank. "Many of the country's foremost political and business leaders," the *New York Times* reported, "are
listening to America through the same small, secretive shop."
They were updating the political machine for the twenty-first
century, providing a place where Bill Clinton and Bill Gates
could each look for advice, blending public service and corporate interests together into one integrated whole.

Penn and Schoen didn't promise a realignment, only a shot
at slogging through one painful win at a time. They didn't believe
government could transform the lives of ordinary Americans,

but they did say it could make getting through the day a little
easier. They didn't want to lead a crusade for the middle class,
but they did promise that people wouldn't have to spend so
much time worrying about politics. They were, in short, New
Democrats—or, rather, what New Democrats had become as
Clinton entered his second term.

   This is what an incomplete victory looked like. If you were
sitting with Penn and Schoen at the top, the view wasn't bad
at all.

Anatomy of a Stalemate

Except it turned out that even this ambition was out of reach.
Impeachment derailed what would have been the signature policy initiative of Clinton's second term—drastic Social Security
reform that could have allowed individuals to invest part of their
accounts in the stock market. With Republicans trying to push
him out of office, Clinton couldn't afford to lose Democratic support by tinkering with the crown jewel of the New Deal.

   Clinton's affair with Monica Lewinsky also, indirectly, cost
Penn and Schoen their contract with the vice president. Gore
fired the pair just a few months into his presidential run, frustrated by their suggestion that he wrap himself around the
Clinton legacy. He steamrolled through the Democratic primary without their help, but by the summer of 2000 he was
lagging behind George W. Bush and fumbling for a campaign
message. That's when, on the recommendation of senior adviser
Bob Shrum, he got in touch with Stan Greenberg.

   It was a predictable choice. Shrum and Greenberg were
partners in the same firm, the chief rival to Penn and Schoen.
Greenberg's public clash with Penn had turned him into the main

82   spokesman for his side of the roiling debate over the Democratic coalition. There was, Greenberg said, "no future for a party competing more and more narrowly for the votes of upscale suburbanites, while grasping at the monied contributions of the well-to-do." Taking on Greenberg was Gore's way of signaling a break with Clinton while gambling that a dose of populism would revive his campaign.

At first it seemed like the bet would pay off. During the Democratic National Convention, Gore unveiled a new slogan, "the people versus the powerful," and moved ahead of Bush for the first time in the race. It was one of the largest post-convention bounces in the history of modern polling, and Gore held on to the lead for over a month. But his margin began shrinking after the first presidential debate, closing to a virtual tie on election day.

Greenberg insisted that Gore's populist conversion had saved the campaign, arguing that a better performance in the debates would have given Democrats a hanging chad—proof majority in the Electoral College. Gore's biggest losses, he pointed out, came with white working-class men put off by his ties to the Clinton scandals, and, more broadly, by the party's increasing association with cultural liberalism and its embrace of globalization. Penn countered in a report for the DLC claiming that Gore had blown the election by alienating "wired workers" of the new economy. Schoen told the *Washington Post* that if Gore had followed Penn's advice, "I'm very confident he would be president-elect today." Meanwhile, he and Penn congratulated themselves on shepherding Hillary Clinton to her Senate victory in New York.

The reality was more complex than either side cared to admit. Greenberg was right to note that Clinton's biggest gains in 1996 and Gore's biggest losses in 2000 had both come from the working class. In 1996, Democrats did better with Americans in the bottom half of the income distribution than at any time since LBJ. Not coincidentally, white voters without a college degree supported the president in greater numbers than their more educated counterparts, just as they had during Clinton's first run for the White House. By 2000, those same voters were drifting away from Democrats. The Perot supporters who once held the key to the next Democratic majority either went for Bush or stayed home, turning the realignment that Greenberg had dreamed of into an electoral stalemate.

But Penn also had a point. Clinton performed well above the historical average for Democrats with the wealthy, and he did better in the suburbs than any Democrat since LBJ, winning nearly a third of the counties that had voted Republican from Eisenhower to Bush. Despite the vice president's populist conversion, Gore lost non-college-educated whites to George W. Bush. Broadsides against the powerful cost Gore with the top of the economic ladder. Bush won the highest-earning 5 percent of voters by over 30 percentage points, just eight years after the same group had almost broken for Clinton.

Overall, Greenberg's analysis of which voters determined the election was still closer to the mark. Yet both sides had to deal with the inconvenient fact that neither had come up with a reliable program for turning out either blue- or white-collar voters. They could pick apart the flaws in the other argument. But the next Democratic majority kept slipping out of their reach.

Schlumbo Rising

Not that Penn seemed to mind. With his days as a twenty-something math geek laboring behind a home-built computer

84   long behind him, Penn rebranded himself as a Washington emi-
nence. He took over as CEO of Burson-Marsteller, a public-
relations firm whose previous clients included the company
responsible for the nuclear disaster at Three Mile Island,
Romanian autocrat Nicolae Ceausescu, and the Saudi Arabian
government after 9/11. "When evil needs public relations,"
Rachel Maddow later told her audience at MSNBC, "evil has
Burson-Marsteller on speed dial."

His friends in the capital had an easy time looking the other
way. He purchased a $5 million mansion in Georgetown with his
wife, Democratic fundraiser Nancy Jacobson. The power couple
became fixtures in the DC social circuit, hosting "issues dinners"
with guests of honor like former Israeli prime minister (and client) Shimon Peres, and book launch parties for friends like *New
Yorker* contributor Jeffrey Goldberg.

Penn picked up the author bug himself, finishing his first
book, *Microtrends*, in time to release it during the run-up to the
2008 presidential election, where it was understood that he
would take a leading part in Hillary Clinton's presidential campaign. A work of pop sociology in the vein of Malcom Gladwell's
The Tipping Point, the book folded Penn's experience in politics
into a larger story about the reinvention of the Democratic Party
as a leading force in a global movement beyond the rigid boundaries imposed by the left and right.

In the globalized and networked society of the future, Penn
argued, individualism would trump ideology. Dozens of new
identities were proliferating—a list of seventy-five examples
included "Powerful Petites" and "Snowed-Under Slobs," along
with a discussion of transgender issues that was surprisingly
nuanced for its time—and political power would go to whichever

party succeeded in piecing together a narrow majority in a fractured society.

Ideological flexibility of a different sort had also become a
hallmark of Schoen's work. While Penn focused on the Clintons,
Schoen cast a wide net, advising clients ranging from Jon Corzine
(who, despite being a former CFO at Goldman Sachs, became one
of the most liberal members of the Senate) to Mike Bloomberg
(first as a Republican, then as an independent). In Italy, he worked
for Silvio Berlusconi, the billionaire tycoon turned prime minister, and harbinger of the rightwing populist wave coming in
the next decade. The common denominator in this politically
mixed crowd was money. Corzine, with an estimated net worth
of $400 million, was the poorest of the bunch.

Schoen had built an impressive, and lucrative, roster, but
it was no match for Penn's role as chief strategist in waiting for
the Hillary Clinton White House. After decades of rough parity
between the two, Penn was now the dominant figure. Tensions in
their partnership had been mounting since the 1996 campaign,
when Penn emerged as the winner of a battle to replace Morris
as the president's favorite strategist. The pair drifted further
apart in the Bush years after selling their firm to WPP Group, a
multinational PR behemoth. Penn thrived in the new arrangement, while Schoen felt like he had become irrelevant to his own
company. In 2007, they formally ended their business relationship when Schoen left the firm with a multimillion-dollar pay-
out, saying that he wanted to spend more time writing.

But thirty years together had left its mark. The two were
heading along different trajectories, but they still looked at
the world in the same way—and it didn't quite fit the picture
that Greenberg (along with critics in a rapidly growing online

86   political ecosystem) drew of them as complacent defenders of the status quo. "Most Americans are profoundly anxious and pessimistic about their economic futures," Schoen warned in 2007, citing Thomas Piketty on the widening income gap. Penn made a similar point in *Microtrends*, drawing on research from Elizabeth Warren, then a professor at Harvard Law School, to discuss the financial crunch that even white-collar dual-earner families were facing—and to say that, with budgets under pressure, "if you are one of those companies holding a lot of subprime loans, watch out."

Troubling economic developments, both predicted, could have major political consequences. Republican gains with working-class whites under George W. Bush were, Schoen said, "a historic—and profoundly worrying—shift." Penn warned that soaring incomes at the top combined with changing campaign finance laws had empowered two distinct groups of donors: a small mega-donor class that could pour millions into advocacy groups and a larger group of elites, still drawn mostly from the wealthiest 1 percent, willing to write a $10,000 check in exchange for a little access to a candidate. "They *have* health care, schools, and houses," he pointed out, dismissing most of the American overclass as a "spoiled" lot who lacked a "respect for the seriousness of life and politics."

Penn brought the same mentality to Hillary Clinton's campaign. In public, he talked about soccer moms and wired workers. He struck a different tone when he stepped away from the microphones. "We are the candidate of people with needs," he wrote in a March 2007 memo outlining his overarching strategy for the race, contrasting their emerging coalition among working- and

middle-class voters with Barack Obama's strong support from
the young and college educated.

When both an election and his reputation were on the line,
even Mark Penn could discover his inner Stan Greenberg. To
explain the dynamic against Obama, Penn reached for a historical analogy the Clintons had heard before. "He may be the JFK in
the race," Penn wrote, "but you are the Bobby."

The Great Forgetting

But Democrats were no longer the party of Bobby Kennedy, or
even the party that nominated Bill Clinton in 1992. In the wake
of Obama's victory, Penn was a key figure in campaign autopsies
that reconstructed his mistakes in detail, from Penn insisting that
Obama was unelectable to urging Clinton not to apologize for
supporting the Iraq War. Penn's most egregious misjudgments,
though, were more fundamental. The most significant was his
assumption that Clinton would stay competitive with Black voters. A close second was his failure to understand how well Obama
fit with the rising Democratic coalition—the same coalition that
Penn had spent years taking credit for bringing into the world.

Greenberg had qualms about where Democrats were heading,
but he did enjoy the irony. In a retrospective on Clinton's loss, he
pointed out that under her husband Democrats had become "the
natural party of young people, virtually all racial and immigrant
minorities, the best-educated women, the most cosmopolitan
and global regions, and increasingly, suburban America." This was
Bill Clinton's legacy, and it cost Hillary Clinton the presidency.

It also left Penn out of a job. He had been forced out of his
position as chief strategist during the primaries, after the *Wall*

Street Journal reported that he had lobbied for a free-trade agreement with Colombia that Clinton opposed. Penn made plenty of enemies on the way down with a take-no-prisoners approach to the race—captured in a cable news appearance where he gleefully mentioned Obama's past cocaine use—that ensured he wouldn't be ushered back into the White House anytime soon.

Yet Greenberg wasn't all that welcome in the Obama camp either. After winning the biggest Democratic victory in forty years on the promise of change, Obama's political team wasn't eager to hear advice from veterans of the Clinton wars. They stood for a failed way of doing politics, a triangulating style that made Democrats complicit in Bush's fiasco in Iraq and helped clear the way for a financial crash that set off the worst economic downturn since the Great Depression.

The indictment went beyond policy. Clintonism made politics into a cynical exercise that turned off the public and prevented Democrats from racking up the electoral margins they needed to push through transformative change. Obama had improved on Clinton's performance with both working-class and white-collar voters, and he did it while driving turnout to the highest level in forty years.

Clintonism's architects seemed to be doing their best to live down to Obama world's expectations. Even before he was forced out of the Clinton campaign, Penn had taken fire from the left for his corporate ties, including his firm's peddling of a "comprehensive communications approach" to "any type of labor situation"—a tactful way of promising to make union troubles disappear. He gave up on a formal role in politics after 2008, taking refuge in the corporate sector with a high-ranking position at Microsoft. But it was widely rumored—and later confirmed—that he remained an active presence behind the scenes as an adviser to No Labels, a centrist group founded in 2010 by his wife, Nancy Jacobson. The effort drew swift condemnation from the left for its business-friendly economic positions, and from Democrats of all ideological stripes who feared it was a stalking-horse for a third-party presidential campaign in 2012.

Schoen kept up the campaign to push Democrats to the right from a perch at Fox News, where he signed on as a contributor in 2009. In his appearances for the network, along with regular contributions to conservative-leaning outlets like the *Wall Street Journal* editorial page, he regularly informed his audience that Democrats were heading toward disaster. If he was trying to rile up the other side, the mission succeeded. "Fake Democratic Pollsters Have Stupid Idea" ran a headline in *Salon* after Schoen and former Jimmy Carter adviser Pat Caddell argued that Obama should drop out of the 2012 race so that Hillary Clinton could take his place at the top of the ticket. After Obama passed on the offer, Schoen cast a ballot for Mitt Romney, his first time voting Republican.

Greenberg's position in Obama's Washington was more complicated. He had failed a key progressive test in the run-up to the Iraq War. Although he eventually came out against the war, he had waffled at first, not wanting to seem like a knee-jerk pacifist. With James Carville, he sent out a strategy memo providing advice for Democrats on both sides of the issue, a textbook case of the business-as-usual politics that Obama had run against.

His closest link to the White House came through Rahm Emanuel, a longtime friend and the incoming chief of staff. But this connection became an early mini-scandal for the administration when journalists discovered that Emanuel had spent five years living rent-free in a DC apartment owned by Greenberg and his wife. That Emanuel had funneled over half a million dollars to Greenberg's firm when he ran the Democratic Congressional Campaign Committee would have been headache enough for the Obama team. More troubling still was the light it cast on Greenberg's extensive list of corporate clients, including Monsanto, Boeing, and British Petroleum—many of whom, as it happened, also worked with Penn and Schoen.

Then there was the matter of Hollywood. In 2002, Greenberg and his partners had agreed to allow documentarian Rachel Boynton to follow their work advising former Bolivian president Gonzalo Sánchez de Lozada, better known as Goni, as he tried to return to power. After winning with just 22 percent of the vote in a multi-candidate race, which Greenberg described as close to the best that could be hoped for in Bolivia's divided electoral system, Goni presided over a military crackdown on protesters that led to sixty deaths. In the uproar that followed, Goni was forced out of office and driven into exile in the United States.

Boynton's film *Our Brand Is Crisis* told the story in vivid detail, juxtaposing video of Bolivians lying dead in the streets with footage of Greenberg's team maneuvering to elect Goni. Critics raved over what they described as a brutal depiction of American arrogance. (A 2015 adaptation starring Sandra Bullock had a more mixed reception.)

Greenberg remained unapologetic, saying that he still believed in Goni's policies, even though their implementation had been disastrous. But what happened after Goni left the presidency was, in a way, an even greater challenge to Greenberg's politics. Breaking with years of narrow victories, Evo Morales

stormed into power with 53.7 percent of the vote at the head of
the MAS Party (Movement for Socialism).

Obama's team didn't dream of revolution, but his rise hinted
at a more modest transformation, a politics where candidates
molded public opinion instead of pandering to it, elections
were decided by surging turnout rather than a bidding war for
a shrinking population of swing voters, and a new progressive
majority broke the electoral stalemate paralyzing Washington.
Even better that the next Democratic coalition reflected the more
tolerant, diverse country that was rushing into existence. "With
New Support Base," a headline in the *National Journal* announced,
"Obama Doesn't Need Right-Leaning Whites Anymore." In the
next America, Democrats wouldn't have to check their proposals with focus groups at the mall, or submit their platform to
Macomb County for approval.

And who listened to focus groups anyway? The data-minded
operatives in Obama world put their trust in analytics. Discontent
with the consultant class had been mounting inside progressive circles for years. Even before Penn's downfall, he had been
Exhibit A in the case against the cult of the guru, with a reputation built around private polls that, his critics said, had a suspi-
cious habit of telling his clients what they wanted to hear. Instead
of bowing to the myth of the all-knowing (and almost always
white and male) strategist, the Obama team followed the science. Randomized control trials replaced focus groups as their
gold standard for message testing, and they built a database with
the names of every potential voter, along with hundreds of pieces
of demographic information, creating statistical models that
projected the results of the 2010 and 2012 elections months in
advance with uncanny accuracy.

92   Conventional polls had good news for progressives, too. By the end of Obama's tenure in the White House, public opinion had moved in their direction on a litany of issues—gay marriage, gun control, immigration, labor rights, belief in systemic racism, and more. The number of Americans identifying as liberal rose to 25 percent, and the change within the Democratic Party was even more drastic. When Bill Clinton was president, almost half of Democrats referred to themselves as moderate; the rest were evenly split between liberals and conservatives. By the time Hillary Clinton was planning her 2016 campaign, liberals were almost a majority in the party, the number of moderates was falling, and barely 10 percent of Democrats called themselves conservatives.

Progressives yearning for a new politics, consultants looking to stay on the cutting edge, pragmatists wanting to stay in the White House's good graces, idealists exhausted with Democrats selling out in Washington—all of them had good reasons for embracing the new era. Governing had required compromises, of course, and that meant staffing the Obama administration with alumni from the last Democratic White House, including the former first lady. But there were plenty of consultants out there who moved easily within the increasingly progressive Democratic Party, plus a next generation of whiz kids who were native speakers in the language of big data. The politics of Clintonism could be safely forgotten, and so could the people who made it.

You Sound Clueless

One advantage of exiling the Democratic old guard to the island of forgotten strategists was that all of them became a lot easier to ignore.

This was simplest for Schoen, whose suggestions for Democrats usually looked like poison pills, and typically appeared in media outlets run by Rupert Murdoch. But decades spent analyzing, often battling, and occasionally abetting rightwing populism gave him a valuable perspective on the ascent of the Tea Party. Schoen's assessment wasn't always reliable—he overstated the importance of fiscal conservatism to the new right, and downplayed the significance of racial grievance—but at a time when progressives were inclined to dismiss the Tea Party as an astroturf campaign ginned up by the Koch brothers and Fox News, Schoen described it as a "genuine grassroots" movement that could transform the Republican Party. "Political elites," he warned, "mistake the anger of populists for ignorance," a failing he had documented at length in his study of Enoch Powell. Forty years later, Democrats were falling into the same trap, blinding them to a growing revolt against the establishment.

Greenberg agreed—most of the time. He spent much of Obama's first term in the White House predicting that Democrats would face an electoral catastrophe if they allowed Republicans to monopolize populist anger with the status quo. His suggestions mixed rhetorical shifts (more attacks on out-of-touch politicians) with substantive moves on policy (higher taxes on the wealthy, a tougher line on immigration). Those concerns faded after Obama's reelection, when he followed the conventional wisdom in assuming that demographic changes were all but handing Democrats a new majority. But he warned that increasing racial diversity would not put an end to the need for class politics. Without a compelling economic message, he argued, the party risked alienating blue-collar voters—white, brown, and Black—who would still determine elections.

His anxieties ratcheted upward during the 2016 campaign. He was a Hillary Clinton supporter from the start, but he recognized early on that Bernie Sanders's crusade against the 1 percent was resonating with the public. His contacts inside the campaign received a barrage of emails urging (and urging, and urging) Clinton to strike a more populist tone.

Clinton never really took the advice. Her message didn't look back to the "Invisible Americans" Penn targeted in her previous run, or the downscale voters at the center of Greenberg's calculations in 1992. She focused on retaining her base of support with older women and adding on the voters who delivered Obama the nomination in 2008, especially African Americans and college graduates. In the Democratic Party of 2016, that was more than enough to clinch the nomination.

Mark Penn pointed out how striking the transformation was shortly before Clinton delivered her acceptance speech at the Democratic National Convention. "In 2008, Hillary had working class voters," he noted, at least among whites and Hispanics. Eight years later, most of those voters broke for Sanders, leaving Clinton with a coalition that was close to the opposite of her first run.

Greenberg saw this change, too, and he worried that it would give Donald Trump an opening. "You sound clueless in blue-collar America," he told Clinton adviser John Podesta shortly after the convention. He kept up the drumbeat during the race, closing with an email to Clinton campaign manager Robby Mook five days before the election saying that a purely anti-Trump message was "not enough."

Mook never replied. Although Greenberg could still get a respectful hearing from old-timers in the Clinton team, among

the younger members of the campaign it was Greenberg who
sounded clueless. Mook had been in middle school when Bill
Clinton was sworn into the presidency, and he was a representative member of the rising cohort of Democratic operatives: a
numbers guy who thought in spreadsheets and won the top job in
Clinton's team because of his track record overseeing low-drama
campaigns and wrangling big egos.

The campaign's most influential strategist wasn't a person at all. It was an algorithm, code-named Ada, that generated
400,000 simulations of the race per day. Ada was the Clinton
operation's secret weapon. Access to its reports on battleground
states was limited to Mook and a handful of other top staffers,
who took quiet comfort in its assurance that key battleground
states like Michigan and Wisconsin were safely in their column.

Ada's public debut was going to be saved for after the election, when it would be trotted out to demonstrate just how out-
matched the shambolic Trump campaign had been. It would have
marked both a victory for Clinton and the final emergence of the
next Democratic majority, with a helpful extra push from the
quants down in analytics. The Clinton team hadn't conjured up
the forces driving this change, but they did their best to speed
the process up. A new era was dawning, and they planned to take
their share of the credit.

In the avalanche of post-election commentary that was about to
fall on the heads of the American public, the Democratic political
class did indeed receive a healthy slice of attention. After years of
soft-focus reporting on the data revolution turning campaigns
into a science, coverage slammed hard into the reverse direction. With Donald Trump about to be sworn into the presidency,

96   it seemed safe to conclude that nobody really knew anything. Consultants in both parties had set the stage for Trump by treating candidates as interchangeable products waiting to be updated for this year's market. Democrats then did Republicans the additional favor of gambling the party's future on well-heeled suburbanites, not just in 2016, but in a strategy that reached back almost half a century.

Veterans of the Clinton wars told a different story. "The Obama years," Greenberg announced, "were the critical juncture when Democratic leaders stopped seeing the working class." Democrats had turned their party into a synthesis of Eugene McCarthy and Jesse Jackson, a rainbow coalition of conscience. The change pushed white voters—still by far the largest racial demographic in the electorate—in opposite directions, driving blue-collar whites to the GOP while college-educated professionals moved toward Democrats. Bill Clinton had managed to hold off the shift in the 1990s, but a gap had opened after his presidency that turned into a chasm in 2016. Schoen distilled the lessons of this history for viewers on Fox News, where he explained, "You can't run a party based on New York, Washington, and Los Angeles, with a little Silicon Valley thrown in."

The number-crunchers in the younger generation of consultants had made real advances over the cocktail of pseudo-science and folklore that too often passed for campaign strategy. ("You know what this campaign needs? More flag pins.") But increasing technical precision came at the expense of deeper political insights.

In Schoen's case, it was a framework for interpreting right-wing populism. It started with outsiders seizing onto a case where the elite consensus was out of step with an issue that was of pressing importance to a significant percentage of the public. That disjuncture gave populists the opportunity to attack a rigged system where the politicians agreed on everything that really mattered and ordinary people were locked out of the process. "Voters must," he wrote in his study of Enoch Powell, "feel that there is some point in the whole game."

Here was another point where Greenberg agreed with his old antagonist. "Voters think they live in a democracy," he wrote early in the Obama years. He urged politicians to take that belief seriously, and he added to it lessons he had gathered during a lifetime of thinking about the strengths and limits of class politics. When political scientists tried to come up with simple ways for evaluating public opinion—the single number that could measure class consciousness, racial resentment, or political ideology—he urged them to listen carefully to what voters said about themselves.

In the report on Macomb that made his reputation, Greenberg had written about a community where race suffused politics, but where voters were also concerned about jobs heading overseas and a college-educated overclass pulling away from the left-behind. Which seems like a point Democrats might have wanted to keep in mind heading into 2016, when Trump flipped Macomb County back into the Republican column at the same time that turnout for Clinton fell in Detroit by 14 percent.

That doesn't mean, of course, that Democrats could have strolled back into the White House if only they had dusted off their playbooks from the 1990s. As the mixed record of Bill Clinton's two terms demonstrated, neither Greenberg nor Schoen had a foolproof strategy. But if they didn't have a complete answer, they did provide a start.

98   And some useful context. In the wake of Clinton's defeat, progressives often turned inward, attributing Trump's rise to uniquely American pathologies. But, as political scientists hurried to point out, nationalist revolts were an international trend.

Greenberg and Schoen witnessed this firsthand. Consulting had taken them around the world, providing front-row seats to a global revolution—and an explanation for why, if you wanted to understand the upheavals roiling American politics, it helped to look across the Atlantic.

A Classless Quality

In the fall of 1992, Philip Gould traveled to Arkansas with a warn-ing. A senior pollster for the British Labour Party, Gould arrived in Clinton campaign headquarters at a low point for his career, and for Labour. He had started off the year hoping for an easy win over a Conservative Party that was running, for the first time in more than a decade, without Margaret Thatcher as its leader. Labour went into the final week of the campaign ahead in the polls, looking like it was about to snap a three-election losing streak. But as the results came in, Gould watched victory melt away. Labour had lost. Again. "It was less an election campaign," he remembered, "and more a collective trauma."

Five months later he received an invitation that changed his life. "Dear Philip," it read, "Stan is anxious to meet you here in Little Rock." Gould had first encountered Stan Greenberg two years earlier during a trip to the United States. Now Greenberg was looking for advice on how Democrats could avoid repeating Labour's mistakes.

100   There were good reasons to be afraid. British and American politics had run along eerily similar tracks for decades: a long stretch of consensus during the postwar economic boom, then a crack-up during the upheavals of the 1960s, followed by discontent and uncertainty in the 1970s, and then conservative dominance in the years of Thatcher and Reagan.

The parallels were even more striking because of how different the countries were in most other respects. One had a government split between the White House and Congress, the other a parliamentary system with no independent executive branch. American politics had been structured around a two-party duopoly since George Washington left the presidency, and no lasting challenger to the Republicans and Democrats had emerged since the Civil War. In the UK, third parties were a much more significant force at the polls, and Labour was less than a century old. The class divide between left and right was even sharper than in the United States. Economic restrictions on voting had only been abolished in 1918, and Labour had since its founding described itself as an explicitly socialist party. The British population was one-fifth the size of the United States, and it was much more racially homogenous. In the 1991 census, 94 percent of the country identified as white, compared to 75 percent in the United States.

None of which stopped Clinton's team in Little Rock from worrying that history was about to repeat itself. George Bush's campaign was borrowing its strategy wholesale from the Tories, flooding the airwaves with ads depicting Clinton as a tax-hiking liberal who spent his formative years dodging the draft and touring the Soviet Union—modified versions of attacks that Gould had just seen take down Labour.

Except it didn't work this time. Gould wound up staying in the United States for five weeks, watching up close as the Clinton operation fought to brand its candidate as a New Democrat. He spent election night in Little Rock, waiting in the cold for Clinton to deliver his victory speech from the Old State House. After celebrating with the campaign the next day, he flew back to London with a plan for reinventing the Labour Party.

Thanks in part to Gould, American and British politics were soon once again running along parallel tracks. In 1997, Labour won an even more resounding victory than Democrats had in either of Clinton's two races, putting the party on a road that eventually led to another striking convergence, in 2016, when both Labour and Democrats were rocked by populist revolts with more than a passing family resemblance.

But all that lay in the future when Gould was soaring over the Atlantic, thrumming with excitement over Clinton's victory. New Democrats had won in the United States, and New Labour could win in the United Kingdom. He could see how to remake the party. And he had a strong suspicion about who could do it.

Social-Ism

Tony Blair said that he liked to call himself a democratic socialist. The problem, he argued, was that most of the country did not.

Blair laid out his case shortly after taking over as head of the Labour Party in a speech marking the fiftieth anniversary of Labour's 1945 landslide victory, the largest in the party's history. With 393 out of 640 seats in parliament, Labour moved to establish a comprehensive welfare state, launching the National Health Service, bolstering protections for workers, and nationalizing industries that totaled about a fifth of the national income.

102   Although the reforms did not deliver the "New Jerusalem" Labour held out as its ideal, let alone a sweeping takeover of the economy, the election was a watershed moment for the country.

It was also the last of its kind. Between 1945 and 1995, Labour had been in power for just fifteen years. During the same period, Democrats in the United States had control of Congress for forty years. Even at the height of Labour's popularity in 1945, only 48 percent of the British electorate cast a ballot for the party of the people. (Conservatives won 40 percent of the vote, with the rest split among smaller parties.) In its entire history, Labour had *never* held two full, consecutive terms in office.

"The truth that we must take seriously," Blair concluded, "is that 1945 was the exception and not the rule." Decades of defeat couldn't be attributed to a chronic case of bad luck. The problem was systemic, and it went to the core of how Labour understood itself.

Most of the country, by definition, didn't belong to the upper classes. Yet Labour had consistently failed to bring potentially anti-Conservative voters into a majority coalition. The party's radical rhetoric—including a party constitution that called for public ownership of the means of production—repelled moderates, but it also set up true believers for disappointment when Labour failed to seize control of the commanding heights of the economy. It was a spokesman for organized labor in a country where two-thirds of workers did not belong to a trade union. Misguided leadership made a difficult situation worse. When the government shifted right under Thatcher, Labour swerved to the left, and it stumbled into the 1990s in a weaker position with both its historic base in the working class and with potential recruits in the broad middle.

Labour needed rescuing, and Blair presented himself as the man for the job. "I am not interested in governing for a term, coming to power on a wave of euphoria, a magnificent edifice of expectations, which dazzles for a while before collapse," he said. "I want to rebuild this Party from its foundations, making sure every stone is put in its rightful place."

It seemed like an odd role for an otherwise exemplary product of Britain's respectable middle class. The son of a lawyer—and devout Tory—Blair had attended an elite Scottish boarding school before enrolling at Oxford, and then following his father into the law, which he used as a springboard into politics. He became a member of the Labour Party only after graduating from Oxford, a fact that his critics on the left would later call a warning of betrayals to come. Blair's politics, the accusation went, came from the head rather than the heart. He knew the arguments for Labour, but he didn't feel the cause in his bones. For true believers, he would always be a convert to the faith.

Blair said that was why Labour needed him. The party had to expand its coalition, and that meant finding a lot more converts. He won his first election to the House of Commons in 1983, during the worst defeat for Labour in sixty years. Blair might not understand what it felt like to have Labour in his blood, but he knew how Tories were made. His father had joined the Conservatives after growing up poor. Becoming a Tory was a sign of how far he had come, and he hoped his children would go even further. Blair wanted to make the Labour Party safe for ambitious strivers. That included children of the working class, like his father, who were looking to climb up a few rungs in the social ladder. It also meant world-class meritocrats, like himself, who were winning the race of life but felt an obligation to the people who had fallen behind.

Most politicians are happy to go through the day without an overarching project. Blair needed one, and he was usually juggling a few. "Politics," he later observed, "is a far more intellectual exercise than people ever think." His diagnosis of the Labour Party was informed not just by his reading of British history but by his interpretation of the underlying challenges facing the modern left in capitalist democracies. Rehabilitating Labour was only a piece of his larger vision. "The ultimate objective," he said, "is a new political consensus of the left-of-centre, based around the key values of democratic socialism."

Along with intellectual zeal, Blair possessed a skill that was, in his telling, even rarer in politics. "The single hardest thing for a practicing politician to understand," he believed, "is that most people most of the time, don't give politics a first thought all day long." He worked to restrain that tendency in himself, maintaining what he called "a normal person's view of politics."

Blair's program for New Labour wove together all the disparate strands in his personality. Shaped by the past but looking to the future, adapting timeless values to a changing present, responding to public opinion while pushing the country forward—he wanted a party that could do it all, and he wanted almost everyone to be part of it: "the self-employed and the unemployed, small business people and their customers, managers and workers, home-owners and council tenants, skilled engineers as well as skilled doctors and teachers."

Which brought him back to the issue of socialism. The Soviet Union was dead, and so, Blair believed, was the orthodox version of socialism represented in the Labour constitution's support for government ownership of the economy's main institutions. Socialist economics was a relic of the past. But another kind of

socialism could live on, a socialism rooted in a moral commitment to others. "The ethical basis of socialism is the only one
that has stood the test of time," he told his audience in 1995. To
distinguish his version from its more familiar counterpart, Blair
called it "social-ism." It was, he said, defined by its commitment
"to fight poverty, prejudice and unemployment, and to create the
conditions in which we can truly build one nation—tolerant, fair,
enterprising, inclusive."

"Social-ism" captured Blair's approach to politics. He wanted
a Labour Party that was rooted in its traditions without being
chained to the past, a movement that drew a sharp distinction
between its values (which were constant) and the means for
achieving them (which should always be open to revision). It
was a program that he defended in meetings with both skeptical
Labour activists and senior executives at Rupert Murdoch's News
Corporation. His appeal to inclusivity catered to liberals, but the
reference to building "one nation" nodded to the Tories' tradition
of "one-nation" conservatism. Blair reached back to Labour's tra-
ditional blue-collar supporters at the same time that he welcomed
upwardly mobile high achievers. You could, he promised, believe
in social justice while taking home a tidy income.

Blair's case for ethics had a practical core. "Socialists have to
be both moralists and empiricists," he said. "If socialism is not
[to] be merely an abstract moralism, it has to be made real in the
world as it is and not as we would like it to be."

In the world as it is, the road to socialism ran through elections. That is why 1945 loomed so large in Blair's mind. Not only
did Labour win, it built a coalition that swept from the country's industrial centers to the expanding suburbs, including the
home district of a young Margaret Thatcher. *That* was Blair's

socialism—a socialism that changed the country because it governed, and that governed because it won, and that won because it brought Margaret Thatcher's neighbors into a national majority.

With this goal in mind, Tony Blair—leader of the Labour Party, face of New Labour, democratic socialist—found that he had a lot to discuss with Philip Gould.

Class Collapse

Gould's crusade to remake the Labour Party began when his flight back from Arkansas touched down at Heathrow. Bill Clinton was a useful example for proving that the left could win, but Gould was focused on the person he credited with devising the 1992 campaign's underlying strategy. "Stanley Greenberg," he said, "broke the new strategic ground." He saw Greenberg as a partner in a shared project. "He was able fully to articulate what I had always instinctively felt," Gould said, adding that Greenberg's writings "became a kind of defining text for me."

And, by extension, for New Labour. Blair had met Greenberg during a trip to Washington in January 1993 as part of a Labour Party delegation. Alongside discussions with policymakers like Alan Greenspan and Larry Summers, Blair's schedule included space to talk politics with Greenberg, over tea at the British embassy. Later in the month, Gould arranged for Greenberg and a handful of other Clinton advisers to speak at a London conference, where Greenberg said his overriding goal for the campaign had been to break the Democrats' reputation as "an elitist and suburban party with contempt for working Americans."

The reception from the audience was mixed, but Gould loved it. "New Labour was always about challenging the assumptions of elitism on both the right and the left," he later explained. That electoral strategy reflected Gould's overall approach to politics, which mapped onto Greenberg's precisely. "I believe in democracy," he said, "almost above everything."

By democracy, Gould meant the same thing as Greenberg: a system for translating public opinion into public policy. "Sometimes the voice of the people can be uncomfortable, sometimes worse than that," he acknowledged. "But each of us has to make a profound and decisive choice: either we trust the people or we don't."

Gould, like Greenberg, believed this democratic orientation should be a guiding star for the left, even when the polls pointed in directions that made progressives cringe. "Every voice, however powerless, however marginalised, sometimes however misguided, has the equal right to be heard," he said. And like his American counterpart, Gould approached the work of interpreting those voices with the kind of missionary zeal that can't be faked. "In many ways," he said, "I felt most happy and fulfilled conducting focus groups"—a confession that would seem like evidence of wildly misplaced life priorities if Gould hadn't delivered it with total sincerity.

It was no surprise that after Blair was chosen to head the Labour Party in 1994, Gould pushed Greenberg to come over to London—effectively, importing a ringer to strengthen Gould's own position within the campaign. Having recently been dropped by the Clinton White House, Greenberg found himself with free time on his hands, and agreed to serve as an unpaid adviser to the Blair team.

In his first report for Blair, Greenberg returned to a favorite theme from the Clinton campaign. "Voters," he said, "need relentless reassurance." The public was growing restless after sixteen years of Conservative government, and Labour's task was to make voting against the incumbent party as easy as possible. Too many people thought Labour was "dangerous"; the party had to make itself "safe." This meant convincing voters looking for a change that Labour would concentrate on "things that matter to people in their lives," not subjects "the public often saw as 'bizarre' issues: homosexuals, immigrants, feminists, lesbians, boroughs putting their money into peculiar things."

Blair was happy to follow this advice. Unlike Clinton, Greenberg noticed, Blair relished a fight. Blair also agreed with the premise of Greenberg's analysis—Labour should be seen as a voice for the public, not a captive to special interests. He had already tangled with trade unions when he pushed Labour to drop its support for public ownership of the means of production from the party constitution. (The new version called instead for both a "dynamic economy" and "a community in which power, wealth and opportunity are in the hands of the many, not the few.") Blair had also taken a stricter rhetorical line on law and order, promising that he would be "tough on crime, tough on the causes of crime."

Ditching socialist economics came out of Blair's desire to make Labour a home for the ambitious and successful. Finding the middle ground on crime was part of his plan to win back working-class voters who leaned to the right on social issues. ("Labour people, certainly our voters," he said, "were far more likely to be tough than soft.") Both fit seamlessly with Greenberg's strategy.

Greenberg's next recommendation, though, was a thornier issue for Blair. Looking over summaries of Labour's focus group research, Greenberg was struck by how often the comments echoed what he heard in the groups he organized for Clinton in 1992. "Ordinary people living through hard times," he said, wanted "to be recognized by those with power." Those responses led Greenberg to an updated version of the approach he urged on Clinton: a populist campaign that told wavering voters the Tories only cared about the rich and powerful. In a survey of potential messages, the best reactions by far were elicited by a prompt saying, "Labour works for all the people. The Conservatives work for the privileged few."

Voters seemed to like—really like—the message. Blair did not. Greenberg thought promising to govern for the *whole* country implied that elites had already been doing just fine, and that the time had come to look after everyone else. Blair saw matters differently. "I didn't want class war," he later explained. "I didn't like division or discord." To Greenberg, he said, "I just don't believe the problem with Britain is the few at the top." He wanted to bring the country together, not drive it farther apart. The best way to do it, he argued, was by running on a simple message: "One Nation."

The impasse left the campaign in an awkward position. Blair's vision of Labour politics that transcended class was popular with his followers inside New Labour, but Greenberg kept insisting that "One Nation" was a guaranteed loser. "I never heard a real voter longing for unity and deploring division," he said. A campaign had to force a choice, and to do that it needed heroes and villains; a message for everyone risked appealing to nobody. Promises to heal abstract wounds in the national psyche didn't offer much to people struggling in their daily lives. Even Gould, who sympathized with Blair's instincts, couldn't find support for the approach in his research. "None of the one-nation themes

110   worked," he wrote in a campaign memo, "because they are not addressing a problem that people think needs solving."

Nailing down a policy platform was just as difficult. Voters were open to the idea of an active government, but this theoretical support was offset by concern that Labour would hike taxes without delivering better schools or strengthening the NHS. Labour's economic team was concerned about spooking financial markets, and the politicos were worried about damaging the party's standing with the business community, including a fragile accord that Blair had reached with Murdoch.

Blair's revolution would have to operate within tight constraints. New Labour policymakers were trying to rebuild the welfare state while keeping an eye on the bottom line, and the campaign was caught between a candidate who longed to move beyond class politics and strategists committed to running against the privileged few. Although Labour was well ahead in the polls, the party had been trained by eighteen years of defeat to expect the worst.

The prospect of an electoral hanging did wonders for the campaign. They ended the message wars by combining broad populism with Blair's politics of ambition, depicting Conservatives as the defenders of an entrenched elite standing in the way of a youthful, striving nation. The goal, Blair said, was "a new age of achievement in which all of the people, not just a few, can share." "Not just" was the key flourish, a way of putting Labour on the side of the many without committing to a direct assault on the few.

Specific policy commitments gave Blair's rhetoric an anchor in everyday life. He promised that income taxes would not be raised and, going even further, that for its first two years in

government Labour would stick to the spending levels that
Conservatives had already proposed. After taking fiscal concerns
off the table, the campaign made what Gould described as a "concrete populist offer"—five promises they handed out on cards
that could fit into a wallet, including lower class sizes, reduced
waiting times at the NHS, and quicker sentencing for juveniles
accused of a crime. "The pledges worked better than anything
else I have ever tested in politics," Gould said.

The day before the election, Greenberg's polls had showed
Labour beating the Tories by 12 points, 43 to 31 percent—a landslide by British standards. When the first exit polls showed Labour
well ahead, Gould almost shut down. "I spent most of the rest
of the day in a state of shock," he remembered. "It was too much
to take in." The final results confirmed Greenberg's predictions
exactly: 43 to 31 percent, the largest margin in Labour's history.

The makeup of Blair's coalition was even more striking
than its size. Early on, Greenberg had noticed that Labour was
assuming a "classless quality" in public opinion. At the time, he
thought this was a change for the better, proof that Labour was
no longer seen as a creature of trade unions. But he grew worried
as the campaign went on. In a presentation to Blair, Greenberg
described a "class collapse" in their polls. Labour was sprinting ahead with white-collar professionals while the Tories were
catching up with working-class voters and the poor. A vocal fac-
tion inside the campaign treated the news as a welcome sign
that New Labour was rising above class. "For some in the team,"
Greenberg realized, "that was more important than maximizing
his vote"—perhaps even for Blair.

Greenberg's fears were overstated, but he was pointing in
the right direction. Support for Labour rose across the board,

112 and voters in the bottom half of the income distribution went for Labour in greater numbers than at any point since the 1970s. But even after those gains Blair still didn't match the party's earlier highs with the working class. New Labour's performance with the top 10 percent of earners, by contrast, was extraordinary. Although the group as a whole remained comfortably Tory, its support for Labour nearly doubled. The party's advances with the most educated slice of the electorate were even more pronounced. In 1997, Labour won college-educated voters for the first time in its history.

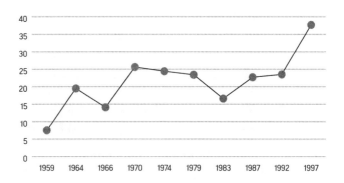

Support for Labour Among College Graduates, 1959–1997

New Labour's coalition fit beautifully with Britain's electoral geography. Strong blue-collar support tightened Labour's grip on working-class seats, while the party's improved performance further up the social scale tipped a number of swing districts in their favor. The result was a landslide that gave Blair the largest parliamentary majority in Labour's history.

But there were signs of trouble, too, for those who cared to look. Turnout fell to 71 percent of eligible voters, still far above the average for the United States, but a 7-point drop from the 1992 campaign. The decline was sharpest in districts that had traditionally gone for Labour, suggesting that many customary Labour supporters weren't sure if they had a place in Blair's party. And with over 40 percent of voters saying they felt little or no attachment with either party, Labour diehards weren't the only people trying to find their place in the shifting political landscape.

In the moment, though, it was hard to argue with success. Five years after watching Bill Clinton deliver his victory speech in Little Rock, Gould saw Tony Blair announce the start of a new era from London. "For the first time," Gould remembered, "I felt exalted." And Blair was triumphant. Labour had reclaimed power by building a new coalition. Now it was time to make a new politics.

Cross-Dressing Is Rampant

Not long after moving into the prime minister's residence at 10 Downing Street, Blair found just the name he had been looking for. The origins of the term "Third Way" are murky, dating back at least to the 1930s, when fascists used it to describe their path beyond capitalism and socialism. Blair shrugged off the historical baggage and resurrected the phrase to describe his program for the next left.

Reaching back to the formula he used to defend New Labour, Blair defined the Third Way as the grand project of adapting the historic values of the left to an era when the debate between state planning and the market had been settled in capitalism's favor.

114   But he also kept revising those supposedly timeless leftwing values. Concepts like equality and solidarity received less attention
than opportunity and efficiency. Not coincidentally, tributes
to the proud tradition of democratic socialism (or social-ism)
dropped out of his rhetoric, replaced by celebrations of a broader
progressive movement.

　　Blair's vision was global, and so was his platform. In 1997,
four years after his pilgrimage to Washington, he invited a delegation headed by Hillary Clinton to a retreat at the prime minister's country estate at Chequers. "We need to brand our politics,"
he told the group, "so we can occupy the territory." Blair was giving the New Democratic project historical depth, intellectual
scope, and an international framing—and the Americans lapped
it up. The event was the first in a series of international sum-
mits of Third Way leaders, at first drawing mostly from Europe,
and then expanding to include representatives from across the
Global South.

　　At home, New Labour acted quickly. The most important
early decision was a surprise move to grant independence to the
Bank of England, giving up political control over monetary policy in the hope—successful, as events turned out—that it would
lead to lower interest rates. The government followed through
on campaign promises to increase spending on the NHS and cut
down on class sizes. Taking a page from the New Democratic
handbook, they had a light touch on regulation. Economic growth
was steady, inflation low, and unemployment falling—all signs,
according to Blair, that Labour was delivering on its pledge to
modernize Britain.

　　The public was more skeptical. Although voters gave Labour
high marks for managing the economy, they wanted more

progress on domestic reforms, especially in improving the NHS. Those frustrations blew up in the winter of 2000 during a flu epidemic that led to a cascade of reports on life-threatening shortages and mounting wait times. Hamstrung by its commitment to budgetary austerity, the government was slow to recognize the scope of the public's anger. Meanwhile, rising gas prices, an uptick in refugees seeking asylum, and anxiety over crime gave critics on the right plenty of material to work with.

Blair said the discontent was proof that the country wasn't changing fast enough. But his pollsters told a different story. Greenberg and Gould had made their partnership official after Labour's victory. They launched a consulting firm in London pitched at "reformist, modernising, and inclusive institutions seeking to adapt to a new era of change," building a roster of clients that included Starbucks, Virgin Media, and the Labour Party.

It all seemed like a quintessential example of life under the Third Way. But Greenberg and Gould had an ambivalent relationship with the term, and with the politics it represented. "Those of us who won elections under that banner," Greenberg said, "understood much of the language was too remote, that real people do not inhabit the 'center,' and that modernization without concrete gains for the middle class loses meaning for voters." As Labour geared up for its reelection campaign, Gould warned Blair that the party was being dragged down by its association with "a whole raft of often confusing and abstract third way messages."

Voters believed Labour was following through on its modernization agenda. They just didn't care that much, especially when they were hearing that hospitals didn't have enough beds. "People feel neglected and ignored," Gould told Blair. "We are

116   outflanked on patriotism and crime; we are suffering from dis-
connection; we have been assailed for spin and broken promises;
we are not believed to have delivered."

In their research, Greenberg and Gould found that simple
messages about strengthening the NHS did much better than
vague promises about meeting the challenges of a new century.
Recognizing Blair's desire to picture himself acting on the largest possible stage, and tapping into his own residual Gramscian
ambitions, Greenberg delivered his recommendations in a memo
with the lofty title, "The New Strategic World: Opportunities for
Hegemony." It was an intellectual case against intellectualized
politics, urging Blair to abandon a "theoretical and obscure" Third
Way and focus on a "battle for real things"—good schools, better
jobs, reliable health care. Gould reinforced the argument with a
list of watchwords for the looming campaign: "On crime we are
tough or for zero tolerance; on the NHS we are for consumers; on
Britain for patriotism."

Blair wasn't thrilled with the idea of running on a mix of
Old Labour economics and centrist social policy. "You were giv-
ing me the right advice for an election," he later told Greenberg.
"It's just that I was choosing not to take it."

The prospect of winning Labour's first back-to-back parliamentary majority—and the fear of blowing the election—
brought him around in time for the reelection campaign in
2001. Blair moved early on immigration, passing the first in a
series of measures to drive down the influx of refugees. In private, he kept up the search for a transformative vision, draft-
ing a fifteen-page memo on New Labour's obligation to unlock
"human potential, economically and as citizens." The campaign
settled on a more conventional promise to boost funding for

public services while pointing to four years of steady economic growth.

Labour was rewarded with a joyless landslide. They won 412 seats, just six fewer than in their 1997 breakthrough. Conservatives only picked up one seat, with the remainder going to the Liberal Democrats, a perennial also-ran whose platform leaned to the right on economics and to the left on culture. But turnout cratered to 59.4 percent, the lowest in almost a century. Yet again, the decline was steepest in working-class districts that were in Labour seats. In a sign of things to come, support for Blair in the bottom half of the income distribution fell by 5 points, while his performance with voters in the top 10 percent was almost unchanged.

And that was before Blair yoked his administration to George W. Bush. Blair's unwavering support for the Iraq War outraged Labour activists and put him on the wrong side of public opinion, where polls consistently showed majorities against intervention. In reports from his focus groups, Gould wrote about a new mood settling over the public. Iraq was damaging enough by itself, but it also exacerbated a larger problem—the sense, already developing in Blair's first term, that the government had stopped listening.

The focus groups were on the right track. Power had given Blair a new confidence in his judgment. Faced with comprehensive public resistance, he later wrote, the Tony Blair of 1997 would have shifted course. Not anymore. "'Being in touch' with opinion was no longer the lodestar," he later explained. "'Doing what was right' had replaced it." He still paid attention to polls, but not with the anxious fixation of his first term—a helpful defense mechanism as his approval ratings plunged.

118   Alongside Blair's growing certainty in his position came an increasing skepticism about the advice he was getting from his political team. Gould's focus group reports were still required reading, but Blair treated them as the ruminations of a sometimes-brilliant partisan rather than as straitlaced analysis. "I used to laugh," Blair remembered, "at how extraordinary the confluence was between his own thoughts and what the groups seemed to say."

Although Gould kept his place in Blair's inner circle, his American counterpart was expendable. As Blair was preparing for his third and final campaign, Bill and Hillary Clinton each suggested he bring Mark Penn onboard. To a prime minister who was increasingly sure of his message, and tired of fighting his pollsters about it, the advice fell on receptive ears.

By the time Greenberg was informed of the revised arrangement, Penn had quietly been advising Blair for months, telling the candidate that he didn't have to apologize for Iraq, and that "married mums" could do for him what "soccer moms" had done for Clinton in 1996. After Greenberg recovered from the shock—his first thought was, "This isn't really happening"—he accepted a diminished place in the race. Repeating his experience with Clinton, he was never formally fired. Instead, he and Penn set up their teams at competing tables in Labour headquarters, with Penn's group just a bit closer to the center. Gould spent the rest of the campaign mediating what he called a "polling war" between the dueling American strategists while working to focus Blair's message on economics and staunch the bleeding from Iraq.

The results were mixed. Labour won a third term, but by the smallest margin yet—a disappointing sixty-six seats in parliament, with 35.2 percent of the popular vote. The returns said more about frustration with Labour than excitement for the Conservatives, who improved on their 2001 performance by just half a point, while the Liberal Democrats came in a strong third with 23 percent. Although turnout bounced back from its nadir in 2001, it was still hovering around historic lows. Once again, the fall was steepest with the working class. Support for Labour in the lower half of the income distribution had fallen by 10 points since Blair's first campaign. Inside the top 10 percent, the drop was just 4 points.

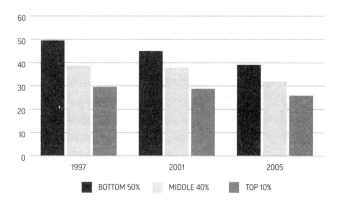

Support for Labour by Income, 1997–2005

Greenberg viewed the numbers as a rational verdict on a botched campaign. In a blistering post-election analysis, he lambasted Penn's research ("biased, self-deluding and overly optimistic") and described the newest version of Labour as an incoherent jumble that, after almost a decade in power, left the public uncertain about the real Tony Blair.

120   To Greenberg, enlisting Penn was a sign that, just like Clinton before him, Blair had lost sight of the difference between a political project that could build a lasting majority and tactics that could scrape together a temporary win. Reflecting on the legacy of New Labour, Greenberg later wrote that Blair "smashed the old class-based politics rooted in the industrial order but failed to substitute a new political choice." Later research backed up Greenberg's thesis, showing that by the 2000s voters were almost evenly split on whether Labour represented the working or middle class.

Glimpses of a new political order were coming into sight. As early as 1999, Gould was telling Blair that opposition to the European Union "gives the opportunity for the Conservatives to reinvent themselves." Gould's reports over the coming years documented the rise of what he called a "politics of grievance," where Euro-skepticism blended with hostility to immigration, crime, and welfare abuse. Personal resentment mingled with a sense of national decline, creating a sense that ordinary voters were being ignored, and that society was coming apart.

These frustrations ran deep with Labour supporters. "Not just intimidating but frightening" was Gould's description of a 2004 focus group with male Labour loyalists. "Their whole of politics was dominated by asylum and immigration," he wrote. "Labour's achievements were just swept away by what was effectively racism."

With distance, Gould came to a more sympathetic perspective. "So much of this is about control, insecurity, and fear," he wrote in a 2011 memoir that he was racing to complete after being diagnosed with terminal cancer. Immigration, in particular, "was not a process over which the electorate felt they had sufficient control or influence. It has left many who had little power in the first place feeling yet more disempowered."

Blair took Gould's warnings seriously. "The one thing that could lose me the next election is immigration," he told a British diplomat after the 2001 campaign. Restrictions on asylum-seeking sent the number of refugees crashing downward. Although Blair was an instinctive supporter of the European Union, he left a decision on whether Britain should ratify a Constitution for Europe up to a national referendum, which was postponed indefinitely after the measure was rejected in France and the Netherlands. While other nations were adopting the euro, the UK stood by the pound.

The politics of grievance required careful maneuvering, but Blair was used to dancing through the raindrops. He believed the tides of history were pulling Britons into a more integrated world—global markets, a stronger European Union, a more diverse population. Labour's task was to shepherd the country down this path one step at a time, giving the public time to reconcile itself to the inevitable.

Critics, including a disillusioned Stan Greenberg, said that Blair had come up empty-handed in his long search for a guiding vision. Inside Labour, the grumbles were becoming louder. Blair had strayed dangerously out of touch with the party, his detractors said, arguing that New Labour had devolved into a mash-up of Bush's foreign policy and Thatcher's economics.

But as the end of his tenure as prime minister was coming into sight, Blair was certain of what the future had in store. In an address to News Corp executives meeting at a resort in Pebble Beach, California—Rupert Murdoch had turned into one of his staunchest backers—Blair announced one last

122   time the vocabulary of left and right was obsolete. "On policy," he said, "cross-dressing is rampant." Yet the exhaustion
of the old ideological conflicts did not bring an end to politics.
The essential struggle of the new era, he said, was no longer a
debate "between socialists and capitalists but instead between
the globalisers and the advocates of protectionism, isolation-
ism and nativism."

The language of left and right might have outlived its
usefulness—Blair certainly thought it didn't apply to him—but
there was still a choice between progressives and conservatives,
one side looking ahead to the open society of the future, the
other looking backward toward an imagined golden age. Blair's
enemies said that he was always trying to please everyone,
but the fact that he had so many enemies was proof of
the opposite. He relished a fight, so long as it was on his
terms. Battle lines were being drawn between globalizing
progressives and nationalist conservatives. Blair knew which side
he would be on—and he liked his odds.

A Coalition of Chaos

Blair would get his fight eventually, but the ride was bumpier
than he imagined. He was pushed into an early retirement shortly
after his address to News Corp, replaced by his Chancellor of the
Exchequer Gordon Brown, who told aides that the performance
in front of Murdoch was "the most disconnected and rootless
speech ever made by a Labour leader." Brown took office just in
time to assume blame for the Great Recession. The slump dealt
a major blow to the reputation for competent economic steward-
ship that had been Blair's chief domestic legacy, and it set Labour
up for a painful reckoning in the next election.

But a funny thing happened in the campaign that followed.
All the candidates running in 2010 promised a change, but they
also seemed to be auditioning for the role of Blair's successor. Brown was the obvious choice, next in line as head of the
Labour Party. But David Cameron treated Blair's rehabilitation of
Labour as a model for how to modernize the Conservatives. ("It's
okay. Blair did the same thing in 1996," his advisers told themselves when they took fire from the old guard.) On substance,
the Liberal Democrats under party leader Nick Clegg—another
youthful Oxbridge type searching for a radical center—looked
more Blairite than Brown's Labour Party.

British voters did little to sort out the confusion. Although
Labour's share of the vote fell to 29 percent, it avoided the nightmare scenario of coming in third behind the Lib Dems. No party
had enough seats to form a parliamentary majority, forcing
Cameron and Clegg to form a coalition government. An administration led by modernizing Conservatives in a legislature where
the balance of power was determined by the Lib Dems wasn't
quite a return to Blairism, but it was awfully close.

After skirting electoral disaster, Labour began plotting
its way back into power with a new leader, Ed Miliband, who
turned to some familiar advisers. Greenberg's firm was back
on Labour's team, with Greenberg as a consultant and his partner James Morris as Miliband's chief pollster. They were a natural fit with Miliband's plan to put economic inequality onto
the agenda. With the country limping through a half-hearted
economic recovery, and Cameron urging more spending cuts,
Miliband was staffing up for a battle over the economy, where
the lines of division between Conservatives and Labour would
be clearer than they had been in a long time.

124   Cameron went into his reelection campaign in 2015 with his own American strategist—Jim Messina, manager of Barack Obama's 2012 race. That Cameron would bring on talent from abroad wasn't surprising, but hiring a Democrat raised eyebrows on both sides of the Atlantic. For Cameron, the surprise was part of the appeal. Messina allowed Cameron to burnish his moderate credentials, borrow some of Obama's glamor, and recruit an adviser skilled in exploiting the data revolution.

Messina offered no apologies for the choice, describing Cameron as part of a global consensus that stretched from Barack Obama and Mike Bloomberg to Cameron's culturally liberal, economically sensible Conservative Party. "Much of his agenda aligns very well with the modern Democratic Party platform," Messina noted, drawing attention to Cameron's support for gay marriage and action on climate change. Like Obama, Messina's Cameron was part of a disruptive movement that was breaking through crusty ideological boundaries. You might even call it a Third Way.

Public polls were tight throughout the campaign, and both sides went into election night convinced they had a shot at winning, with the odds favoring another coalition government. Miliband prepared two speeches, one for a Labour victory, the other if it looked like the Liberal Democrats would form another government with the Tories.

He didn't get a chance to deliver either. Conservatives won a clean majority in parliament. Labour trailed behind in a distant second, and the Lib Dems collapsed, ending the night with just eight seats, down from fifty-seven in the previous election.

Messina saw the results as confirmation of what he had already been saying about Cameron, and about politics after the financial crisis. "In all major elections after the Great Recession," he argued, "the candidate who provided the clearest economic vision looking ahead prevailed." Cameron and Obama had worked from the same playbook, running with an economic platform that looked toward the future. Miliband sounded too much like the past, a Labour revivalist who didn't realize the congregation had tired of jeremiads against the rich and powerful.

Greenberg agreed that Cameron was part of an international movement that might be the wave of the future, but he doubted that Messina would like where it was heading. Sunny economic messages had exasperated the voters in Greenberg's focus groups, and technocratic centrism didn't have a mass public constituency. But there was a market for nationalism, and Conservatives tapped into it. First, they promised a referendum on whether Britain would remain in the European Union. Then, in the final weeks of the campaign, they warned that in a hung parliament Labour could sneak into power by striking a deal with the Scottish National Party, forming a "coalition of chaos" that might break up the United Kingdom. The accusation dominated media coverage in the run-up to the vote, strengthening the Conservative position with two distinct groups—white-collar voters who might otherwise be tempted to vote for the Liberal Democrats again, and working-class voters drawn toward Nigel Farage's rightwing UK Independence Party.

"The lesson," Greenberg concluded, "is that playing the nationalist card works electorally." (Although as he made this argument in May 2015, Greenberg insisted the strategy

126   wouldn't work in the United States. "America is a genuinely exceptional nation that embraces its multiculturalism," he argued, one month before Donald Trump kicked off his presidential campaign.)

Greenberg was refighting the Clinton Wars, this time with Messina in Mark Penn's role. And once again, each side had a point. The Conservatives had closed the campaign with a hard nationalist turn, and it made the difference in crucial swing seats. But the coalitions for the two parties remained split along economic lines, with Labour doing best in blue-collar regions, and Conservatives running strongest in districts with few working-class voters.

Conservatives were reaching out to modernizers and nationalists at the same time. The two-and-a-half party system of the Blair years had broken down, and minor parties were vying to become power brokers in a fractious parliament. Yet through all the upheavals that followed the Great Recession, the basic class division between Labour and the Conservatives would have been recognizable to a time traveler who dropped in from the Churchill years.

The situation, in short, was confusing. Thanks to Brexit, it was about to get a lot simpler.

Normal People

For Tony Blair, politics always came back to ambition. It was the through line of his biography, the thread connecting the youngest prime minister in modern British history to an upwardly mobile father who had lifted himself up from poverty. It was also the key to his strategy for transforming Britain—to build a Labour coalition that linked strivers of all social classes, and a country

where talent would always be rewarded. "You can be successful
and care," he insisted. "Ambitious and compassionate; a meritocrat and a progressive."

Alexander Boris de Pfeffel Johnson didn't have to worry
about climbing the ladder. He was born into Britain's ruling
class, and clever enough that not even a herculean capacity for
self-destruction could endanger his place at the top. If Blair was
a model meritocrat, Johnson was a picture-perfect aristocratic
rogue.

Which is why he was so quick to see the advantages of populism. Johnson looked down from above on the elite that Blair
was so desperate to climb into. When technocrats said that globalization was inevitable, Johnson told voters they always had
a choice. "Democracy matters," he argued when he came out
in favor of the campaign to leave the European Union in 2016.
"The public can see all too plainly the impotence of their own
elected politicians," he said. "We are seeing an alienation of the
people from the power they should hold."

Critics of Brexit played into Johnson's strategy when they
reacted with visceral disdain to what they saw in the public, like
the Labour MP caught on mike in small-town England saying,
"The very first person I come to is a horrible racist. I'm never
coming back to wherever this is."

Johnson and Blair were on opposite sides of a debate over
policy, but there was an eerie symmetry in their view of politics.
They agreed that the choice between globalizers and nationalists was the central division of their times. When Johnson talked
about the public having a right to decide who came into the country, he sounded like Enoch Powell (minus the references to the
Black man having the whip hand over the white man). But he also

128   repeated points that Blair had seen in his reports from Gould and
Greenberg more than a decade earlier.

The resemblance wasn't accidental. Blair said that maintaining "a normal person's view of politics" had been one of his
greatest strengths, allowing him to transcend the conventional
left-right divide. Dominic Cummings, Johnson's chief strategist
and the architect of the Brexit campaign, used exactly the same
language. "The party system does not map to how normal people
think," he said. "Swing voters are more communist than lots of
Labour MPs, in terms of how they think about things like taxing
the rich. And they're more fascists in terms of things like violent crime and punishments for violent criminals and sex criminals than almost anybody."

With Cummings at his side, Johnson set out to bring those
swing voters into a new Conservative majority. "Our campaign
was pitched in this place that doesn't make sense on a left/right
axis," Cummings explained. "On the one hand, we talked about
immigration, but we also allied ourself with the NHS, which
completely bamboozled the media." Where Blair moved right on
economics and aligned with progressives on culture, Johnson
ditched Cameron's austerity while draping himself in the flag.

Here was a Tory plan for transcending class politics. A half
century after Enoch Powell had demonstrated the electoral
potency of rightwing populism, and a generation after Blair drew
educated achievers into Labour, Johnson told frustrated workers they belonged on the right. Brexit had proven this approach
could work in the twenty-first century, delivering a narrow victory to Leave in a referendum with higher turnout than any election since 1992. After replacing Theresa May as prime minister
in 2019, Johnson set out to realign the parties along the divisions

set by Brexit. Although the strategy risked alienating cosmopolitan city-dwellers, those losses would be more than compensated for by gains in heartland Labour seats that had voted Leave. The numbers were in their favor, and the geography was even better, with Remain voters concentrated in a smaller number of urban seats, and Leave voters spread more evenly across the country.

But first he had to deal with Labour's Jeremy Corbyn. While Johnson was developing a kind of inverted Blairism—flipping the approach to policy, borrowing its understanding of politics—Corbyn offered a straightforward repudiation.

Fifteen years older than Johnson, Corbyn joined the House of Commons after the same 1983 Thatcher landslide that also swept in Tony Blair. He spent the next three decades advocating for the orthodox leftism that New Labour was designed to marginalize. When he entered the contest to succeed Miliband as Labour leader in 2015, oddsmakers gave him a hundred-to-one chance. During the Blair years, Corbyn was treated by the prime minister's allies as something between a minor irritation and, in the words of one Blair adviser, "a slightly quaint irrelevance."

That opposition—to Bush's foreign policy before Iraq, to financial deregulation before the 2008 crash, to searching for the center before thinking about principles—was exactly what Labour activists went looking for in 2015. Membership in the party more than doubled, climbing to 550,000, and the new arrivals sided decisively with Corbyn. He carried 59.5 percent of the vote in the leadership election, beating even Blair's total in 1994, while earning just twenty endorsements from Labour's 230 MPs.

With Johnson as his foil, Corbyn aimed to jolt class politics back to life. There was no denying the obstacles in his path:

130   a party still divided over Brexit, a Labour establishment that viewed him as a dangerous ideologue (and possible anti-Semite), polls that showed persistent doubts about whether he could manage a government. But those same barriers existed during his campaign against Theresa May in 2017, when Labour defied expectations with its narrow loss.

Running against a candidate who embodied the upper-crust toff, Corbyn set out a clear vision—a massive expansion of the welfare state, sweeping extension of workers' rights, and major tax increases on the rich. "No more tinkering around the edges," he declared. "Together, we'll take on the privileged, and put the people in power."

The electorate declined Corbyn's offer. Although the Tories improved a bit on their performance from 2017, the real story was Labour's collapse. Conservatives carried the popular vote by 12 points and did even better in parliament thanks to the twists of electoral geography. Johnson demolished Labour's so-called "red wall," flipping fifty-four seats that stuck with Corbyn in 2017, including several that Labour had held for generations, and one that the party had never lost in a contested election. With Labour's coalition now heavily concentrated in urban areas, Corbyn's party of the people wound up with fewer seats than at any time since 1935.

Johnson won by focusing the election on Brexit and consolidating the Leave vote in his camp. The strategy all but abolished the economic divide between the parties, leaving the Tories with a coalition that was older, whiter, and considerably more downscale than Cameron's had been just four years earlier.

When voters couldn't bring themselves to cast a ballot for a Tory, many opted to sit out the race. Turnout dipped slightly from 2017, although it remained well above Blair's two reelection campaigns. The decline was larger for Labour seats than for Conservatives, with the biggest fall coming in Labour seats that supported Brexit.

Labour's record with the upper classes was more complicated. Over the last decade, the party had lost ground with the affluent while holding its own with the most educated. That marked an important contrast with the United States, where Democrats improved with both high-earning and high-education voters. If the British electorate in 2019 had been restricted to voters without a bachelor's degree, Johnson's victory would have been even larger. If it had been limited to college graduates, Corbyn would have won. Instead of moving together, the two wings of the British elite—one filled with credentialed meritocrats, the other dominated by the truly wealthy—were drifting apart.

A realignment whose origins stretched back decades had entered a critical new phase. The country had taken a major step beyond class politics, and the results were a disaster for Labour. Corbyn, the party's most leftwing leader in a generation, had achieved a nightmarish version of Blair's dream.

Labour's warring factions would have plenty of time to reflect on this irony during their extended tour in the minority. With only 202 seats, Labour's caucus was even smaller than after the 1983 massacre that brought Corbyn and Blair into the House of Commons. "It is one thing to lose an election," an analysis from a team of political scientists observed. "It is quite another to lose your advantage in the very working-class communities which the Labour movement was founded to represent."

The results were also disappointing for the Liberal Democrats, and for one of the party's most high-profile

132   strategists—Stan Greenberg. The pollster's defection caused a minor stir when it was announced in the summer of 2019 that one of the architects behind Tony Blair's victory would be joining up with the Lib Dems. "In my bones I am a supporter of Labour and I want to see them succeed," Greenberg insisted at the time. But as an opponent of Brexit and a critic of Corbyn, he felt obligated to help the Lib Dems put together an anti-Conservative majority. The hope was that if the Lib Dems held the balance of power they could strike a deal with Labour to drop Corbyn as part of a coalition government. Although the party improved on its performance in the popular vote by 4 points, that still amounted to just 11.6 percent of the total vote. Because their support was concentrated in a handful of districts, the Lib Dems ended the night down one seat in Parliament, ensuring they would remain a marginal presence.

With the Tories in command, Johnson embarked on a victory lap through the ruins of Labour's red wall. "I know that people may have been breaking the voting habits of generations to vote for us," Johnson said during a speech at Sedgefield, the first stop on his tour, and the sweetest victory in the election. Sedgefield was a historic win for the Conservatives, and a personal one. Labour MPs had won every election in the seat for eighty-four years. For twenty-four of those years, it was represented by Tony Blair.

Six weeks after Johnson's visit to Sedgefield, the first patients in Britain tested positive for COVID-19, setting off a pandemic that led to over 200,000 deaths in the UK, including a near miss for Johnson, who was rushed to an intensive care unit and forced to hand over temporary responsibility as prime minister to a deputy. Johnson made a full recovery, only to be forced to resign when it was discovered that he had opened government offices to host parties for his staffers during lockdowns.

After a short-lived attempt to revive Thatcherism under Liz Truss, whose proposals to slash taxes for the wealthy sparked both a backlash with voters and a panic in financial markets, Conservatives elected Rishi Sunak as their leader. A child of Indian immigrants, Sunak became the first person of color to serve as prime minister. He was also a Goldman Sachs alumnus and, through his wife, heir to a fortune estimated in the billions, making him the wealthiest resident of 10 Downing Street in British history.

The turbulence of the period—three prime ministers in two months—was due partly to personal defects (like Johnson's hubris) and the pressure of events (like a once-in-a-century pandemic). But the underlying problem was structural. Judged by the standards of the pre-Brexit era, Sunak and Truss were both exemplary Conservatives. Yet coming after Johnson's landslide, their elevations were a sign of a party in crisis, caught between its increasingly blue-collar coalition and a Tory establishment that yearned for a return to the Cameron years. So long as that divide persisted, the political situation was unlikely to remain stable.

Labour moved to take advantage of the opening. The party's new leader, Keir Starmer, made reconnecting with working people a top priority. Starmer used a playbook familiar to veterans of the Blair years, combining a broadly populist economic agenda (stronger labor laws, higher taxes on private equity earnings) with a shift to the center on immigration, crime, and foreign policy. The clearest signal of Starmer's intent was delivered in March

134 2023, when Corbyn was barred from running as a Labour candidate by the party's National Executive Committee.

Although Labour insiders welcomed the shift from Corbyn, they complained that Starmer's tactical maneuvers didn't get the party any closer to having a political vision. "The question is," one asked, "what's the point of a Labour government?"

The party's longest-serving prime minister had thoughts. "The takeover of the Labour Party by the far left," Blair said after Johnson's victory, "turned it into a glorified protest movement with cult trimmings."

But Blair's approval ratings weren't anything to boast about either. After he was knighted in 2022, a poll found that only 14 percent of the country approved of the decision. Although he was the face of a philanthropic network—including the Tony Blair Sports Foundation, the Tony Blair Faith Foundation, and the Tony Blair Institute for Global Change—he was just as likely to appear in the news tinged with scandal. His name popped up in Jeffrey Epstein's "little black book," and he was linked to the dissolution of his ex-friend Rupert Murdoch's marriage when journalists discovered steamy notes about a "Tony" written by Murdoch's former wife Wendi Deng. ("He has really really good legs [and] Butt.") As Starmer worked to strengthen Labour's blue-collar credentials, images circulated online of Blair speaking at a conference in the Bahamas hosted by soon-to-be-discredited crypto kingpin Sam Bankman-Fried.

If voters held Blair's decisions against Labour, it wasn't reflected in the polls. When Sunak called a national election in 2024, forecasts showed Conservatives headed for a crushing defeat, with Labour running far ahead, and the Tories battling for second place against Reform UK, a rightwing populist party founded in 2018. Labour might lack an overarching vision, but it could trounce a divided right.

Even though victory was in reach with a strategy ripped from the pages of the New Labour handbook, the country was a long way from the political revolution that Blair promised a generation earlier, the "new political consensus of the left-of-centre, based around the key values of democratic socialism." Judged by the standards that ambitious young man set for himself, Labour had failed.

But the party's track record, like Democrats in the US, looked better when placed in a larger context. Because during the same period when Labour was floundering, parties on the left around the world were collapsing. After the cautious optimism of the nineties, the twenty-first century had delivered a simple lesson to the left: things could always get worse.

A lot worse.

How to Break the Left

One of the few things about politics that Israelis agree on is that their country is special. Other people complain about taxes and interest rates; they deal with matters of life and death. The government declared a state of emergency in the first week of its existence, and it has never lapsed. When a visit to the wrong holy site can set off armed riots, there's no way to draw a clear line between purely symbolic debates and existential conflicts. Israel doesn't have a constitution because fundamental questions about how to define a Jewish state have never been resolved, including who counts as Jewish. In its fragmented political system, with dozens of parties fighting for a seat at the table, no single party has ever won an outright majority.

Look past the heightened stakes and the unstable alliances, though, and you can see that Israel falls into a larger pattern. It was a stronghold for social democracy when the international left's fortunes were at their peak in the middle of the twentieth century. A coalition headed by what became known as the Labor Party held power from the country's founding in 1948 down to

1977, just when other left parties around the world were running into serious headwinds. Labor's first defeat was followed by decades of trench warfare with the leading rightwing party, Likud, where control of the government flipped back and forth after agonizingly close elections.

In the twenty-first century, during the age of Trump and Brexit, the battle has been resolved in the right's favor. Under the leadership of Benjamin Netanyahu, Likud has become the dominant force in Israeli politics over the last generation. Although opposition to Netanyahu persisted throughout this period—and would soar in the aftermath of the October 7 terrorist attacks—Labor has imploded. By 2022, the party that had towered over Israel was reduced to just 4 seats out of 120 in the Knesset, Israel's national legislature.

This dismal result marked the end point of a shift decades in the making. What had been the far right became the new conservative establishment. The old conservatives were the new center. The old center was the new left. And the old left dropped off a cliff.

Put Labor's decline on a graph, and it looks like a company spiraling into bankruptcy—or like the collapse of established socialist parties throughout much of Europe. The trend is so widespread that disgruntled leftists have a name for it: "Pasokification," after the breakdown of Greece's once formidable PASOK party. Here, for example, is the number of seats held by Labor in the Knesset since the 1960s.

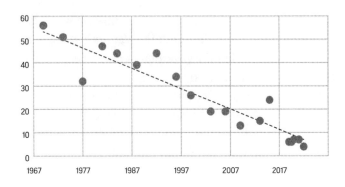

If the trajectory is familiar, so is the history that accompanies it. Following economic turmoil in the 1970s, Labor and Likud converged on a program that shifted policy to the right, turning the land of collectivist kibbutzim into a startup nation. Per capita GDP rose to some of the highest levels in the world; so did the gap between the rich and the poor. Voters often say that kitchen-table issues are their top priorities, and majorities tell pollsters they would prefer a more socialist approach to the economy than a capitalist one. (That's even true for members of Likud.) But economic debates find little traction in a political climate dominated by the connected issues of national security and the Israeli occupation of Palestinian territories. Like many other countries, Israel has seen a battle over national identity transform the right and left, sending working-class voters in one direction and the most educated in another.

But there is one way Israel stands out. The absence of a formal constitution is not just a sign of unsettled arguments over the meaning of a Jewish state. It also reflects the extraordinary gamble that Israelis placed on democracy—so long as Jews were in the majority. David Ben-Gurion, the driving force behind Israel's founding and the country's first prime minister, was a voluble critic of the American constitution, which he described as "a conservative, reactionary institution that stands against the will of the people." To Ben-Gurion, checks and balances were just wrenches thrown into the gears of the democratic machine. In his government, and in Israel to this day, the only structural limit on a parliamentary majority was the guarantee of another election.

Which was easy for Ben-Gurion to defend when he thought his broadly socialist party would always come out on top. Labor's faith in the people was shaken by the crack-up of its majority in the 1970s, and it never fully recovered. With the right on the ascent, Labor politicians warned that democracy itself might crumble. It was an early instance of a framing—democracy on one side, apocalypse on the other—that later became ubiquitous in countries dealing with rightwing populist revolts. Yet the threat wasn't coming from a tiny cadre of elites. It came from voters, confronting Israeli leftists with the knotty challenge of saving democracy from a public it could not entirely trust.

The effort began in earnest in 1981, when Likud faced its first reelection campaign, and Israelis were thrown headlong into the age of polarized politics—a country torn between an embattled left and a nationalist right, where both sides claim to be fighting a war for the soul of the nation. It was a searing experience, terrifying for some, exhilarating for others.

It's also when Doug Schoen and Mark Penn decided they should take a trip to the Holy Land.

140 **Begin, King of Israel**

The connection to Israel came through David Garth, Schoen and Penn's boss in the Ed Koch 1977 mayoral campaign. A partner in Garth's firm was friends with one of Menachem Begin's senior advisers. The economy was in trouble, with growth slipping and the price level more than doubling each year, while polls showed Labor running far ahead. Although Garth was a Democrat, anxious Likudniks reached out to him for assistance. Soon, he was flying off to Israel with his young protégés in tow.

They landed in a country that was still recovering from what Israelis called "the revolution." Until the 1970s, parties on the left regularly earned almost twice as many votes as the combined forces of the right. "We are 100 percent Zionists," Ben-Gurion said, "and we are 100 percent socialists." Labor was not seriously challenged in Israel's first thirty years of existence, and its influence spread far beyond electoral politics.

Membership in a political party could determine your job, your home, even your doctor. The Histadrut, the largest labor organization, controlled much of the economy, and it was controlled by Labor. More than a conventional union, the Histadrut was Israel's largest employer and, for its members—around 80 percent of the workforce in the 1970s—also their bank and healthcare provider. (Resistance from the Histadrut is one of the chief reasons that Israel did not have a universal health insurance system until 1995.)

Labor's experience was a textbook case of hegemony, with far-reaching consequences for Israeli life. Opposition movements were protected in law but grudgingly accepted in practice. Intelligence officials spied on parties from both the right and the far left. In its early years, the country had two radio stations, both overseen by the government, and not a single television network. Although newspapers were privately owned, a military censorship office, along with a broader culture of self-policing, set firm limits to the public conversation—limits that were even more constricting for the Arabic-language press.

By the time Schoen and Penn arrived in Tel Aviv, however, Labor's dominance was a rapidly fading memory. It's not unusual for countries to be governed by a single party in the first generation after winning independence, but that kind of control is almost impossible to maintain over the long run outside of authoritarian regimes.

The breakdown of Labor's hegemony came right on schedule. It began in 1973, just as Ben-Gurion's generation was aging out of politics, when the government was caught flat-footed by the attacks that launched the Yom Kippur War. The debacle unleashed frustrations with the political establishment that had been building for years across the ideological spectrum. In addition to familiar complaints from the more radical socialist left, Labor faced opposition from a new party, Dash, demanding greater civil liberties and more open markets. Dash's individualist bent challenged Labor's collectivist orientation. "Civil rights," noted leftwing politician Haim Oron, "was an alien idea to socialists." At the same time, a virulently anti-Arab movement was gathering around the Orthodox (and American-born) Rabbi Meir Kahane, known for pronouncements such as, "There is no coexistence with cancer, and Arabs are a metastasizing cancer!"

Inside Labor, Likud didn't look much better than Kahane. Ben-Gurion called the party's leader, Menachem Begin, "a classically Hitlerist type." A onetime leader of the Zionist paramilitary group Irgun, Begin was still viewed by many as a terrorist

142   for his role in the bombing of the King David Hotel in 1946, along
with the massacre of more than 100 Palestinians in Dayr Yasin,
a village outside Jerusalem, in April 1948. At a 1952 demonstration against a proposed reparations agreement with Germany,
Begin told the audience they were part of a "war to the death."
Taking him literally, the crowd surged toward the Knesset, where
the debate unfolded to the sound of rioters fighting to break
through the police.

Battling with the right, then, was nothing new for Labor.
Losing to them was. Labor was supposed to set policy in the
Knesset while the protesters bellowed from the outside. When
Begin took power in 1977, it felt like the mob had won.

How Labor's coalition broke apart made the defeat even more
painful. Begin focused his campaign on a widening divide between
Ashkenazi Jews (Central and Eastern European) and Mizrahi Jews
(North African and Middle Eastern). Ashkenazim were the favorite children of the Labor government, and therefore of Israeli society, creating a Mizrahi underclass packed into urban slums. To
Schoen, the gap between the two groups "sometimes seemed as
large as the distance between New Yorkers and Mississippians."

Although Begin was Ashkenazi, he recognized the explosive potential of the cultural resentments and economic frustration that was building among the Mizrahim. Speaking to
working-class audiences, he promised to take the country back
from a clueless Ashkenazi elite that had Labor in the palm of its
hand. Likud's platform mixed a cautiously conservative economic policy—in favor of both cutting taxes and increasing
social spending—with a hawkish line on foreign policy and a
maximalist approach to colonization of the West Bank and Gaza.

Four years later, Schoen and Penn saw how effective the combination could be firsthand, although they didn't do much more than watch. Begin's advisers guarded their influence jealously, and the Americans had to satisfy themselves with tweaking the campaign on the margins. But as Penn and Schoen sifted through polling data from their room at the Sheraton Hotel, working from the same homemade computer Penn built for Koch's 1977 campaign, they witnessed Begin launch a historic comeback.

Scrambling to make up for lost ground, Begin returned to the strategy that had worked for him last time. Begin cast himself as an outsider taking on craven elites—Labor at home, liberal internationalists abroad—who refused to put Israel first.

Schoen had analyzed rightwing populism in his dissertation on Enoch Powell, but this was his first time working for the other side. "The tone of the campaign was vicious," Schoen remembered, later saying it was one of the toughest in his career. Begin said his opponents were flirting with treason and called Labor leader Shimon Peres a liar. Likudniks disrupted Labor rallies, hurling tomatoes at Peres while chanting "Begin, King of Israel." (Language typically used for national icons that originated with the biblical "David, King of Israel.") Shops with Labor posters had their windows smashed, and cars were spray-painted with the words "traitor, traitor, traitor."

With Peres's lead shrinking in the polls, Labor said that democracy was on the line. "I see the battle today as being over Israel's democratic soul," Peres announced. The mayor of Jerusalem accused Begin of fostering "a hysterical personality cult," and a former cabinet member said Likud was trying to "pave the way toward fascism in public life."

144   Begin's team shrugged off the charges. "Everything is blown out of proportion," one of his top staffers insisted. Likud spokesman Ehud Olmert offered a perfunctory, "We dissociate ourselves from the violence." Begin condemned the attacks, called for peace, and then resumed barnstorming through Mizrahi neighborhoods.

Labor supporters treated the rote dismissals as proof of their suspicions. They viewed Begin's campaign as a natural extension of his time in government, when Likud delivered slaps on the wrists to settler vigilantes terrorizing Arabs in the West Bank. "There's been a sort of demonization of the enemy," an instructor at Haifa University complained, "a mystification of the whole Palestinian problem, where it can't be dealt with rationally."

Jacobo Timerman, a journalist and human rights activist who had fled Argentina after being tortured under its military dictatorship, warned that Israel could head down a similar path. "You will always have elections here," he said, but added, "there is always a democratic way to elect a fascist government."

And a democratic way to split the difference. Likud eked out a win by the slimmest of margins, beating Labor 37.1 percent to 36.6 percent in the popular vote, which translated into a single seat advantage in the Knesset (enough for Begin to cobble together a majority coalition with a handful of smaller parties). Although Penn and Schoen couldn't take credit for the result, they considered Begin's victory proof that the techniques they were developing in the United States could travel abroad. Reliable polling and good messaging could bring candidates back from the dead, especially when they had a condescending establishment to run against.

But as the Americans packed their bags for the return flight home, Israelis were faced with a more complicated set of lessons.

The campaign had kicked off a fight the election could not resolve.
The war for the country's soul had ended, for now, in a stalemate.

Both sides would have to get used to it.

You Live in Fear

Deadlock was the new keyword in Israeli politics. Labor's hegemony was finished, but neither party could forge a lasting successor. Begin struggled in his second term, and resigned abruptly
in 1983, shortly after the death of his wife, amid whispers that he
was too depressed to eat. Labor won a narrow plurality in the next
campaign, running again with Peres as leader. But after Labor
proved unable to build a majority coalition in the Knesset, Peres
was obliged to form a national unity government with Likud.
The positions flipped in 1988, when Likud failed to turn its slender plurality into a Knesset majority, and was forced to join up
with Labor again, all while smaller parties continued to vie for
influence.

Bitter polarization produced almost a decade of mandatory
unity between the two warring factions, with Labor and Likud
alternating leadership positions in two-year terms. Both sides
were able to find some areas of common ground, especially on
economic policy. "There is very little difference between the two
major parties or any of the others these days on economic matters," political scientist Daniel Elazar observed in 1992. "They
are all in favor of the principle of a free market, but none of them
want Cousin Mordechai to be unemployed."

Labor's shift was the most striking, and consequential.
It was under Peres that the government finally took decisive
steps to crush the soaring inflation rate, which was approaching 400 percent by 1984. Labor's eclectic program mixed

146   conventional leftwing tactics like price controls with sharp interest rate hikes and drastic cuts to government spending.

Inflation plummeted, and the effects spread far beyond the price level. Young Labor politicians turned away from the socialist ethos of their forerunners—which had long been violated in practice—and set to work dismantling the quasi-public institutions that underpinned the party's earlier hegemony. The Histadrut was the greatest victim of the change. Membership plunged, and key assets were sold off to private investors. The introduction of national health insurance, supported by both Labor and Likud, dealt another blow. Although still an important player in Israeli society, the Histadrut never regained its earlier standing.

A rough consensus on economics cleared the way for an even more ferocious struggle over national identity. The debate over the Israeli occupation became the chief dividing line between the left and right, with surveys showing that for the public Labor was defined by its association with peace, and Likud by its nationalism. "In Israel, the level of your leftness used to be measured by how close you are to Karl Marx," said Amnon Rubinstein, one of the country's most influential legal thinkers. "Today it's measured by how close you are to Yasser Arafat," head of the Palestine Liberation Organization (PLO).

Not that Labor wanted to be seen as cozy with Arafat. The party might no longer be filled with, as Ben-Gurion had put it, "100 percent socialists," but it was still for "100 percent Zionists." Even a two-state solution was a nonstarter at the time. But Labor's tentative moves toward negotiating with the PLO and its opposition to expanding settlements marked it as the comparatively dovish alternative to Likud. Although critics further to the left dismissed those differences as merely symbolic, mere symbols can have enormous political repercussions, and there was no denying the significance of the underlying question. The longer Israel held on to the occupied territories, the more likely it would be forced to choose between recognizing Palestinians as equal citizens or establishing its own version of apartheid. The first meant giving up the country's identity as a Jewish state, the second its claim to being a democracy.

Rising tensions between Israelis and Palestinians kept the issue at the center of the debate. A new party, Meretz, staked out a position at the far left of acceptable Zionist opinion, declaring in its platform, "We must choose between protracted war with the Arab world and economic and social burden, and peace, welfare, and achievement." Another leftwing party, Hadash, ran both Jewish and Arab candidates. But support was also growing for Meir Kahane's far-right Kach Party, which won its first seat in the Knesset in 1984. Four years later, with polls saying that Kach had a chance of picking up eleven seats, making it the third largest party in the Knesset, it was prohibited from competing in the election by a law banning parties that incited racism.

Government orders could slow down Kahane's movement, but they didn't stop it. Polls demonstrated that a majority of Israeli Jews wanted Palestinians consigned to permanent second-class citizenship, at best. In one survey, 44 percent said that Arabs in the occupied territories should not have the right to vote, and an additional 15 percent favored deportation. "I think he is the right medicine," an eighteen-year-old Kahane supporter told a reporter. "Maybe a bit drastic, but the right medicine." It was a popular opinion in his demographic. According to one poll, 42 percent of high schoolers approved of Kahane's program.

148   The changing ideological landscape, with the parties con-
verging on economics as the occupation rose in salience, super-
charged the electoral realignment. Voters who identified as lower
class moved to the right, while the affluent and educated moved
left, opening a gap that persists down to the present.

Shifting coalitions, rancorous campaigns, and evenly split
elections were all symptoms of Israel's freshly polarized politics,
and they created a boom market for American political consultants. Labor and Likud both recruited help from abroad, desperate
for any advantage they could get. Reports on the outsiders helping to transform Israeli politics became mainstays of campaign
coverage. One of Likud's favorite consultants, Arthur Finkelstein,
became a fixture in media coverage, with one story describing
him as a "modern-day Rasputin."

Although Penn and Schoen didn't have Finkelstein's noto-
riety, they kept a close eye on events in Jerusalem. They were
admirers of Ariel Sharon, who they met during Begin's campaign, and considered one of the only Likudniks who recognized the significance of polling. (Sharon asked them to find
out whether voters would be more likely to support Begin if he
appointed Sharon as defense minister. The surveys said yes, and
Sharon's appointment followed in due course.) During the 1984
campaign, they worked for the moderate party Yahad, headed by
a former Likud minister who had adopted a more dovish position on the West Bank and Gaza. Yahad only won three seats
in the election, but it set an important precedent for later—
much more successful—centrist movements.

Then Labor came calling. The stalemate between the parties
had finally broken in 1992, when Labor patched together a majority under Yitzhak Rabin, the first party leader chosen through

a primary election. Labor had beaten Likud by 10 points, while Meretz placed a respectable third. A former general who rose to the highest rank in the Israeli military, Rabin cast himself as a reluctant dove who could be trusted to make peace. He pledged to negotiate with Palestinians, and he received qualified backing from two mostly Arab parties. (They didn't join his coalition, but they agreed to back his government if it was put up to a vote of no confidence.) Hopes for Rabin seemed to be vindicated with the signing of the Oslo Accords, an agreement with Arafat's PLO where both sides committed to find peace—eventually. But Oslo left the key disputes between Israelis and Palestinians unresolved, promising only that future talks would reach a compromise. In the meantime, the settler population in the West Bank continued to rise. While Rabin was being feted as a peacemaker, Israel's occupation was gaining strength on the ground.

Rabin's legacy would be determined by how the unsettled questions of Oslo were resolved, and he needed public opinion on his side to bargain from a position of strength. In 1995, with his reelection campaign approaching, Rabin brought Penn and Schoen onto his team. They had just finished their first poll for Labor when they learned that Rabin had been shot by a rightwing extremist during a peace demonstration in Tel Aviv.

Rabin died the next day, and he was quickly succeeded by Shimon Peres. Support for Labor soared in the wake of Rabin's assassination, and a confident Peres decided to keep Penn and Schoen on board, overlooking the minor role Penn and Schoen played in his 1981 defeat.

With polls giving him a lead of almost 20 percentage points, Peres could afford to be generous. For the first time, the prime minister was going to be chosen on a separate ballot from the

150   rest of the Knesset, and Peres regarded Likud's candidate, Benjamin Netanyahu, as a joke. At seventy-two years old, Peres was Netanyahu's senior by almost three decades. He welcomed the contrast with an opponent he considered too extreme, too shallow, and too inexperienced to mount a plausible campaign. "I can't lose to somebody like that," he assured Schoen.

Peres's confidence evaporated when dozens of Israelis were killed by a string of Palestinian suicide bombings, sending approval for the peace process into free fall. Memories of Begin's victory were still fresh for Penn and Schoen, who advised Peres to steal a page from his old enemy and run as an uncompromising defender of Israel's security, putting aside the peace process to wage a relentless campaign against terrorism.

The strategy was an awkward match for Peres, who had won a Nobel Peace Prize for his role negotiating the Oslo Accords, and Labor wound up with the worst of both options. Peres was denounced as a butcher after an attack on the militant group Hezbollah caused the deaths of 106 Lebanese civilians. But journalists questioned the sincerity of his hawkish conversion, while Likud used grisly footage from the bombings in their television ads. "I know that many of you live in fear," Netanyahu said. "I'll never compromise on security."

After the bloodiest campaign in Israeli history, the country returned to its stalemate. Netanyahu beat Peres by a whisker, 50.5 to 49.5 percent, while Labor edged out Likud in the Knesset. In a conversation with one of his advisers the day after the election, Peres broke down and wept.

Politics Without Limits

Ehud Barak often referred back to a favorite quote from David
Ben-Gurion. "I don't know what the people want," the country's
founding father said, "but I know what is needed by the people
of Israel."

Which might have been worrying to hear from Labor's new
leader, except that not being a conventional politician was one
of Barak's most appealing qualities. He spent his early career
in the military, where he rose to become chief of staff in the
Army, like his mentor Yitzhak Rabin. He entered politics in 1995,
when Rabin appointed him Minister of Internal Affairs. After
Peres's defeat, Barak was elected head of the Labor Party, just a
few months after winning a seat in the Knesset. It was his first
campaign, ever.

Barak approached his new career with the same habits of
thought—thorough, systemic, keenly analytical—that he honed
as a master's student in engineering at Stanford and during a
brief career in the business world after retiring from the military,
and before joining Rabin's cabinet. It was during his corporate
period, when he was consulting for the diet company SlimFast,
that Barak first met Schoen, who was advising the brand on marketing. "For a former military man," Schoen recalled, "he had
an extraordinarily instinctive understanding of how to sell diet
products."

Finishing Rabin's work became the overriding purpose
of Barak's life. Like Rabin, Barak saw himself a warrior turned
peacemaker. On economics, his views fell squarely into the Third
Way—for markets and efficiency, against wasteful spending
and high inflation. But finding peace on terms that guaranteed
Israeli security came first for Barak, and second place wasn't

152   close. "We'll have an intelligent, moral opposition leading in one direct way," he promised: "toward peace."

But he recognized that to have a chance at fulfilling Rabin's legacy—a modus vivendi with Israel's neighbors in the Middle East and a lasting settlement over the West Bank and Gaza—he would have to solve a political problem. Although Rabin had broken through the stalemate that defined Israeli politics for over a decade, Labor's coalition had come up short in the next election, and even Rabin's victory did not look nearly as impressive when compared to the party's earlier majorities.

Policy was easy for Barak. Politics was harder. (Herbert Hoover, another Stanford-trained engineer, had the same problem, which was not an encouraging sign for things to come.) "I don't feel like a politician, even now," Barak told a journalist after three years at the head of Labor.

There were good reasons for the decline. The institutional basis of Labor's earlier hegemony had been demolished, thanks in good part to decisions made by the party's own leaders. Labor had not found a way to win back the Mizrahim, and its standing with Arabs had plunged under Peres. Meanwhile, Israel's demographics were changing thanks to a massive influx of immigrants from the former Soviet Union—about a million people in a country of five million—and the new arrivals did not have fond memories of socialism.

Barak saw Labor's problems as significant, but not all that exceptional. Center-left parties around the world were struggling to reclaim lost majorities, and there was a recent success story he wanted to learn from. In his first month as party leader, he flew to England to meet with the team behind New Labour. At a weekend workshop put together by Philip Gould and Stan Greenberg,

Barak and his advisers were given a behind-the-scenes tour of the Clinton and Blair campaigns. Although Gould was preoccupied with domestic politics in the UK, Greenberg was well on his way to becoming a global brand. His latest client, Gerhard Schröder, was set to become Germany's first Social Democratic chancellor in sixteen years.

Three substantial wins were good enough for Barak. Clinton's election offered convincing proof that Greenberg knew what he was doing, while Blair's and Schröder's suggested that the methods could travel across borders. Barak hired Greenberg and his two high-profile American partners—James Carville and long-time Democratic wordsmith Bob Shrum—to help guide Labor out of the wilderness.

The American trio made its debut with a media tour that included a wobbly press conference where journalists pressed the outsiders on their sometimes-shaky grasp on the details of the Israeli political scene. "I don't know how much this guy Greenberg is familiar with Israel politics," Netanyahu poked at Barak during a debate in the Knesset, "[but] if your speech today is a result of his advice, you had better improve fast."

Despite their rocky introduction, the Americans were confident in their take on the big picture. Following the same basic method he used back home, Greenberg brought together polls and (translated) focus groups to produce a composite portrait of the Israeli electorate. He found a country that lived up to its reputation for conflict, where the constant threat of violence produced what he called a "politics without limits"—including legal ones, as Greenberg discovered when his offices in Washington, DC, were broken into (twice) by burglars assumed to be veterans of Israeli special forces.

The relentless pressure of Israeli politics was like nothing Greenberg had experienced before. It could be exhilarating, especially when you could leave it behind with a flight back home. But he thought voters were sick of it. After spending time in the country, Greenberg came to one overarching conclusion: "Israelis longed for Israel to be normal." The subjects that came up in conversations with voters were the same ones he had seen with focus groups in the US and UK—jobs, schools, pensions. "Normal things," Greenberg said. "That's all they wanted."

Confronted with a familiar set of problems, Greenberg came up with a familiar response—a campaign to persuade Israelis that Labor had changed. It started with reassuring voters that Labor would keep them safe, a promise that was easier to make for a candidate with Barak's military résumé. Then Greenberg urged Barak to repair Labor's relationship with potential swing voters. Barak started with a public apology for Labor's neglect of the Mizrahim, a move that irritated key members of the Labor establishment, including Peres. (The Americans were not unhappy with Peres's reaction. After a dinner with Peres, where the elder statesman suggested that Barak call for "open borders" in the Middle East, Carville grumbled, "he wants us to lose.")

To underscore Labor's transformation, Barak brought the party into a formal coalition with two other parties in the run-up to the election, dubbing the new organization "One Israel"— Barak's counterpart to Clinton's New Democrats and Blair's New Labour.

According to Greenberg, reassurance and apologies were only the first half of a two-part strategy. They were means to an end, ways of getting voters to listen to Barak so that he could seal the deal with a strong economic message—in this case, one that addressed popular frustration with an economy where incomes were flatlining and unemployment had spiked to 11 percent.

Greenberg was accustomed to getting a frosty reception when he pushed for economic populism. But with Barak and his advisers the problem wasn't opposition. It was indifference. "The campaign had no economic plan and none in the works," Greenberg remembered. "Labor leaders just couldn't get themselves to take the economy seriously."

The final part of Greenberg's strategy was the most controversial of all within the campaign. In parliamentary systems with many parties, narrowly divided elections can turn small factions into kingmakers. In Israel, that role had been played by the Shas Party, a vehicle for the ultra-Orthodox, also known as Haredim. The split between religious and secular Jews had run through Israeli politics from the start, and resentment had escalated under Netanyahu. Shas had used its status as a crucial member of Likud's coalition to increase funding for Haredi schools and force the government to double down on a commitment to exempting yeshiva students from compulsory military service.

Labor's voters bristled at this outsized influence, but so did most of the country, including Soviet immigrants who complained that they were being "treated like half-people." Leaping at the opportunity to put the left on the winning side of the culture war for once, Greenberg encouraged Barak to frame the election as an opportunity to choose a "government that works for all, not just the extremist groups."

Greenberg borrowed the "not just" phrasing from Tony Blair's promise to deliver prosperity "in which all of the people—not just a few but all of the people—can share." But he was now looking beyond economics to a broader message about unity.

156   Greenberg was drawing on some of the same fears about democracy that Labor had tapped into during the campaigns against
Begin, while grounding the argument in everyday concerns that
more abstract warnings about fascism could obscure. "The aspiration for unity," he said, "was an aspiration for a government
that would address normal problems and work for the whole
country."

His rationale had an appealing simplicity. A nation held captive to extremists couldn't get anything done—couldn't manage
the economy, couldn't fund the education system, couldn't make
peace with Palestinians. Most important of all, it couldn't end
the permanent crisis that politics had devolved into. It couldn't
make Israel a normal country. But it did leave an opportunity for
Barak to align himself with the public on an issue where debate
had been stifled by a political class that was desperate to avoid
sparking an explosive debate over religion.

That potential, though, is exactly why Greenberg's proposal
was shot down. Barak was willing to challenge the Haredim on
select issues—for instance, a targeted rollback of the military
service exemption—but he was not going to call for a reckoning over religion's place in the public sphere. Instead, the campaign settled for a softer approach: opposed to extremism of all
types, heavy on Barak's military record, insistent on the need
to get the country moving, and filled with just enough details
on policy—including an eventual economic program aimed at
reducing unemployment and narrowing income inequality—to
give the public a sense of what they were voting for.

Barak's strategy was a rough approximation of what
Greenberg had recommended. But it was also a synthesis of advice
that Barak was getting from two other teams of consultants that

he had quietly recruited. One was a French group. The other was Penn and Schoen. News of the relationship came as a surprise to Greenberg's team, who didn't find out until the story leaked in the last week of the campaign. For Barak, though, it was just common sense. No general liked going into battle without a comprehensive view of the terrain, and he did not want to be bound by a single perspective on the race.

Penn and Schoen endorsed the broad strokes of what he was hearing from Greenberg, including the importance of courting the Mizrahim and Soviet immigrants, along with the value of calibrated attacks on Haredim. The biggest difference came down to a question of emphasis. In their telling, Barak was a secondary factor in the election. His biggest asset was not being Netanyahu at a time when two-thirds of voters said the country was on the wrong track. So long as Barak continued to not be Netanyahu—and the laws of biology being what they are, that was a safe bet—the election was his to lose.

And he didn't lose it. But he didn't entirely win it either. On the favorable side of the ledger, he trounced Netanyahu by 12 points in the head-to-head matchup. Barak's call for peace had brought out the left, and his economic message had made up lost ground with the working class. He received more than 90 percent of the Arab vote and a majority of the Jewish vote. Barak held on to Labor's Ashkenazi base while improving with both Soviet immigrants and the Mizrahim, narrowing the gap between Mizrahi and Ashkenazi that opened during the realignment of the 1970s.

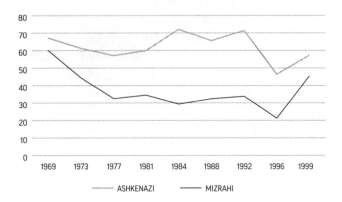

Support for Left, Center, and Arab Parties by Ethnicity, 1969–1999

Despite Barak's landslide, the results in the Knesset were a mixed bag. One Israel's share of the popular vote fell by 6.5 points from what Labor received under Peres in 1996. Well short of a Knesset majority, Barak was forced to look for partners, and he narrowed his choice to two options: creating a national unity coalition with Likud or striking a bargain with the third-place finisher, which just happened to be the ultra-Orthodox Shas. (Another option—including Arab parties and excluding both Likud and Shas—was never attempted.)

To Greenberg, the decision was obvious. "You can't form a government with Shas," he told Barak. Bringing Shas into his coalition meant giving up on his pledge to curb the Haredim's influence. The problem, for Barak, was that joining with Likud meant abandoning the search for a resolution to the Israeli-Palestinian conflict. With Shas, and only with Shas, he would have a chance at fulfilling Rabin's legacy.

Barak still wasn't sure of what the people of Israeli wanted. But he was certain of what they needed. Which meant Shas wasn't going anywhere.

You Are Going to Lose

Barak was willing to gamble everything he had, and more—not just his reputation, but the future of the Labor Party, and the Israeli left. He came away with less than nothing.

The turning point arrived in 2000, when he traveled to Camp David for a summit with Arafat presided over by Bill Clinton. Barak was losing ground before the talks got underway, and his support nosedived when they ended in failure. "The public has completely lost confidence in the current government on all fronts," Greenberg told him in a memo. Two months later, a Palestinian uprising broke out after Likud leader Ariel Sharon walked along the Temple Mount (an incendiary move because the site is sacred for both Jews and Muslims). A survey of the West Bank and Gaza by Greenberg's team informed Barak that three-quarters of Palestinians opposed his framework for peace; even if Arafat had been inclined to compromise, bargaining on Israel's terms could have ended his political career. At the same time, the economy was heading into a recession, handing Barak responsibility for presiding over the worst economic downturn in almost half a century.

With pressure mounting to hold a special election, Barak organized a call with his trio of American advisers. "I'm not sure that I can win," he admitted. According to Greenberg, the Americans responded, in unison, "You are going to lose the election." The debacle at Camp David had dispirited Labor and enraged Likud. Israeli Arabs were calling for a boycott of the election. Most damaging of all, Greenberg said, the voters who gave Barak his majority felt that he had betrayed their trust, first by bringing Shas into his coalition, then by letting the peace process take over the government while the economy spiraled into recession.

Voters took their revenge at the polls, delivering Sharon an almost two-to-one margin over Barak. The participation rate among Arabs plunged to 18 percent, down from 75 percent in the previous election. Although turnout bounced back to 62 percent in the next campaign, it has remained persistently below the overall average. Meanwhile, Soviet immigrants and the Mizrahim sprinted away from Labor. During the next round of Knesset elections in 2003, support for rightwing and ultra-Orthodox parties jumped 6 points among middle- and upper-class voters. Among working- and lower-class voters, it rose by an astonishing 45 points.

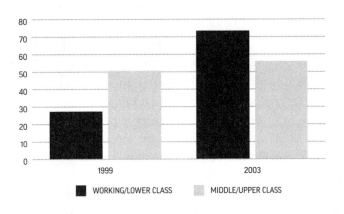

Support for Rightwing and Ultra-Orthodox
Parties by Class Identification

Labor was left with a minority coalition skewed toward the top, setting a pattern that has repeated itself in every subsequent election.

Barak hoped that his government would be a crossroads for Labor. He got his wish, but it turned out the road led into an abyss. "Barak finished off the peace narrative," future Labor leader Merav Michaeli observed many years later. Instead of signaling the party's return to dominance, Barak offered Labor one last chance at power before ushering in a prolonged decline. After holding on to its second-place standing in the next two legislative elections, Labor fell to an unprecedented fourth place in 2009. It staged a minor rally in the next decade—with Greenberg providing occasional advice—only to break apart in 2019, winning just six seats. The results three years later were even more embarrassing: four seats total, making Labor the tenth-largest party in the Knesset.

Labor's breakdown took place in tandem with the emergence of new centrist parties. With parties rocketing into prominence and receding just as quickly, unlikely alliances became the norm. The most dramatic moment in the early days of the upheaval was the announcement that Sharon was departing Likud to launch a centrist party, Kadima—and that he would be joined by Shimon Peres. Before reaching the decision, Peres commissioned a poll from an old acquaintance, Doug Schoen, whose findings showed broad support for a centrist coalition headed by the two men.

The plans for a grand coalition between two elder statesmen fell apart when Sharon slipped into a coma after suffering a massive stroke. In his place as head of Kadima stepped Ehud Olmert, a Likud member of long enough standing that, like Sharon, he had worked for Begin in the campaign against Peres. Olmert brought

Schoen onto Kadima's payroll, where the American said he was "shocked to find that the economy and jobs as well as poverty were right behind terrorism and security as top concerns among Israeli voters." Like Greenberg before him, Schoen described himself as pushing for a clear economic message only to collide with a wall of indifference. When Kadima underperformed at the polls—they won the most seats but were forced into a coalition with Labor—Schoen pinned the blame on Olmert's neglect of pocketbook politics, calling it "the hidden issue of the campaign."

In other words, Schoen thought a critical mass of Israelis still yearned for a normal life. But in a political system where the rules were being rewritten by the day, one thing seemed certain: normality wasn't coming anytime soon.

Bibi, King of Israel

Labor's agonies and the emergence of a viable moderate alternative were bound up with a larger transformation—a story where the crisis of the left and the rise of the center were both signs of a political culture that was speeding to the right. By 2023, 62 percent of Israeli Jews identified as rightwing, compared to 24 percent for centrists, and just 11 percent for the left. The right posted its best numbers among the young, with 73 percent of eighteen-to-twenty-four-year-olds placing themselves on the right.

This change looks all the more remarkable when you consider how weak the right appeared not that long ago. In the 2006 election, Likud fell to fourth place in the popular vote, its worst performance in decades, and a black mark for Netanyahu, who had returned as party leader after Sharon's resignation.

Netanyahu was rescued by his opponents. First, Olmert stumbled in office. A bid to revive the peace process failed, and then, in 2008, he was forced to resign by corruption allegations that eventually landed him in prison. With Kadima reeling, Netanyahu scraped back into power in the next elections. He has been there ever since, except for a single eighteen-month interval. In 2019, Netanyahu surpassed Ben-Gurion as the longest-serving prime minister in Israeli history, a fitting symbol of Likud's dominance, and a tribute to the man whose supporters had long ago taken to chanting "Bibi, King of Israel."

The echo of "Begin, King of Israel" was intentional, and appropriate. More so than either Sharon or Olmert, Netanyahu was the heir to the populist rightwing politics that broke Labor's grip on voters in the 1970s—and then, after decades of struggle, gave Likud its enduring majority.

The right's political revolution was made possible by mounting skepticism about the two-state solution, along with slow-rolling demographic change and skillful maneuvering at the top. According to one poll, taken in 2021, almost 60 percent of Jewish Israelis opposed having the government start negotiations with the Palestinians. Meanwhile, with Orthodox Jews having three times as many children as their secular counterparts, the population was slowly becoming more religious over time.

Netanyahu played to these strengths—favorable public opinion on a crucial issue, plus improving demographics—by redoubling his commitment to a nationalist politics that drew support from the Mizrahim, Soviet immigrants, and the ultra-Orthodox. The public heard less about his belief in the free market and more about leftwing parties busing Arab voters to the polls. He also

164   proved to be an exceptional coalition-builder, encouraging right-wing parties to forge a united front, even when it meant striking alliances with groups that were once seen as toxic with the mainstream.

The only interruption to the reign of King Bibi came when eight parties opposed to Netanyahu took back the Knesset by the barest of margins—60 seats out of 120, with one abstention. The coalition brought together a rightwing party headed by Netanyahu's former chief of staff with the first Arab party to ever become the formal member of a governing majority.

But resistance to Likud wasn't much of a unifying principle, and the government fell apart after a year. Netanyahu stormed back into office, this time with support from a party—Otzma Yehudit, literally "Jewish Power"—descended from the far-right Kach Party that was banned from taking part in the 1988 election after violating a law against racial incitement. Under Netanyahu, the head of Jewish Power, who referred to Kach founder Rabbi Meir Kahane as a "saint," became national-security minister.

Contempt for elite institutions is the lifeblood of populist politics, and the government moved swiftly against one of its favorite targets. The Supreme Court had been a recurring irritant for the right—a rival center of power that was ready to strike down legislation it saw as a violation of the country's norms. With Netanyahu facing multiple charges of corruption, a hostile legal system was more than just a threat to his legislative agenda. Emboldened by his victory in the election, Netanyahu pushed for an overhaul of the judiciary that would allow the Knesset to override the Supreme Court's rulings and decide who served on the bench. (Under the existing system, judges were chosen by a committee where a majority were either Supreme Court justices or members of the Israeli Bar Association.)

The proposal spurred a backlash that threatened to grind the country to a halt. Tens of thousands of demonstrators poured into the streets, turning massive protests into a weekly ritual. Members of the Air Force reserve stopped showing up for duty, and the Histadrut threatened a general strike. Polls showed that overwhelming majorities were opposed to the plan, and legal experts issued dire predictions about the damage that an untrammeled government could inflict. "The concern is unrestrained political majorities doing whatever they want," explained a professor of constitutional law. "And, of course, who's going to be the victim? Probably Palestinians, women generally, asylum seekers, Israeli Palestinian citizens, LGBTQ, religious minorities, Reform, Conservative."

Those fears were well grounded, but they were also a sign of how much the Israeli left had changed since the days when Ben-Gurion dismissed judicial review as a reactionary constraint on the will of the people. Just underneath the surface of the left's resistance to Netanyahu's judicial reform was the anxiety that this could be the last chance to set up the floodwall before the hurricane crashed onto shore. They landed on a classically conservative solution to a dilemma that Alexander Hamilton would have recognized—an independent judiciary to limit the dangers posed by an unchecked majority.

Which isn't an ideal framing for a popular movement. So it's no surprise that protesters landed on a different slogan. Week after week, they returned to a single chant: "democracy!"

166   Almost a quarter century earlier, Stan Greenberg came away from
his time in Israel certain that voters were exhausted with fighting. They just wanted to be normal.

The irony was that by the time Netanyahu took the reins of
the most rightwing government in the country's history, Israel
was normal—not because it had become more like the rest of the
world, but because the rest of the world had become more like
Israel. Wars for the national soul were breaking out across the
globe. Israel wasn't the exception. It was just ahead of the curve.

Although polarization had blown apart the left's old majorities, it didn't guarantee the triumph of the right. The country
went through four elections between April 2019 and March 2021
because Netanyahu wasn't able to form a lasting majority. Even in
the campaign that sealed his grip on power in 2022, the popular
vote was almost evenly split between pro- and anti-Netanyahu
forces. The problem, for the left, was that the anti-Netanyahu
side included a substantial number of conservatives who supported Likud's policies but didn't like the cloud of accusations
surrounding its leader.

Looming over Israel's internal debate was the blunt demographic fact that when you counted all the residents in the land
it controlled, including the occupied territories, the Jewish and
Arab populations were about equal in size. A group with power
on its side and numbers against it is always going to be fearful. So
long as the left could not build majority support for a response
to that challenge, the right was going to have the upper hand.

Not even the worst day in Jewish history since the Holocaust
could change that. The terrorist attacks of October 7, 2023, were
a tragedy for Israel, and a disaster for Netanyahu. But as his
approval ratings plummeted, the framework that he had done so

much to place around Israeli politics remained intact. Palestine had slipped out of public focus in the run-up to the attacks because both Netanyahu and his critics had stopped treating the occupation as a problem that demanded immediate attention. Hamas's assault shattered that illusion, but as the bodies were being counted it was harder than ever to see a plausible path for reviving the two-state solution. If one had ever existed at all.

Although supermajorities told pollsters they wanted Netanyahu to resign as soon as the war ended, his most likely replacements were figures of the center-right promising a more competent version of his strategy. "The sense of being so lonely, so weird, so misunderstood, and so illegitimate—this, to me, is new," said the leftwing academic Yael Berda. King Bibi's days might have been numbered. His kingdom would live on.

It would also be a lonelier place. At home, the left was isolated. Globally, however, it was Israel that stood apart. As the death toll in Gaza reached staggering heights, the international outpouring of sympathy for Israel that followed October 7 gave way to a backlash that left the country with few allies on the world stage and led to a trial for genocide in the International Court of Justice. It was a cruel turn of events for a nation whose founding was bound up with the twentieth century's greatest atrocity, and it gained even greater force because of the country that took the lead in pressing the formal accusation—South Africa, still associated around the world with the triumph over apartheid, a term it was becoming more and more common to see applied to Israel.

There was an irony here, too. While Israel had been moving sharply to the right over the last generation, South Africa had been undergoing the reverse journey. The end of apartheid was

168   followed by the inauguration of a proudly leftwing government
        that held power in an uninterrupted streak for decades, occupy-
        ing an influence not unlike what Labor once held in Israel. But
        it turns out that the story of liberated South Africa, which hap-
        pens to feature some familiar characters from this book, comes
        with warnings of its own.

A Better Life for All

Nelson Mandela walked out of prison in February 1990 with a message for South Africa, and the world. At seventy-one years old, he was grayer than the man who had gone into confinement over 10,000 days earlier. But his vision for South Africa was the same one that Mandela said he was willing to die for when he stood trial for resisting apartheid. Almost three decades later, it brought thousands of his supporters to Cape Town City Hall, where an overflowing crowd spent hours in the roasting sun waiting to hear from their hero. "I greet you all," Mandela declared, "in the name of peace, democracy, and freedom for all."

"Freedom" was an important word for someone with painful experience of what its absence felt like, and Mandela had a particular definition of the term in mind—not just for himself, but for South Africa. Dismantling apartheid was only the beginning. The next step, and the harder one, was stamping out its legacy, creating a united country where the fruits of prosperity were widely shared. "We have waited too long for our freedom," he told the crowd. "We can no longer wait."

170   And it didn't seem like they would have to. In South Africa, Mandela's liberation symbolized the impending demise of a brutal regime grounded in racial domination, where a Black majority was ruled over by a white minority. (The voting-age population was about 70 percent Black and 20 percent white. The remaining 10 percent were either South Asian or "coloured," the South African term for people of mixed racial backgrounds.) But looked at from abroad, the last days of apartheid fit into a global patten. The Berlin Wall had fallen three months before Mandela's release from prison, and the collapse of the Soviet Union would follow one year later. Apartheid's implosion was the other side of the end of history, proof that authoritarian regimes of the right and left belonged to the past. Mandela represented hope for South Africa, and South Africa represented hope for the world.

That's no longer the case today. After thirty years of continuous rule by Mandela's party, the African National Congress (ANC), almost 90 percent of South Africans believe the country is going in the wrong direction. Although the country has made enormous progress in securing formal equality, and there have been real benefits for a growing Black upper and middle class, the gap between the rich and the poor has widened under the ANC's watch, producing some of the highest levels of income inequality in the world. By 2024, the unemployment rate had soared to 32 percent, worse than what the United States experienced during the worst days of the Great Depression. Widespread corruption has undermined the government's ability to provide basic services—clean streets, drinkable water, reliable electricity—in what was once Africa's most advanced economy. A senior member of the ANC has publicly admitted that the country risks becoming a failed state. When a sixty-nine-year-old Black woman living on the outskirts of Cape Town was asked what a generation of freedom had done for her, she replied, "I've gone from a shack to a shack."

Yet only now has the ANC's grip on power begun to slip. In a country where race and class are still tightly bound together, the ANC has stayed in office by winning massive support from poor Black voters. South Africa has one of the most racially and economically polarized electorates in the world. It also has a government that, for decades, has called for a sweeping overhaul of the social order. ("Radical economic transformation" was the mantra under former president Jacob Zuma.) In practice, the greatest rewards from ANC rule have gone to a narrow elite that remains disproportionately white. Instead of realizing Mandela's dream of a rainbow nation marching forward together, the ANC has presided over the creation of a multiracial ruling class that enriches itself while the poor wait for the lights to come back on.

If Israel offers a case study in how hegemony breaks down, turning a bastion for social democracy into a poster child for reactionary populism, South Africa tells the opposite story—how a leftwing movement toppled a racist regime, built a lasting electoral majority grounded in the poorest members of society, and then delivered new (yet somehow quite familiar) kinds of disappointment.

It's a case of point-by-point contrasts, with almost no overlap between the two. Except for the people who saw both histories unfold firsthand.

172   The People Shall Govern!

If Stan Greenberg had stayed quiet, he might have been in Cape Town to celebrate Mandela's liberation. Ever since his first visit to South Africa in 1973, no country outside the United States had fascinated him more. As his academic career was going sideways in the early 1980s, it briefly looked as if Greenberg would reinvent himself as a South Africa hand. The Rockefeller Foundation asked him to join a commission on US relations with the country, and he became co-director of a research program on South Africa funded by the Ford Foundation.

Greenberg's advance was stymied by the apartheid government after a recording of him denouncing the regime in private made its way into official hands. With the South African ambassador threatening to withhold visas to the entire Rockefeller commission, Greenberg was forced out of his position—and, eventually, into politics.

He kept a close eye on South Africa as the years went on. Mandela had long been a hero to Greenberg, who called the campaign against apartheid "fundamental to everything I have done as an adult." He saw Mandela as the leading example on the world stage of the tradition that he associated with RFK in the United States, a builder of multiracial coalitions that could shift the balance of power toward the poor and working class.

Mandela's politics were inseparable from the ANC. Established in 1912 to defend the rights of Black South Africans, the ANC had long considered itself, in Mandela's words, "not as a political party . . . but as a Parliament of the African people." It was an ideologically mixed organization drawn together by the battle against apartheid, with a membership that ranged from aspiring capitalists to orthodox Marxists, all claiming to

represent an overwhelmingly Christian country where social
conservatism runs deep.

The leadership class of the ANC skewed toward the radical end of this spectrum, and the evidence strongly suggests that, like many in the upper ranks of the ANC, the young Mandela was a member of the South African Communist Party. But his most enduring commitments were to the principles outlined in the ANC's official statement of principles, known as the Freedom Charter. Released in 1955, the document committed the ANC to forging a movement across racial lines that would launch a comprehensive program of social reconstruction, including nationalizing industry and redistributing land. Although the details were left intentionally fuzzy, the importance of a simple credo came through clearly: "the people shall govern!"

Almost four decades later, the time had come for the ANC to fill in the blanks. Radicals in the group had assumed that the death of apartheid would take place alongside a larger crisis of capitalism, laying the groundwork for a rapid transition to socialism. The ANC had long maintained an alliance with the country's largest trade union federation (COSATU, the Congress of South African Trade Unions) and the Communist Party. All three had worked together to overthrow apartheid, and they agreed to go into the elections under the ANC's banner.

But the regime's final days had not played out according to script. The economy was in trouble—average incomes had been falling steadily since the 1970s—due in good measure to the success of a global anti-apartheid movement that had choked off the flow of capital to South Africa, pushing the country to the brink of default. Now that victory was in sight, sanctions were going to lift, raising the possibility that money would start

174   pouring into the economy just as the left was about to take charge.

The social picture was just as murky. Legal discrimination had been abolished, but the National Party—the same party that had created the apartheid regime and held power continually since 1948—was still running the government. The first elections with universal suffrage were not going to take place until 1994, leaving the country suspended between worlds. Bands of paramilitary groups, both white and Black, roamed the streets. Political violence surged, resulting in almost 10,000 deaths between 1991 and 1994. With crime also on the upswing, the euphoria among Black South Africans that followed Mandela's release gave way to frustration with how little had changed—all before the ANC had its first day in power.

Mandela began calibrating expectations well before the election. Speaking in 1992 to the World Economic Forum at Davos, an annual meeting ground for the global elite, he performed a careful balancing act. It's easy to imagine brows furrowing in the crowd when he said that economic development in sub-Saharan Africa required "a massive transfer of resources" from the global North. But Mandela quickly pivoted to reassuring the audience that the ANC would "establish the political and social climate which is necessary to ensure business confidence." He called for a mixed economy with public spending levels comparable to Germany or France, balanced by a government that recognized the importance of a robust private sector. Mandela then closed by urging his listeners to recognize their common humanity with the great mass of people striving to rise out of poverty.

He was more straightforward back home at a meeting of the ANC's economic policy conference. "There is a political reality facing us," he said. "The business community worldwide is not going to have any truck with a government that wants to nationalize; it's a reality. Do you want to fly in the face of this reality? You can't do it."

But to do anything at all, the ANC had to win. The National Party, headed by President F. W. de Klerk, had not given up on retaining power in free and fair elections. Although Black voters were about 70 percent of the electorate, that left 30 percent who were either white, coloured, or South Asian. If discord within the Black population lured enough voters away from the ANC, de Klerk might just sneak through.

Although de Klerk's plan was the longest of long shots, the legitimacy of Mandela's government would be shaped by the size and makeup of his coalition. A crushing majority that transcended racial lines would give him a mandate for change; a smaller victory owed exclusively to Black voters riven by internal divisions would hamstring the administration before it began. With the country's most prominent Zulu politician talking openly about civil war—a threat to be taken seriously given that Zulus were the largest ethnic group among Black South Africans—the possibility could not be dismissed that the ANC would break under the pressure of the moment, and take the country down with it.

Pushed in one direction by the audience at Davos, pulled in the other by radicals at home, facing off against an incumbent with no intention of going quietly into retirement, straining to fend off a civil war—with all of this in mind, the Mandela team began to plan a campaign.

Just as they set to work, a special issue of *Newsweek* came across the desk of Popo Molefe, chair of the ANC's election

176   division. The issue was devoted to a behind-the-scenes retrospective on the 1992 US presidential race, giving heaping piles of
credit to the strategists it praised for masterminding Clinton's
rise. "We would like to work with these people," Molefe told a
nonprofit group that had offered to bring in outside consultants
for the ANC. Calls were made, and soon Greenberg was on a flight
to Johannesburg.

Newsweek hadn't mentioned that Greenberg—"a Yale
prof turned pollster who understood the mood of the embattled middle class"—had been thinking about South Africa for
twenty years, but it didn't matter. Winning is what counted,
and Mandela's advisers thought they had found just the man to
help them do it.

Now Is the Time?

For almost half a century, the ANC's reason for existence was
obvious: ending apartheid. Now that job was over, and South
Africa was becoming a genuine democracy. To take the next
step—to truly remake the country—the ANC had to change, too,
growing from a liberation movement into the voice of a nation.
And to do that, it had to become a political party that could piece
together a national majority.

It didn't take long for Greenberg to come up with a plan.
After an initial meeting with Mandela's team in June 1993,
he quickly fell into a routine. While keeping up his work for
Clinton, he began flying to South Africa every two weeks, taking the red-eye out of New York on Thursday and arriving back
in DC by Monday morning.

A few points were obvious from the start. First off, the stakes
were high. "I was here in a country on a precipice," Greenberg

realized during his first trip. Although Mandela's team welcomed assistance, they were not looking to follow orders. Resisting apartheid had not made for an easy life. The government had banned the ANC from 1960 to 1990, and many of the movement's leaders had only just returned from decades of exile. Commitment to the cause had sustained them during long years abroad. Finally back home, they were jealous guardians of the ANC's ideological purity—"I assumed that all the returning ANC white exiles were communists," Greenberg said—who were not about to hand over their life's work to an American interloper.

ANC veterans had moral authority, but the campaign's organizational muscle was provided by COSATU. To Greenberg, the strength of labor made for a notable contrast with the United States, where his time in Democratic politics had accustomed him to "check-the-box meeting with unions that lack the energy to organize anybody." COSATU's 800,000 members gave the group an imposing presence within the campaign. They, too, worried about the ANC betraying its socialist principles. But they also wanted to win. One high-ranking official in COSATU had even made a pilgrimage to Arkansas during the 1992 campaign to study the Clinton operation in person.

Then there were the pollsters the ANC had already hired—three groups in all, including a team headed by one of Greenberg's former graduate students at Yale. They were natural partners for Greenberg, and what they found was troubling. The ANC was struggling to crack 50 percent of the vote nationally and was in danger of losing the country's major urban areas. Even more alarming, disappointment with life after apartheid was bleeding into perceptions of the ANC, which many South Africans were already coming to see as a cloistered elite cut off from everyday life.

Although coming from the outside had its drawbacks, it allowed Greenberg to play the role of neutral observer rising above the campaign's rival factions. He used that position to make the case for tailoring Mandela's message to fit what he was seeing in the research on public opinion. It was the South African version of a battle he was used to fighting in the United States, with the ANC leadership taking the place of a well-intentioned but out-of-touch Democratic establishment.

Inside the campaign, the battle crystallized itself in a debate over slogans. The ANC had settled on "Now Is the Time," a favorite chant with activists, including Mandela. It was a declaration of victory in battle against white supremacy that framed the election as the culmination of a liberation movement decades in the making.

Greenberg hated it. "I want you to consider," he told a meeting of key campaign staffers, "that the phrase means exactly what it says: 'Africans are going to seize power after years of powerlessness.'" That didn't offer much to coloured and South Asian voters, let alone whites, and it even left many Black South Africans feeling cold. They were anxious about the future, and the ANC was looking backward. Whatever hopes for revolution were harbored by the ANC's ideological vanguard would have to take second place to addressing the more immediate challenge facing a country where violence was rising and the poverty rate among Blacks topped 50 percent.

"Apartheid," Greenberg insisted, "is a trap." He recognized, of course, that apartheid had been the central fact of South African life for decades, and that its legacy pervaded the country—which was only to be expected for a system that was still in the process of being torn down. But running to vindicate the rights of

Blacks after centuries of oppression would draw the ANC back into the past, allowing the NP to monopolize the subjects that were on the top of voters' minds: unemployment, crime, education, housing, electricity, the water supply.

"This election is about making life better for people," Greenberg said, "not theoretical or abstract things." And even in South Africa in 1994, a reckoning over apartheid counted as an "abstract thing."

In place of "Now Is the Time," Greenberg nominated "A Better Life for All." The phrasing was borrowed from a cliché one of his colleagues had used in a US Senate campaign. It had the pre-chewed feeling of a slogan born out of focus groups—which, of course, it was. But what mattered to Greenberg was that, in South Africa, the focus groups *loved* it. "'Now Is the Time' was okay but did not light up the room," he recalled. "A Better Life for All," by contrast, "lifted the spirits in the room. It was as if someone gave them permission to hope for something better."

Mandela went along, reluctantly, with Greenberg's suggestion. It was only his latest compromise on the way to power. The most important concession had already been made. It had, in fact, been the precondition for ending apartheid. Without either side explicitly acknowledging the arrangement, the NP had agreed to gamble on democratic elections, knowing that it would probably lose, in return for the ANC giving up on seizing wealth from an almost entirely white capitalist elite. In this negotiated surrender, whites would hand over the government so they could retain control of the economy.

The challenge for the ANC was to prove that they had chosen wisely. The party set out a simple standard in a campaign manifesto. The ANC's performance, like democracy itself, "must be measured by the quality of life of ordinary people." Mandela's team paired "A Better Life for All" with another slogan that made the promise more concrete: "Jobs, jobs, jobs." (Plus a loftier counterpart, "Jobs, peace, and freedom.") The campaign manifesto promised to cut taxes for the poor, build a million new homes, expand access to electricity and clean water for millions more, establish universal health care for children under five—and to create 2.5 million new jobs (jobs, jobs). Instead of reaching for historical significance, the pledges brought the campaign down to earth, where voters could see how it might change their lives.

Mandela did not act as if the NP had emerged from decades of enforced racial domination with clean hands, but he did pick his battles. When he attacked de Klerk, it was for continuing to discriminate against Blacks in the present, not for crimes of the past. Mandela accused the government of looking the other way while ANC supporters were being murdered by the hundreds, but the campaign ran advertisements saying that all South Africans, including the ANC, had a responsibility to end the violence. The promise took on extra significance one month before the election, when nineteen Zulu protesters were shot down by security guards at ANC headquarters.

The violence kept going into the election. On the last day of campaigning, a 150-pound car bomb set by white terrorists exploded in downtown Johannesburg. The blast killed nine people and injured almost a hundred, tearing open a waist-deep crater just outside the offices of the ANC. A second bomb exploded at a taxi stand later the same day, followed by another outside Jan Smuts Airport on the first of the four days set aside for voting. After voting began, the Mandela team kept track of incoming stories about ANC staffers being driven out of polling sites in the mostly Zulu province of KwaZulu-Natal. "The reports," Greenberg said, "read more like appeals to the world by prisoners behind enemy lines."

But the votes were eventually counted—at least most of them—and when the returns came in, the Mandela team was ready to celebrate. The ANC dominated with 62.5 percent of the vote, just ahead of the campaign's internal goal of 60 percent, and more than 40 points ahead of the NP.

To nobody's surprise, the parties were sharply divided by race. If only whites had been allowed to vote, the NP would have won in a landslide, and the ANC would have been an asterisk, with less than 2 percent of the white vote. But under the new rules, almost three-quarters of the electorate was Black, and over 80 percent cast a ballot for Mandela. The ANC also made inroads with coloured and South Asian voters, carrying almost 30 percent of both groups. And despite the chaos in the run-up to the election, turnout was stratospheric, almost hitting 90 percent.

What stuck with Greenberg, though, were his memories of watching focus groups with undecided voters before the election. His record in the United States prepared him for a dour experience. People who stay on the fence late into a campaign typically do so because they don't pay much attention to politics, and in South Africa most of the participants in the discussion would not even know how to read. Yet Greenberg came away deeply impressed by what he saw. "Nowhere else do people read the material world so accurately, and in such a nuanced way," he later said.

South Africans knew what the ANC was promising, and they wanted to believe Mandela could deliver it—jobs, peace, and freedom, along with drinkable water and a functioning toilet. "Elites ought to be compelled to listen to these people," Greenberg told himself, "so they could learn some of their wisdom."

What held the group back wasn't opposition to Mandela, or his platform. They wanted a better life for all, but they didn't know if the ANC could deliver, and they were afraid of being disappointed. Which was, indeed, wise.

Fight Back

The inauguration of South Africa's first Black president was a global event, with a guest list that included Bill Clinton, Fidel Castro, and almost sixty other heads of state. "The time to build is upon us," Mandela declared shortly before fighter jets soared overhead with the colors of the country's new flag—black, red, green, gold, and blue—trailing in their wake. It was a stunning display, and a tribute to Mandela, the former leader of the ANC's guerrilla army turned commander-in-chief of the South African military.

But after the foreign dignitaries flew home and the jets returned to ground, the new government was left to confront the same structural challenges that helped bring down the NP, including widespread poverty, a shrinking economy, and a ballooning deficit.

Mandela left most of the daily work of governing to others. He would be eighty by the end of his term, and he had no intention of running for a second. His achievements were substantial but chiefly symbolic. Mandela's job was, mostly, to be Mandela, living testimony to the possibility of national reconciliation.

The task of implementing the ANC's platform fell to Mandela's second-in-command, Thabo Mbeki. Although Mbeki's title was deputy president, he was closer to a de facto prime

minister. It was a remarkable ascent for Mbeki, a veteran of the
apartheid resistance who had spent most of his life abroad. He
had left South Africa in 1962 shortly after the ANC was driven
underground and spent almost thirty years in exile until the ban
on the group was lifted in 1990.

During his travels, Mbeki became a kind of roving ambassador for the ANC, picking up a master's degree in economics
from the University of Sussex and developing a reputation as an
intellectual. He was also a former member of the South African
Communist Party who, after graduating from Sussex, enrolled
at the Lenin Institute in Soviet Moscow.

Mbeki's leftist credentials made what happened next even
more surprising. After two years in power, with the deficit still
rising and inflation rates climbing above 8 percent, he announced
a pivot toward austerity—lowering the deficit, tightening monetary policy, reducing tariffs, and privatizing state-owned enter-
prises. Mbeki said that the measures were a precondition for
raising growth rates over the long run, and he framed the program in radical terms, describing it as an effort to rescue South
Africa from a default that would hand the government over to
the IMF. But it was also, undeniably, a retreat from the ANC's
promises in 1994.

The results were muddled. Although the deficit and inflation
both fell, unemployment rose, and the economy grew at an anemic rate of 0.5 percent in 1998. Resistance from the left stopped
Mbeki from pushing through the entire package, and the ANC
did not abandon its campaign agenda wholesale. Thousands of
new homes were built, and millions of people had clean water
and electricity for the first time. Meanwhile, a concerted effort
to create an African economic elite led to an increasing number

of Black businessmen and professionals, along with greater representation on corporate boards—a move that could be seen as either a triumph for a more equitable capitalism, or as a step toward creating an African bourgeoisie that would eventually midwife the transition to socialism.

When Greenberg returned to South Africa in 1998 to help plan the ANC's next campaign, this time with Mbeki as its leader, he didn't encounter many people mourning the government's failure to institute socialism, but he did find a pervasive dissatisfaction with the ANC. Support for the party was threatening to dip below 50 percent, and its approval ratings among coloureds and South Asians had collapsed. The ANC's own polls showed that 80 percent of voters believed unemployment was getting worse, and 70 percent said the same thing about crime.

The transcripts from the focus groups were even uglier. Voters concentrated their anger on the ANC, saying that party leaders had shut themselves off from ordinary South Africans. "They have forgotten us—the very people who have elected them," a Johannesburg resident complained. "The best thing is for me not to vote at all, because they are getting richer and I am poorer," another said. "When it rains, I don't know where to go because I do not have a house."

Disillusionment with the ANC raised the possibility—remote, but not unthinkable—that a viable opposition party could emerge. The NP was a nonstarter. Despite placing second in the election, the party went into free fall after the campaign, its first defeat since 1948. The NP's breakdown cleared the way for white voters to consolidate behind a party that wasn't burdened with the legacy of apartheid.

That's where the Democratic Party saw its chance. The DP
came out of the chief liberal party under apartheid, with "liberal" here meaning support for a modest welfare state, cautious market regulations, and racial equality—a voice for whites who opposed apartheid but worked inside the system to end it. In 1994, that legacy earned the DP a whopping 1.7 percent of the vote. The question they confronted under Mandela was how to bring in NP supporters without betraying their liberal principles. It was a delicate task, and for help the party turned to a political operative with years of experience handling questions like this.

Doug Schoen's name came to the DP through R. W. Johnson, one of the party's leading intellectuals, and, as it happened, Schoen's supervisor at Oxford. (Johnson had grown up in South Africa and returned to the country in 1995.) Schoen urged the DP to make itself a home for all of the ANC's opponents. His approach was captured by the slogan he recommended for the campaign: "Fight Back." To liberals, it could be a fight against corruption and misgovernment. To whites who had not yet recovered from the end of apartheid, it could be a fight against Black political domination.

According to Schoen, "Fight Back" was just good politics. He had learned a long time ago that everyone was looking for their piece of the pie. It was natural that whites, along with coloureds and South Asians, would doubt that the ANC was governing with their interests in mind. And if South Africa was going to avoid becoming a one-party state, it needed an opposition movement with a broad base in the electorate. Coming off an election where fewer than one in fifty voters had cast a ballot in their favor, the DP could not afford to be choosy.

Mbeki's team had a different view. "We understood it then as pandering to racism," said Melissa Levin, a pollster who was known within the campaign as "little Stan Greenberg." Thanks to the DP, she said, "a new language of racism had emerged disguised in terms palatable to liberal democracy." In response to the ubiquitous "Fight Back" posters, the ANC put up its own posters saying, "Don't Fight Black."

Which is exactly what Schoen wanted. The ANC's pushback drew further attention to the campaign's message. It ratified the DP's position as the chief alternative to the status quo and allowed the party to cast itself as a consistent opponent of racial preferences before and after apartheid. In the run-up to the vote, a national poll reported that a plurality of whites believed the DP cared about people like them. Only 4 percent said the same about the ANC.

The good news for Mbeki was that in the same poll just 1 percent of Blacks said the DP was on their side. There was no danger of the ANC losing. But inside the campaign, Greenberg warned that public disillusionment with the ANC could lead to "a racially polarized and dispiriting election." It was crucial for the party's legitimacy, he argued, to maintain respectable levels of support with coloured and South Asian voters. And even if Blacks wouldn't defect to the DP, they might stay home—a political setback that would also render a moral judgment on the ANC. "There is poignancy," Greenberg said, "in the perception of a government that does little about poverty and starvation, but is at the same time wasting money, driving in fancy cars, and 'no longer live here.'"

In the end, the ANC got what it needed from the campaign. GDP growth ticked upward in 1999, and surveys showed increasing satisfaction with the government's record on schools, housing, and health care—good enough for Mbeki to claim that progress was being made, even if there was a long way to go. The ANC came out of the election with 66 percent of the vote, even better than in 1994. Turnout beat the already stratospheric levels of the first campaign, almost reaching 90 percent. Although the party lost ground with coloured and South Asian voters, and its performance with whites continued to be abysmal, it more than compensated by increasing its margin with Blacks. In an even more racially polarized electorate, the ANC had a tight grip on the only demographic with the numbers to make a majority.

But the DP also had a story to tell. The party came in a distant but clear second, quintupling its share of the vote to 9.6 percent. Its gains came at the expense of the NP—now going under the name "New National Party"—which fell to a distant fourth place. The DP was nowhere close to taking power, but as the official opposition party it had a license to make trouble for the ANC. And there would be plenty of opportunities to use it.

Until Jesus Comes

It's hard to imagine a graduate of the Lenin Institute benefiting more from global capitalism than Thabo Mbeki. Fueled by an international commodity boom, the economic recovery that began under Mandela roared ahead on Mbeki's watch. Inflation plummeted, unemployment drifted steadily downward, and the budget deficit turned into a tidy surplus. The sunny fiscal picture allowed the government to shift away from austerity. By 2006, over 70 percent of households had running water, and more than 80 percent had electricity. Basic education was free and 90 percent of children were in school. Poverty was falling thanks to generous welfare payments that raised incomes for the elderly, parents, and the disabled.

Mbeki said that South Africa was leading a continental renaissance, and the ANC claimed vindication in the battle to deliver a better life for all. The argument was plausible enough for the party to post its best numbers to date with non-Black voters when Mbeki ran for a second term in 2004, driving racial polarization to historic lows.

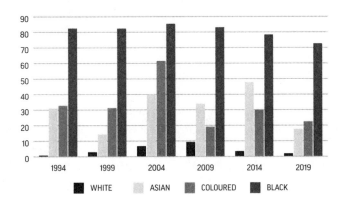

Support for ANC by Race, 1994—2019

Then the boom came to an abrupt halt. With the global economy reeling from the financial crisis, a painful recession hit South Africa in 2009. Although the overall growth rate bounced back the next year, it never returned to pre-crash levels, and per capita GDP went into a decade-long decline. Unemployment retook its place as the central question in South African politics, and income inequality resumed its upward march.

Economic stagnation is the problem that makes everything else worse, like a heat wave raising the temperature on every social controversy. The most tragic was the AIDS epidemic. Mbeki's disastrous response—he questioned the link between HIV and AIDS while blocking the use of lifesaving drugs—led to over 300,000 premature deaths and shaved nine years off the average lifespan. Corruption siphoned off billions that was meant to be spent on public works projects, which were routinely interrupted by a "construction mafia" intent on grabbing its share of the funds. Unable to keep up with needed repairs, the country's infrastructure decayed. After years of expanding access to electricity, rolling blackouts became the norm—which further lowered GDP, exacerbating every other problem in turn. By 2013, South Africans had less trust in parliament, police, and the courts than under apartheid.

This slow-rolling structural breakdown was punctuated by outbreaks of brutal violence. In 2012, almost three dozen striking mineworkers in the town of Marikana were killed by police, the bloodiest use of state power since apartheid. Labor conflicts, though, were a less persistent source of tension than immigration. South Africa's economy was struggling, but it was still one of the wealthiest economies on the continent, and therefore a magnet for workers. Already in 2008, a wave of riots targeting migrants from Zimbabwe caused over sixty deaths and drove thousands more to seek refuge in churches and police stations. And that was before the immigrant population doubled over the next decade. By 2019, according to a Pew Research poll, over 60 percent of South Africans viewed the new arrivals as a burden on the country, blaming them

190   for taking jobs, raising crime rates, and increasing the risk of terrorism.

Although the ANC retained its majority, the party was able to shuffle discredited leaders out of power. Mbeki's bid for a third term was derailed by Jacob Zuma. Unlike the polished Mbeki, who often seemed to be auditioning for the role of philosopher-king—and amateur epidemiologist—Zuma was a charismatic populist. He was a natural campaigner with a platform that reached out to the left and right simultaneously, endorsing both prayer in schools and land expropriation.

Even before the election, a confident Zuma predicted that the ANC would hold power "until Jesus comes." Zuma's bond with his supporters was strong enough for him to weather indictments for racketeering, fraud, and money laundering. He had already been acquitted of rape in a 2006 trial, where he said that after having sex with an HIV-positive woman he took a shower to minimize the chance of infection.

With Zuma at the head of the party, the ANC racked up almost two-thirds of the vote in the 2009 campaign, making Zuma into South Africa's latest Black president, and its first with multiple wives. (He came into office with three, and added a fourth in 2012.)

Elites scoffed, but they continued to benefit the most from ANC rule. While Zuma railed against "white monopoly capital," the gap between the rich and the poor continued to widen. The upper echelons of the business and financial community were slowly diversifying, but the rewards did not trickle down to the wider population. Through it all, the ANC could still count on support from the organizations that had long represented the South African left, including COSATU and the Communist Party.

By the time Zuma was forced to resign in 2018—the corruption charges finally caught up with him—polls showed that two-thirds of South Africans were unhappy with the state of their democracy. Almost as many, including a majority of Blacks, said that the average person's economic condition was either worse off than under Mandela or unchanged. Approval for the ANC had collapsed among coloured, South Asian, and white voters. The party retained its hold on the loyalties of Blacks, but even there a stark decline in turnout hinted at growing disaffection. Participation among Blacks fell from the astonishing 87 percent reached in Mandela's campaign to just over 50 percent in 2014. The abstention rate was almost three times higher than for whites, and nine times higher than for coloureds. The ANC's electoral base wasn't ready to abandon the party en masse, but it was having a tougher time ginning up the energy to trudge to the polls.

Signs of weakness for the ANC coincided with a period of increasing strength for its main opponent. After the DP changed its name in 2003 to the Democratic Alliance, the rebranded party gained ground in each succeeding election, climbing to 22.3 percent in 2014. The DA's growth was driven by a combination of near unanimous backing from whites and growing support from coloureds and South Asians. What held the party back from becoming a true competitor with the ANC was its dreadful performance with Blacks, where its support remained stuck in the single digits.

The DA set out to change that dynamic in earnest after 2014. In its rise, the party focused on consolidating the non-Black vote. Now, it aimed to break inside the ANC's base—and finally

transcend the color line that ran through South African politics. The DA nominated its first Black leader, Mmusi Maimane, a
thirty-five-year-old pastor who made his reputation with a fiery
speech describing Zuma as "a broken man presiding over a broken
society." To help shape the party's new message, Maimane's team
recruited an international cadre of political consultants, mostly
from the center-right, with one notable exception.

Stan Greenberg had steered clear of South African politics
for more than a decade after working on Mbeki's first campaign.
When the DA announced that Mandela's celebrity American
pollster had defected, howls went up from the ANC. "My Little
Stan Greenberg heart broke," said his former deputy Melissa
Levin. But to Greenberg, the ANC's record in office was all the
explanation he needed.

Greenberg was accustomed to urging once-dominant parties to show that they had changed by making a public break
with the left wing of their coalitions: Bill Clinton's Sister Souljah
moment, Tony Blair renouncing state ownership of the means of
production, Ehud Barak apologizing for Labour's treatment of the
Mizrahim. The DA's challenges were different. Instead of winning
back lost voters, it had to bring an entirely new group on board.
But Greenberg believed that turning Maimane into the party's
face gave the DA a chance to prove that a new sheriff was in town.

The details of Maimane's strategy would have come as a surprise to Democratic insiders who associated Greenberg with
marginalizing the activist left to appease blue-collar whites
stewing over racial grievances. In South Africa, frustrated Blacks
were the main target, and Greenberg urged Maimane to punch
right. "Greenberg said we were never going to make a breakthrough among Black voters unless there is a disruptive moment,"

complained one member of the DA old guard. Former party leader Helen Zille was more pointed. "Stan Greenberg," she said, "tried to turn the DA 'woke.'"

Voters didn't buy it. The ANC did leave the 2019 election in a weaker position. The party's share of the vote dipped below 60 percent, its worst performance to date, and participation rates dropped to their lowest levels since the end of apartheid. But support for the DA slumped, too, marking the first time it lost ground in a general election since beginning its upward ascent in 1994.

Maimane's outreach made close to zero difference with Blacks, who continued to view the DA with suspicion—Zille's Twitter account was a recurring source of tension—while costing the party with its base. Turnout among whites tumbled by almost 10 percentage points, and a good number of those who showed up cast a ballot for the rightwing Freedom Front Plus Party, which trumpeted its opposition to affirmative action and land expropriation. Although FF+ was a sideshow in the election, with just 2.4 percent of the vote, it experienced the largest percentage rise of any party, and its gains came out of the DA's hide. FF+ leader Pieter Groenewald credited the improvement to the party's slogan, which he said came to him on a drive to the airport: "Fight Back South Africa."

Instead of a new majority taking shape around a transformed consensus, the two parties of the establishment—the ANC and the DA—were outflanked by populist rivals pushing from the extremes, breaking the electorate into a proliferating array of microfactions. In the DA's case, FF+ was the main culprit. For the ANC, it was the leftwing Economic Freedom Fighters. Led by a former president of the ANC Youth League, the EFF won

10.8 percent of the vote after running on a platform that combined ethno-nationalism with tributes to Marx and Lenin.

And still the ANC remained on top. In the twenty-five years since Mandela's first campaign, the underlying framework of South African politics maintained an eerie stability. The ANC's vote had stayed within a narrow band, never rising above 70 percent, and bottoming out in 2019 with 57.5 percent. The DA replaced the NP as the main white opposition party, but their combined share of the electorate was almost exactly the same: 20.4 percent for the NP in 1994, 20.8 percent for the DA in 2019.

You can see the continuity in this graph of election results in South Africa since 1994, where the DA and NP votes are merged together.

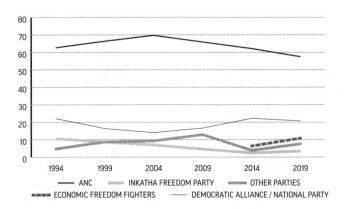

With the ANC slowly losing legitimacy, and no viable alternative ready to emerge, South Africans confronted a distinctive kind of democratic breakdown. The basic structural features were familiar: mounting inequality, collapsing infrastructure, rising social disorder. But here they were presided over by a government that owed its power to the poor and working class. The ANC hasn't delivered a better life for all, but it had created a more racially diverse elite that could buy its way out of the problems facing the rest of society—private schools for their children, hired guards for their neighborhoods, personal generators for their homes. Those who can't afford a ticket to this country within a country face a grimmer calculus. As an immigrant from Zimbabwe explained, if South Africa failed, "The whites will all leave but the Blacks will all die."

Time is the greatest threat to the ANC today. It's the same problem that the Labor Party in Israel encountered in the 1970s. Successful liberation movements often turn into their country's dominant political party, but hegemony comes with an expiration date. The average age in South Africa is twenty-eight, meaning that most people in the country were born after the end of apartheid. They come into politics with a different set of concerns, and without the loyalties of their elders. "They're just showing up Mandela's face again," a twenty-two-year-old researcher in Johannesburg complained in 2023. "Maybe the old people are still buying it, but we're not."

In Israel, Labor's first major defeat took place after twenty-nine years in power. In South Africa, the ANC lasted for thirty, coming up short of a majority for the first time in the 2024 elections, when a spoiler campaign from Zuma drove the ANC down to 40.2 percent of the vote—still a plurality but low enough to require an unprecedented national unity government. The second-place DA became the ANC's chief partner in a coalition that included eleven total parties. But the DA broke into office because of the

ANC's weakness, not its own strength. With 21.8 percent of the vote, the party actually did worse than in 2019. All of which underlined the central dilemma: the ANC might be losing its grip on power, but no coherent majority was ready to take its place.

It was difficult to see this problem resolving itself anytime soon. Black voters were leaving the ANC, but most came from the upper and middle class—ironically, the greatest beneficiaries of ANC rule. In 1994, the highest-earning 10 percent of Black voters were 4 percentage points more likely to back the ANC than the bottom 90 percent. By 2019, they were 25 percentage points less likely to do so.

The ANC's strong performance with the poor and working class wasn't an inevitable product of the laws of political physics. In Israel, the revolt against Labor turned into a majority movement when the Mizrahi underclass bolted to Likud. To millions of people who counted on government payments to make ends meet, the ANC was a line of defense against an even worse outcome. In harsh economic conditions, the assistance became still more precious, especially when the main opposition party could not shed its reputation as a defender of white interests. "We want money and we want jobs," a Soweto woman said. "That's why we go for the ANC."

With the prospect of a better life for all slipping out of reach, the country that had commanded the world's attention during the battle against apartheid fell out of the spotlight. Occasionally, stories would break into foreign media—riots following the imprisonment of Zuma that resulted in 354 deaths and billions of dollars in property damage; an outgoing power utility executive who claimed to have been poisoned with cyanide in his coffee as blackouts climbed to record highs. But these were short-lived exceptions to the rule of indifference, and the rest of the world quickly moved on.

So did Stan Greenberg. In another life, he might have wound up spending his career on South Africa. In this one, he said that the battle against apartheid was fundamental to everything in his work. But after Maimane's disappointing performance in 2019, the DA old guard reclaimed its influence, and Greenberg's advice was no longer welcome.

There wasn't anything more for Greenberg to do—at least, nothing that he could think of. When he was asked in the summer of 2023 about his views on the country, he said that he had stopped following the news.

Conclusion

Not long into the Biden administration, a debate broke out in Democratic circles over how to win elections. It wasn't an issue that progressives had expected to worry about. They had spent the Trump years focused on the problem of minority rule—an Electoral College that kept putting the loser of the popular vote in the White House; a Supreme Court moving swiftly to the right; a Senate biased in favor of sparsely populated, rural states; and a Republican campaign to tighten restrictions on voting. Conservatives were supposed to be mounting a last stand against demographic change, while progressives were tearing down barriers that stood in the way of a rising multiracial majority.

In 2020, the story took a surprising turn. The Democratic margin was close enough that victory felt weirdly like defeat—a squeaker for Joe Biden in the Electoral College, plus a fifty-fifty split in the Senate, and a thirteen-seat loss in the House. Turnout surged to the highest levels in over a century, but that included millions of new Republican voters. When all the ballots were counted, Joe Biden emerged with 51.3 percent of the vote. Eight years earlier, Barack Obama had received 51.1 percent. Instead of a realignment, Democrats had to settle for yet again scratching out a victory at the margins.

Just under the surface, however, dramatic changes were taking place. After years of being denounced as a white supremacist, Donald Trump posted significant gains with Hispanic voters and slightly improved his performance with African Americans. The only racial demographic where Trump lost ground was among whites, where his share of the two-party vote was lower than any Republican since John McCain was steamrolled by the financial crisis in 2008.

In the less racially polarized electorate of 2020, Biden's most significant gains came from white college graduates. Even during the Obama years, the education gap had been close to a nonfactor in national politics. In 2012, Democrats did just 1 point worse among voters without a college degree. By 2020, that had turned into a 12-point deficit. There had been a Democratic realignment, but it had only taken place among BA-holders, where the party won 59 percent of the vote—12 points better than its performance with non-college graduates.

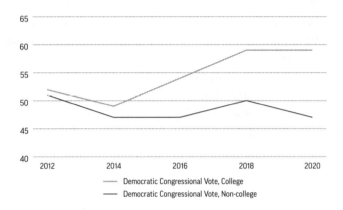

Democrats went into election night ready to slam the door shut on Trumpism. They left it confronting a Republican Party that was more racially diverse, a Democratic Party that was more affluent, and a country that was almost evenly split between the two. Combined, it raised the possibility that the true challenge for democracy wasn't minority rule imposed by the right. It was an electorate that Democrats didn't understand as well as they thought.

An early and influential explanation for the party's underwhelming performance came from David Shor, a Democratic data guru and former Obama campaign whiz kid. According to Shor, Democrats were losing ground because the views of party insiders—politicians, staffers, activists—were out of step with public opinion. Shor's solution was for Democrats to tread carefully on issues where most voters leaned to the center or right (typically connected to the subjects grouped under the heading "culture war") and emphasize their most popular positions (often focused on economics, but also including abortion rights after the demise of *Roe v. Wade*).

Center-left journalist Matthew Yglesias dubbed the approach "popularism," and it briefly became one of the most controversial topics in Democratic politics. Critics accused Shor of telling Democrats to cave into bigotry, supporters said that progressives were refusing to face up to the realities of public opinion, and both sides charged the other with manipulating the data.

The controversy was so bitter because it cut to the core of how Democrats imagined themselves. No question was more painful to contemplate than what the gentrification of the Democratic coalition meant for the party of Franklin Roosevelt. Because education and class are tightly linked, Democrats have found themselves representing most of the wealthiest districts in the country, while Republicans dominate in districts below the median income.

Marcy Kaptur, a congresswoman from Ohio, and one of just 71 Democrats in the House elected from a district with an income beneath the national average—compared to 152 for Republicans—put the dilemma in stark terms. "How is it possible that Republicans are representing the majority of people who struggle? How is that possible?"

If this book has done its job, you'll have a good sense of the answer by now. But before wrapping up the story, it's worth taking another look at the big picture.

The best place to start is by recognizing that Democrats have company. The transformation of the left is an international phenomenon, and compared to many of their counterparts abroad—just think about Israel—Democrats have weathered the

202   transformation well. But there are plenty of countries that don't fit neatly within this pattern, and even among those that do there is still considerable room for variation.

In the United States, the reshuffling of the electorate began more than fifty years ago. By the time Richard Nixon was sworn into the presidency, cultural polarization had already broken the New Deal coalition, and the climate has only become friendlier to polarizers over the decades. Rising education levels have created an electorate that is more likely to search for ideological consistency. Partisan media has shredded the monoculture of the postwar era. Small-time donors who get riled up by what they see on cable news have become the key to building a campaign war chest. Even incumbents in safe seats live in fear of angering primary voters whose priorities diverge sharply from the general electorate. State and local party machines have atrophied. They have largely been replaced by a permanent political class based in Washington, DC, funded by a tiny number of high-rolling donors, and employed by an overlapping network of foundations, think tanks, and activist groups—what you might call a swamp.

At the same time, the evisceration of organized labor has gutted the institution most responsible for linking blue-collar voters to Democrats. As union influence dwindled, the Fortune 500 wing of the Democratic Party gained in stature. Absent the counterweight supplied by a vigorous labor movement, it was easy for policymakers to defer to the will of the market, as interpreted by whichever Goldman Sachs alum happened to be in the room at the time. This shifting balance of power led to policies that lowered deficits, loosened regulations, and reduced trade barriers—until the Great Recession spurred a revolt against a rigged economy and the politicians who made it.

Polarization has made finding a stable partisan home easier for both progressives and conservatives. But as the distance between Republicans and Democrats widened, support for both parties nosedived. As voters braced for the 2024 campaign, almost half of the country described itself as independent, the highest in polling history. Most Americans considered both sides too extreme, and almost two-thirds said that just thinking about politics was exhausting.

Looking at the results of polarized politics over the long run—a country that is both more progressive on social issues and more economically divided—it's clear that the main beneficiaries are the comparatively small number of voters who lean to the right on economics and to the left on culture. The greatest losers are the much more sizable group of economically progressive and socially conservative (or even just moderate) voters who don't have a place in either party and have landed on the wrong side of the two most important changes in American life over the last half century. A politics split between almost evenly matched red and blue teams has delivered its biggest victories to white-collar neoliberals while fostering a deep-seated cynicism among working-class populists, who get the least from the system even though their votes regularly decide elections. This anger has taken a toll on both parties, but one side has paid the greatest price. "The Democrats are more dangerous because they act like they're for you—like they're for the working people," a retired steelworker told researchers from Harvard. "But they're not."

Most historical changes worth studying aren't the product of a single overriding cause, and the remaking of the left is no exception. Some of the factors that have reshuffled party coalitions in the United States can be found abroad, but others can't.

204   The two-party system, for instance, is often blamed for driving workers away from Democrats by turning campaigns into a zero-sum contest over divisive social issues. But polarization is even more intense in Israel, where dozens of parties regularly compete for power.

Even though each country's experience is distinctive, a common thread runs through this larger history. No matter the time or place, the most important question in politics is always the same: Whose side are you on? Like other parties on the left around the world, Democrats used to have a simple answer. They were defenders of working people. The choice was clear, and voters sorted themselves accordingly.

Today, Democrats are closer an alliance between professionals and the poor, with the balance of power weighted toward the top. These voters are disproportionately white and well-educated, with social views to the left of the wider electorate, an inconsistent record on populist economics, and a tendency to view politics as a crusade against the forces of darkness. Although they are still far from a majority, the political system gives them—along with the politicians they love, the media they consume, and the nonprofits they fund—an outsized voice. Which makes it even more difficult to imagine key members of the Democratic coalition accepting the compromises that could build a bottom-up majority committed above all to standing with workers.

And that, more or less, is why Republicans—like rightwing parties around much of the globe—now represent so many of the people who struggle.

But there's one part of this transformation that hasn't received the attention it deserves. That's the story I've tried to tell in this

book, the story of the battle that Democrats, along with parties
on the left around the world, fought against polarization in the
years between the early crisis for class-based voting in the 1960s
and the potential realignment of our time.

The key word in the last sentence is "battle." It's not a history of a speedy and inevitable backlash to the civil rights revolution of the 1960s, or about a Democratic elite that sometime
in the 1970s abandoned the working class in a bid to win over
white-collar professionals.

It's not, in other words, the story I expected to find when
I started researching this book, which happened to be around
the time that Democrats were taking sides in the debate over
populism. The shadow of Clintonian triangulation loomed
over the back-and-forth, but the description of Clinton's
strategy that I saw in the commentary was close to caricature,
treating the quest for soccer moms as the entirety of Clinton's
politics. The real strategy behind the Clinton campaign, the
decades of earlier arguments, and the way this dispute had
played out far beyond the United States might as well not
have existed.

That silence was striking because, with this earlier history in
mind, you can't help noticing how familiar the arguments from
the Biden era should have been. The particulars in Shor's analysis were new, but the basic assumptions were part of the founding brief for the DLC and of Tony Blair's case for New Labour, to
name two of its most important precursors.

Without understanding this background, it's impossible
to grasp the dilemma facing the left today. The breakdown of
economically polarized voting wasn't the result of a deliber-
ate strategy to court upscale votes at the expense of the left's

working-class base, at least not entirely. It was pushed forward at decisive moments by politicians trying to have it all, winning back workers at the same time they courted white-collar suburbanites—and then laying the groundwork for a populist backlash by failing to deliver on their promises.

Yet the simplified version of this history—the one with clueless neoliberals tutting over deplorables while their majorities crumbled—didn't come out of nowhere. Even if the origins of the left's troubles were complex, key players in the story were looking more and more like the caricatures their critics drew for them.

Consider, for instance, Doug Schoen and Mark Penn. Schoen spent the early part of 2020 working as a pollster for Mike Bloomberg's presidential run, where his advice helped net Bloomberg a princely 6.9 percent of the national vote after spending almost $1 billion on the campaign. After Bloomberg's implosion, Schoen resumed his role as a recurring character in the Murdoch extended universe, assuring Fox News viewers that Democrats were making a grave mistake by veering to the left.

Penn, too, had become a regular face on the network. He began making appearances during the Trump administration, when he described the impeachment push as a witch hunt and met privately with the president in the Oval Office. In the run-up to the 2024 campaign, rumors circulated in Washington that Penn was masterminding a third-party presidential bid that would sink Biden's chance at reelection. Although Penn denied the reports, the controversy provided more evidence that he was not going to be welcomed back into mainstream Democratic circles anytime soon. (Not that his views were altogether absent. In Congress, Josh Gottheimer—a Penn protégé, Democratic representative from suburban New Jersey, and co-chair of the centrist

Problem Solvers Caucus—ensured that business-friendly moderation would have a champion in the party.)

Schoen and Penn had lost the Clinton wars, but their old nemesis didn't feel like a winner. Now in his seventies, Stan Greenberg feared that the goal he had given his life to was slipping even further away. Although his assessment of Trump was brutal—he said the candidate's rallies "sounded more like a 'race war' than a conventional campaign"—the pollster had developed a grudging respect for Trump's dedication to winning blue-collar votes. He still believed that Democrats could forge an updated version of the RFK coalition that he had glimpsed while sifting through primary returns back in 1968, a bottom-up majority dominated by working people. But turning the class project into an electoral reality demanded a total commitment that he thought was conspicuously absent inside the Democratic establishment.

Greenberg's pessimism had been building for some time. One of the best explanations for the problems confronting Democrats in the Biden administration came from a memoir that Greenberg had finished just as the Obama era was getting underway. Near the end of the book, which came and went without much notice in 2009, Greenberg paused to take stock of a pattern that he had noticed in his work.

Time and again, Greenberg helped candidates on the center-left win by running on a broadly populist platform. Then he watched those same clients take a neoliberal turn when the polls were closed. "After every one of these elections, these big, sometimes historic, leaders had a 'come-to-Jesus' meeting with the principal managers of the economy," he said. "Without even being in the meeting, I knew the content: 'That was all well and good for the campaign, but you need to understand that

208   the economy is at great risk, deficits are out of control, invest-
        ment will not be forthcoming, austerity and fiscal balance has
        to be your first priority.'" The people had spoken at the ballot
        box, and now they were expected to sit quietly while the adults
        got to work.

        Then came what Greenberg described as the inevitable next
        step. Even if economic growth picked up over the long run, the
        gap between the many and the few continued to widen. Defensive
        politicians turned into apologists for the status quo, asserting in
        public that things were getting better, then grumbling in private
        about ungrateful voters. Rather than take on economic power-
        brokers, center-left governments focused on cultural battles they
        stood a better chance of winning. Disillusionment settled over
        voters, especially in the working class. Frustration might curdle
        into apathy, which showed itself in plunging turnout. Or it could
        mutate into grievances that played into the hands of the right.

        The disjuncture between the populist campaigns and neo-
        liberal governments created the opening for a different kind of
        politics—the kind that for Greenberg was personified by Penn
        and Schoen. They were the consultants who told presidents and
        prime ministers not to worry about the compromises. Ideology
        was dead, and so was class warfare. Instead of a strategy for
        changing the country, they supplied tactics for surviving an elec-
        tion; rather than providing a coherent vision, they came up with
        a grab bag of issues that tested well.

        Pollsters said this was realism, but they were shaping real-
        ity, making politics smaller than it had to be. The main winners
        of this game were the wealthy and powerful people who liked
        the system just as it was, followed closely by the consultants.
        Liberated from the burden of a conscience, campaign experts

could flit across the globe, selling their services to whoever could
pay the bills.

"I have come to appreciate that in virtually all these countries that there are forces at play not always visible and direct, that work to preclude messages and strategies that highlight class, equity, or fairness," Greenberg wrote, "even when the survey tests well, [and] 'the facts' repeatedly take you to that message."

Maybe a different kind of leader could have brought the class project to fruition, but none of his clients came close. They could speak the language of class politics, but they rarely felt the music of it, and their real ambitions lay elsewhere. For Bill Clinton, son of the Jim Crow South, it was healing a nation scarred by centuries of racial oppression. For Tony Blair, it was making a Labour Party that welcomed upwardly mobile strivers like his father (and himself). For Ehud Barak, it was ushering the peace process to a successful resolution. For Nelson Mandela, it was moving South Africans beyond apartheid while the details of governing were largely sorted out by others. Whatever the merits of those projects, they weren't the same as Greenberg's. When the time came to decide which to put at the front of the line, the choice didn't take long.

The question on Greenberg's mind at the start of the Obama administration was whether Democrats could find a way out of this trap. Instead, he saw the promise of hope and change turn into a point-by-point replay of the old routine. Dreams for a second New Deal were replaced by a shift to deficit reduction after Democrats were trounced in the 2010 midterms. Next up was a grinding reelection campaign where Obama squeaked out a narrow victory after running as a defender of the middle class against Mitt Romney's vulture capitalism. In Obama's second

210 term, assurances that America was Already Great drowned out complaints about the lingering damage from the Great Recession, handing Donald Trump the makings of a campaign that pushed the country even closer to a full-blown realignment. Then, after Republicans lost by the slimmest of margins in 2020, Greenberg got to watch the next generation of Democratic operatives brood over the mystery of how the party had lost the working class.

Which raises an obvious question: What comes next?

Here, the prospect isn't quite as bleak as Greenberg's formula suggests. Although a cycle that recurs across decades in multiple continents can't just be a product of bad luck and individual mistakes, there is always room for contingency in politics. A world where Bill Clinton had never met Monica Lewinsky, Tony Blair had not hitched New Labour to the Iraq War, and Ehud Barak had not gambled his career on striking a bargain with Yasser Arafat might look quite different from the one we live in today. South Africa's ordeal is the result of a more comprehensive betrayal by the ANC, but even that failure can't be reduced to a simple story about the ravages of neoliberalism.

To some extent, Democrats have already broken out of the cycle that Greenberg identified. Although the party has struggled under Biden, its dismal poll numbers have more to do with the rising cost of living (fueled, in part, by over $2 trillion in new federal spending) than with a neoliberal pivot (which never arrived).

Looking ahead, it's important to recognize that conservatives face plenty of challenges, too. Populists on the right have been predicting the coming of a working-class majority for decades, only to see their realignment pushed back into the indefinite future. Although class conflict sells on the campaign trail, business and financial leaders rarely struggle to get a hearing from conservative politicians in office. The clash between rightwing elites and their own voters can be even fiercer that its analog on the left, and it has to be managed by increasingly populist parties that, unsurprisingly, tend to attract more than their fair share of bomb-throwers. With the percentage of college graduates in the electorate set to rise over the coming decades, the right is also betting on a demographic whose numbers are heading in the wrong direction.

There will, then, be opportunities for the left. The question is how they can be exploited. While there's no guaranteed formula, there are a few guiding principles. Everything starts from the premise that democracy is a machine for turning the views of ordinary people into government policy. Those views can change, especially over the long run, and determining the exact contours of public opinion will always take a mix of art and science. But it's possible to know what voters think, and those opinions are unlikely to shift much over the course of an election. The most effective candidates move within the limits set by the public. Those who don't run the risk of a speedy punishment from the electorate. And the refusal of both the left and right to take these lessons seriously—a refusal encouraged by the logic of polarization—has pushed democracy to the breaking point.

Democrats looking to turn those broad principles into a strategy for cobbling together 50.1 percent of the vote have a number of options. Candidates like Gretchen Whitmer in Michigan, Raphael Warnock in Georgia, and Mark Kelly in Arizona have shown that the standard Democratic playbook can, in the right circumstances, keep down the party's losses with blue-collar voters while driving up its numbers with the

212   educated and affluent. Kentucky Democrat Andy Beshear has made himself into one of the country's most popular governors, thanks in good measure to a genial presence and nonconfrontational style that could have come out of a memo from Penn and Schoen during the Reagan era. Meanwhile, John Fetterman proved in Pennsylvania that Democrats could make headway in Trump country—he beat Biden's performance in rural counties, at times by double digits—after running a populist campaign whose ads included a pledge to "make more sh*t in America," a line it's easy to imagine killing with Greenberg's focus groups in Macomb almost forty years earlier.

So Democrats can count on more than the occasional good election night. The problem is that piecemeal victories aren't enough for any of the party's disparate factions. Moderates say that rightwing extremism is putting the political system at risk, while the left calls for a fundamental overhaul of American life. But whether the goal is saving democracy or changing the country, neither side will come close to getting what it wants until Democrats forge a large and durable majority—the kind of majority that could force Republicans to move back toward the center or risk electoral oblivion, and that could push serious progressive reforms through Congress. And there's no way to build that majority without restoring the party's connection to a broad swathe of the working and middle class.

Recent studies of these voters have shown that a familiar set of tactics can get the job done. In surveys conducted by the left-leaning Center for Working Class Politics, voters without college degrees responded best to candidates with blue-collar backgrounds, populist economic messages, and platforms that prioritized kitchen table issues. Those conclusions were backed up in a lengthy report conducted by the nonprofit group American Family Voices, which found that voters in struggling Midwestern communities (still) viewed Republicans as the party of business, (still) thought that the system was rigged in favor of the wealthy, and (still) wanted politicians to take on the top 1 percent.

But if attacking the millionaires and billionaires was enough to win back the working class, Bernie Sanders would be sitting in the White House today planning his next summit with Prime Minister Jeremy Corbyn. The old formulation from the 1992 Clinton campaign still applies: voters want a candidate who will promote their interests *and* honor their values. That doesn't mean trying to roll the clock back to the stone age, but it does require finding a position on questions like crime and immigration that fits within the broad center of public opinion—a center whose death has been conveniently exaggerated by polarizers of the left and right.

Landing on the right message is just the beginning. Effective campaigns shape the public's view of a particular race. But realignments take place when perceptions change about an entire party. No single candidate can force that shift, especially when voters are primed to believe that politicians will say anything to get elected. It takes a movement with a consistent vision supported by candidates up and down the ballot who deliver on their promises after taking office. For the left, that means raising living standards in the short term while using the government to build worker power over the long run.

There's no denying that the odds against this project succeeding are long. The old class politics drew upon reservoirs of social solidarity that have long since run dry. Resurrecting it for our time demands a frontal assault on a polarized political system that has built up over decades, and it runs against the grain of a capitalist economic order that reaches back centuries. But it would create a country where ordinary Americans had more—a great deal more—say over their lives. Another name for that is democracy.

Don't you want to see what it looks like?

Left Adrift uses stories about specific people to make an argument about a larger historical change. If you've made it this far, then you know that the larger historical change in question is the transformation of the left around much of the world over the last half century or so. The clearest guide I've found to that subject is Amory Gethin, Clara Martínez-Toledano, and Thomas Piketty's edited volume, *Political Cleavages and Social Inequalities: A Study of Fifty Democracies, 1948–2020* (Cambridge: Harvard University Press, 2021). Maybe the best thing to be said about this remarkable piece of scholarship is that it delivers on the promise of its title. Drawing on detailed electoral surveys produced over decades, it uses rigorous statistical work to illuminate political shifts in dozens of countries, pointing out both common trends and deviations from the norm. Gethin, Martínez-Toledano, and Piketty then did all of us the additional favor of putting their data online in easily accessible form. The World Political Cleavages and Inequality Database, available at https://wpid.world, is an extraordinary resource, one of the best time sinks on the internet, and the source for most of the charts in this book.

Knowing how the left has changed over the years gave me a new appreciation for analysts who were perceptive enough to see it coming, starting with Ronald Inglehart. *The Silent Revolution: Changing Values and Political Styles Among Western Publics* (Princeton: Princeton University Press, 1977) didn't get everything right, but it was close enough to earn Inglehart the victory lap that he took with co-author Pippa Norris in *Cultural Backlash: Trump, Brexit, and Authoritarian Populism* (Cambridge:

Cambridge University Press, 2019). For retrospective summaries, see Russell Dalton's *Political Realignment: Economics, Culture, and Electoral Change* (Oxford: Oxford University Press, 2018) and Thomas Piketty, *Capital and Ideology* (Cambridge: Harvard University Press, 2020).

Although the shifts discussed in these works have enormous significance, they're not where this book got its start. That came when I picked up Stan Greenberg's memoir and found that I just couldn't put it down. *Dispatches from the War Room* (New York: St. Martin's Press, 2009) changed how I thought about the making of the modern Democratic Party, and it opened my eyes to an international history that I had not spent nearly enough time thinking about. It also led to me reading everything by Greenberg that I could get my hands on, starting with his early, explicitly radical academic work: *Politics and Poverty: Modernization and Response in Five Poor Neighborhoods* (New York: John Wiley and Sons, 1974) and *Race and State in Capitalist Development: Comparative Perspectives* (New Haven: Yale University Press, 1980).

There's more continuity than I would have guessed between Greenberg's early writing and the books published at the peak of his influence over Democratic politics—*Middle Class Dreams: The Politics and Power of the New American Majority* (New York: Times Books, 1995); *The New Majority: Toward a Popular Progressive Politics* (New Haven: Yale University Press, 1997), coedited with Theda Skocpol; and *The Two Americas: Our Current Political Deadlock and How to Break It* (New York: St. Martin's Press, 2004). You can get a sense of Greenberg's shifting views on the Democratic Party's future during the Obama and Trump years from the titles of two of his later works: *It's the Middle Class, Stupid!* (New York: Penguin Group, 2012), co-authored with James Carville, and *RIP GOP: How the New America Is Dooming the Republicans* (New York: St. Martin's Press, 2019). In the first book, Greenberg sounds the alarm for Democrats, warning that the party has veered dangerously off course and needs to redis-cover its populist roots pronto. (Sample chapter title: "The Elites Deplore Class Warfare, but What About the Voters?") Seven years later, with Donald Trump in the White House, it was Republicans who needed the course correction before they were steamrolled by a multicultural majority.

I was fascinated by Greenberg's trajectory, but I wasn't con-vinced there was a book here until I found Doug Schoen's story. His first memoir, *The Power of the Vote: Electing Presidents, Overthrowing Dictators, and Promoting Democracy Around the World* (New York: Harper, 2009), doesn't match Greenberg's for insight or candor, but it's much better than it needs to be, and it led me to his brilliant first book, *Enoch Powell and the Powellites* (New York: St. Martin's Press, 1977). Although none of the many books he went on to write would live up to this early standard, a consistent worldview runs through the best of them, including *Pat: A Biography of Daniel Patrick Moynihan* (New York: Harper & Row, 1979) and *The Nixon Effect: How Richard Nixon's Presidency Fundamentally Transformed American Politics* (New York: Encounter Books, 2016). His second memoir, *Power: The 50 Truths* (New York: Regan Arts, 2023), doesn't live up to its pre-decessor, but it rounds out his story (and in some cases repeats it). Also worth reading is Mark Penn's *Microtrends: The Small Forces Behind Tomorrow's Big Changes* (New York: Grand Central

Publishing, 2007), co-written with E. Kinney Zalesne and a more nuanced work than his press coverage had primed me to expect.

Richard Scammon and Ben Wattenberg's *The Real Majority* (New York: Coward-McCann, 1970) diagnosed the coming revolution even earlier than Inglehart, and gave Schoen a step ahead of the competition. If Scammon and Wattenberg have a successor today, it's probably Ruy Teixiera and John Judis, as you can see in both *The Emerging Democratic Majority* (New York: Simon and Schuster, 2002) and *Where Have All the Democrats Gone?: The Soul of the Party in the Age of Extremes* (New York: Henry Holt and Company, 2023). It might not be pure happenstance, then, that Teixiera's résumé includes a stint as vice president of Penn and Schoen Associates. On the emergence of the industry that made it possible for Greenberg and Schoen to earn a living as campaign operatives—and quite a generous one at that—see Adam Sheingate, *Building a Business of Politics: The Rise of Political Consulting and the Transformation of American Democracy* (New York: Oxford University Press, 2016) and Dennis W. Johnson, *Democracy for Hire: A History of American Political Consulting* (New York, 2017). James Harding, *Alpha Dogs: The Americans Who Turned Political Spin into a Global Business* (New York: Farrar, Straus and Giroux, 2007), follows the American consultant class abroad, and Sasha Issenberg, *The Victory Lab: The Secret Science of Winning Campaigns* (New York: Broadway Books, 2012), updates the story for the age of big data—although the advances that Issenberg discusses don't look quite so momentous these days.

So much for the individual stories. The question now is how to weave together these personal journeys with the political upheavals that restructured electorates around the world. Given Antonio Gramsci's early and enduring importance to Greenberg, the three volumes of *The Prison Notebooks*, ed. and trans. Joseph Buttigieg (New York: Columbia University Press, 2011), are a useful place to start. Adam Przeworski and John Sprague's *Paper Stones: A History of Electoral Socialism* (Chicago: University of Chicago Press, 1986) is the kind of incisive analysis of left politics that the young Greenberg would have spent a lot of time thinking about. For a more recent treatment of the subject, see Line Rennwald and Jonas Pontusson, "*Paper Stones* Revisited: Class Voting, Unionization and the Electoral Decline of the Mainstream Left," *Perspectives on Politics* 19, no. 1 (2021), 36–54. There's also an essay to be written contrasting Greenberg's use of Gramsci with Stuart Hall's, which you can see on display in *The Hard Road to Renewal: Thatcherism and the Crisis of the Left* (London: Verso, 1988). For an unsparing account of Greenberg's place on the left, and in American politics more generally, see David Roediger, *The Sinking Middle Class: A Political History of Debt, Misery, and the Drift to the Right* (Chicago: Haymarket Books, 2022). Roediger's analysis isn't mine, but there's no doubt that it's worth wrestling with.

Greenberg's and Schoen's careers are inseparable from the making of the Third Way, where the best place to start reading is Stephanie Mudge's *Leftism Reinvented: Western Parties from Socialism to Neoliberalism* (Cambridge: Harvard University Press, 2018). Frances Fox Piven, ed., *Labor Parties in Postindustrial Societies* (New York: Oxford University Press, 1991), captures these pivotal institutions at a moment of transition; it deserves a sequel.

220   Then there's the question of the Democratic Party's role in this story. For contrasting accounts, see Lily Geismer, *Left Behind: The Democrats' Failed Attempt to Solve Inequality* (New York: Public Affairs, 2022) and Kenneth Baer, *Reinventing Democrats: The Politics of Liberalism from Reagan to Clinton* (Lawrence: Kansas University Press, 2000). Geismer provides the case for the prosecution, Baer for the defense. Michael Kazin's *What It Took to Win: A History of the Democratic Party* (New York: Farrar, Straus and Giroux, 2022) ably situates these recent developments against the many evolutions of the Democrats over the party's long life. Ryan Grim, *The Squad: AOC and the Hope of a Political Revolution* (New York: Henry Holt and Company, 2023), and Joshua Green, *The Rebels: Elizabeth Warren, Bernie Sanders, Alexandria Ocasio-Cortez, and the Struggle for a New American Politics* (New York: Penguin Publishing Group, 2024), take this story down to the present. Nelson Lichtenstein and Judith Stein's *A Fabulous Failure: The Clinton Presidency and the Transformation of American Capitalism* (Princeton: Princeton University Press, 2023) is the best overall account we have of liberalism in the 1990s; its summary of the Clinton White House's neoliberal turn matches perfectly with the transition from Greenberg and Carville to Penn and Schoen. Lainey Newman and Theda Skocpol, *Rust Belt Union Blues: Why Working-Class Voters Are Turning Away from the Democratic Party* (New York: Columbia University Press, 2023), brilliantly explores these changes from the bottom up. For the view from the top, see Sam Zacher, "Polarization of the Rich: The New Democratic Allegiance of Affluent Americans and the Politics of Redistribution," *Perspectives on Politics* (published online, 2023), 1–19. I also benefited from reading early versions of two books that have not yet gone to press as I write: Daniel Schlozman and

Sam Rosenfeld's *The Hollow Parties: The Many Pasts and Disordered Present of American Party Politics* (Princeton: Princeton University Press, 2024) and Lily Geismer and Brent Cebul's edited volume *Mastery and Drift: Professional-Class Liberals Since the 1960s* (Chicago: University of Chicago Press, 2025).

On the British side of this history, start with another fantastic political memoir: Philip Gould, *The Unfinished Revolution: How New Labour Changed British Politics Forever*, rev. ed. (London: Abacus, 2011), where Gould's aching sincerity comes through on every page. For more on Gould—truly an indelible figure—see Dennis Kavanagh, ed., *Philip Gould: An Unfinished Life* (Basingstoke: Palgrave Macmillan, 2012). Following Tony Blair's evolution from ruminating on democratic social-ism in pamphlets for the Fabian Society to holding forth on the Third Way in front of Rupert Murdoch was one of most rewarding detours in this research. Blair tells his side of the story in *A Journey: My Political Life* (New York: Knopf, 2010), but also see Anthony Seldon with Chris Ballinger, Daniel Collings, and Peter Snowdon, *Blair* (London: The Free Press, 2004), and Seldon with Snowdon and Collings, *Blair Unbound* (London: Simon and Schuster, 2007). For a more scholarly treatment of New Labour's origins, see Colm Murphy, *Futures of Socialism: "Modernisation" the Labour Party, and the British Left, 1973–1997* (Cambridge: Cambridge University Press, 2023). Geoffrey Evans and James Tilley, *The New Politics of Class: The Political Exclusion of the Working Class* (Oxford: Oxford University Press, 2014), take the long view on the campaign to move beyond class politics. Richard Carr, *March of the Moderates: Bill Clinton, Tony Blair, and the Rebirth of Progressive Politics* (London: I. B. Taurus, 2019),

222   provides a transatlantic sequel to Baer's sympathetic interpretation of the DLC. Steve Richards, *Whatever It Takes: The Real
Story of Gordon Brown and New Labour* (London: Fourth Estate,
2010), and Gabriel Pogrund and Patrick Maguire, *Left Out: The
Inside Story of Labour Under Corbyn* (London: The Bodley Head,
2020), give the juicy details on the battle for Labour after Blair
left the stage. On the potentially short-lived electoral revolution of 2019, see David Cutts, Matthew Goodwin, Oliver Heath,
and Paula Surridge, "General Election and the Realignment of
British Politics," *Political Quarterly* 91, no. 1 (March 2020), 7–23.

Dahlia Scheindlin's *The Crooked Timber of Democracy in Israel:
Promises Unfulfilled* (Boston: De Gruyter, 2023) landed on my
doorstep at just the right time. I can't imagine a better starting
point for American readers—like, for instance, me—looking for
a guide through the notoriously complex landscape of Israeli
politics. The book pairs beautifully with the ongoing series *The
Elections in Israel*, which has been putting campaigns under the
microscope for more than fifty years. That Scheindlin got her
start in politics working for Stan Greenberg feels somehow
appropriate. My GW colleague Shira Robinson's interpretation of Israel's founding, *Citizen Strangers: Palestinians and the
Birth of Israel's Liberal Settler State* (Stanford: Stanford University
Press, 2013), shaped how I understood everything that came after.
There are worse ways to think about Israel's political transformation than to spend time with the lives of the two figures who
loom over the country's history. For the founding generation,
that's David Ben-Gurion, on which see Tom Segev, *A State at Any
Cost: The Life of David Ben-Gurion*, trans. Haim Watzman (New
York: Farrar, Straus and Giroux, 2019). In the last generation, it's

Benjamin Netanyahu. Although that story is not yet complete, see Anshel Pfeffer, *Bibi: The Turbulent Life and Times of Benjamin Netanyahu* (London: Hurst, 2018). Arie Krampf's *The Israeli Path to Neoliberalism: The State, Continuity and Change* (New York: Routledge, 2018) and Shaul Magid's *Meir Kahane: The Public Life and Political Thought of an American Jewish Radical* (Princeton: Princeton University Press, 2021) highlight two important stops on the road from Ben-Gurion to Bibi. For a defense of liberal Zionism that reckons with the distance between promise and reality, see Ari Shavit, *My Promised Land: The Triumph and Tragedy of Israel* (New York: Spiegel and Grau, 2013). David Shipler's reporting during his stint as Jerusalem bureau chief for the *New York Times* from 1979 to 1984 captured history in the making at a turning point for Israel. His book, *Arab and Jew: Wounded Spirits in a Promised Land* (New York: Times Books, 1986), is even better. Rashid Khalidi, *The Hundred Years War on Palestine: A History of Settler Colonialism and Resistance* (New York: Henry Holt and Company, 2020), helps explain why the effort to isolate the occupation of Palestine from Israeli politics was doomed to fail, while Gal Ariely's *Israel's Regime Untangled: Between Democracy and Apartheid* (Cambridge: Cambridge University Press, 2021) addresses a hot-button subject with rigor.

If apartheid looms over Israel's future, its legacy is unavoidable in discussions of South Africa. Roger Southall is an unfailingly balanced guide to the country's past and present. Three works of his were especially useful for this book: *Liberation Movements in Power Party & State in Southern Africa* (Rochester: Boydell and Brewer, 2013); *The New Black Middle Class in South Africa* (Rochester: Boydell and Brewer, 2016); and *Whites and Democracy*

224   *in South Africa* (Rochester: Boydell and Brewer, 2022). J. Bleck and
      N. van de Walle, *Electoral Politics in Africa Since 1990: Continuity
      in Change* (Cambridge: Cambridge University Press, 2018), pro-
      vide helpful comparative background on South Africa's experi-
      ence since liberation. Adam Branch and Zachariah Mampilly shift
      the focus to popular movements growing out of discontent with
      electoral politics in *Africa Uprising: Popular Protest and Political
      Change* (London: Zed Books, 2015). That R. W. Johnson, one of
      the most prolific critics of the ANC, also happens to have been
      Schoen's mentor at Oxford is yet another of the coincidences
      that piled up in my research. His most significant work on the
      subject—*South Africa's Brave New World: The Beloved Country
      Since the End of Apartheid* (New York: Overlook Press, 2009)—
      is marred by a weakness for rumor-mongering that occasion-
      ally veers into the fantastical. (If Robert Mugabe was indeed
      warned ahead of time about 9/11, as Johnson claims, I haven't
      been able to find independent verification of it.) But the book
      has also been, in crucial respects, tragically prescient. André
      Odendaal, *The Founders: The Origins of the ANC and the Struggle
      for Democracy in South Africa* (Lexington: University Press of
      Kentucky, 2013), ably chronicles the spirit of the early ANC.
      The ambitions of the party's first years in power come through
      clearly in Thabo Mbeki's *Africa: The Time Has Come: Selected
      Speeches* (Tafelberg: Cape Town, 1998). For a moving account of
      how the dreams that accompanied liberation have gone unful-
      filled, written by an American with an international audience in
      mind, see Eve Fairbanks, *The Inheritors: An Intimate Portrait of
      South Africa's Racial Reckoning* (New York: Simon and Schuster,
      2022). Despite Fairbanks's often melancholy tone, her assess-
      ment of South Africa is ultimately hopeful. So is Evan Liberman's

vigorously argued *Until We Have Won Our Liberty: South Africa After Apartheid* (Princeton: Princeton University Press, 2022). Combined, the two provide a valuable counterweight to the fatalism that runs through much commentary on South Africa today.

But did any of the political strategizing in this book matter? Critics of the consultant class say that today's political-industrial complex rests on a hodgepodge of myths and superstitions, with no discernible impact on the outcome of elections, and they have an impressive body of scholarship to back up the argument. My favorite is Christopher Achens and Larry Bartels, *Democracy for Realists: Why Elections Do Not Produce Responsive Government* (Princeton: Princeton University Press, 2016), the best summary of the case against an even semi-rational voter, and a blistering takedown of what the authors call the folk theory of democracy. Bartels takes the same zest for mythbusting to the crisis of democracy literature in *Democracy Erodes from the Top: Leaders, Citizens, and the Challenge of Populism in Europe* (Princeton: Princeton University Press, 2016). It's a compelling argument, but I'm still inclined toward a more generous view. In recent years, Anthony Fowler has been a forceful defender of this interpretation. See, for instance, "Partisan Intoxication or Policy Voting?" *Quarterly Journal of Political Science* 15, no. 2 (2020), 141–179, and Anthony Fowler, Seth Hill, Jeffrey Lewis, Chris Tausanovitch, Lynn Vavreck, and Christopher Warshaw, "Moderates," *American Political Science Review* 117, no. 2 (2023), 643–660. But if I had to pick just one case for the defense, it would be V. O. Key Jr.'s *The Responsible Electorate* (Cambridge: Harvard University Press, 1966). Almost sixty years after its publication, it's still one of the wisest books ever written on American politics. Check it out.

ACKNOWLEDGMENTS

This little book needed a lot of friends along the way. It began with a request from Mason Williams, Lily Geismer, and Brent Cebul to write a chapter on "Topic TBD" for an edited volume on liberalism since the 1960s. With their help, I landed on a question—how did Bill Clinton become president, anyway?—that I thought could be answered with a few weeks of work. Talking with Stan Greenberg and Doug Schoen persuaded me that there was much more to the story. Although both men are more than capable of speaking for themselves, my understanding of their work is far deeper because they agreed to speak with me. Fast-forward a couple months and a brief chapter on the politics of Clintonism had turned into a monster draft, and I still felt like there was more to say. That's when Nick Lemann and Jimmy So gave this book a home at Columbia Global Reports. Over the next two years, they pushed me to reach for big arguments grounded in characters and backed up by hard facts. Other publishers, take note: this is how the job is done.

At GW, Eric Arnesen told me this was a risk worth taking, and two department chairs—first Daniel Schwartz, then Denver Brunsman—provided essential backup. Students in my under-graduate seminar "How to Win Elections" stuck with me for an entire semester as I took them through a guided tour of modern political history as seen through the eyes of Greenberg and Schoen. Alexis Doe, Jennifer Ham, Samir Iqbal, and Jed Sutton deserve extra credit for staying around with me for multiple courses where the questions in this book were never far from my mind.

Those same questions have a way of coming up in my work as an editor at *Dissent*. It's a privilege to be part of a magazine that has earned its place in the history of the left. But it's even better to spend my semi-free time talking—and talking, and talking, and talking—about politics with Natasha Lewis, Nick Serpe, and Mark Levinson.

My former *Dissent* coeditor, Michael Kazin, read the manuscript in full and provided characteristically brilliant comments. So did, late in the game, Daniel Schlozman and my GW colleague James Hershberg. Peter Mandler, Shira Robinson, and Roger Southall gave me the benefit of their expertise as I moved into British, Israeli, and South African history, shaping my interpretation on matters big and small while saving me from some truly howling screwups along the way. Leigh Grossman then gave the resulting manuscript the rigorous copy editing it needed.

Finally, there's my family, who had nothing to do with the writing of this book, except for being the reason I want to do anything at all. That I'm able to get anything done with three small children at home depends on enormous amounts of help. Doraikannu and Leelavathi Regunathan have racked up more than their fair share of emergency childcare hours. They have been joined in grandparenting duty by my mom, Meg Hawco, who taught me close to everything that matters. Most of the rest I learned alongside Renu Regunathan-Shenk, who built a life with me, and makes it worth living. But one lesson I've picked up from our kids—Nikhil, Adi, and Easha—is the beauty in recognizing how little we know. For making me a parent, and everything that's come after, this book belongs to Nikhil.

A NOTE ON LANGUAGE

14 **"Liberalism was a dirty word to us":** Anshel Pfeffer, "The Strange Death and Curious Rebirth of the Israeli Left," *Jewish Quarterly* 246 (2021), 25.

15   **"Roosevelt did not carry out the socialist platform":** Arthur Schlesinger Jr., *The Age of Roosevelt, Vol. 3: The Politics of Upheaval, 1935–1936* (Boston: Houghton Mifflin, 1960), 562.

INTRODUCTION

16   **erosion of class-based voting is real:** For a summary of class divides in the Democratic coalition, see Sam Zacher, "Polarization of the Rich: The New Democratic Allegiance of Affluent Americans and the Politics of Redistribution," *Perspectives on Politics* (2023), 1–19. On how these shifts have played out (or not) elsewhere in the world, see Amory Gethin, Clara Martínez-Toledano, and Thomas Piketty, eds., *Political Cleavages and Social Inequalities: A Study of Fifty Democracies, 1948–2020* (Cambridge: Harvard University Press, 2021).

17   **are divided by levels of education:** Calculations for the graph are based on analysis of data from American National Election Studies, available at www.electionstudies.org.

18   **retained their firm base of support with voters who hadn't graduated from high school:** Thomas Piketty, "Brahmin Left Versus Merchant Right: Rising Inequality and the Changing Structure of Political Conflict in France, the United States, and the United Kingdom, 1948–2020" in *Political Cleavages and Social Inequalities: A Study of Fifty Democracies, 1948–2020,* eds., Amory Gethin, Clara Martínez-Toledano, and Thomas Piketty, 113.

19   **"beautiful health care":** "Trump Promises 'Brand New Beautiful Health Care,' Offers No Details," NBC News, October 22, 2020, available at www.youtube.com.

21   **the last Democratic nominee to do better in West Virginia:** *Congressional Quarterly's Guide to U.S. Elections,* vol. 1, 6th ed. (Washington, DC, 2010), 798.

22   **how the left's coalition has evolved in France:** "Vote for Left-Wing Parties (SFIO/PS, PCF, Radicals, Greens, Other Left) by Education Level, France," World Political Cleavages and Inequality Database, available at https://wpid.world.

22   **a lot like what has occurred in Italy:** "Vote for Left-Wing Parties (PSU/PSDI/PCI/PD/PDS/Green/Other Left) and M5S by Education Level, Italy," World Political

Cleavages and Inequality Database, available at https://wpid.world.

23   Denmark, which is often called a bastion of social democracy: "Vote for Left-Wing parties (Social Democratic / Socialist / Social-Liberal / Communist / Green) by Education Level, Denmark," World Political Cleavages and Inequality Database, available at https://wpid.world.

24   as different as Brazil, India, and the Philippines: The case of Brazil is especially interesting. By the 1990s, support for its chief left party was skewed toward the most educated voters. That dynamic reversed after Luiz Inácio Lula da Silva was elected president in 2002, giving a sharp economic polarization to the Brazilian electorate. When Lula ran for a third term against Jair Bolsonaro in 2022, he was still able to count on solid support from the poor, but his support fell in many of the states with the highest levels of poverty. Lula compensated for this weakness by improving on his performance in wealthier parts of the country, including São Paulo and Rio de Janeiro. For more, see Wendy Hunter and Timothy Power, "Lula's Second Act," *Journal of Democracy* 34, no. 1 (2023), 126–140.

24   it only made sense that class warfare would lose its bite: Ronald Inglehart, *The Silent Revolution: Changing Values and Political Styles*

Among Western Publics (Princeton: Princeton University Press, 1977).   **229**

25   not usually the most important: Jefferson Cowie, *The Great Exception: The New Deal and the Limits of American Politics* (Princeton: Princeton University Press, 2016), nicely illuminates key factors behind the rise and fall of the New Deal's version of class politics. But placing the United States in a global context reveals that among wealthy countries the American experience of class dealignment was not all that exceptional.

25   economic inequality began its upward climb not long after: See, for example, Florian Hoffmann, David Lee, and Thomas Lemieux, "Growing Income Inequality in the United States and Other Advanced Economies," *Journal of Economic Perspectives* 34, no. 4 (2020), 70–76.

26   some of the states with the highest income gaps in the country are also the most reliably blue: "The Unequal States of America: Income Inequality in the United States," Economic Policy Institute, available at https://www.epi.org/multimedia/unequal-states-of-america/.

28   quick and easy path toward becoming a caricature of yourself: For how a snapshot of the profession right before Donald Trump's election would deliver another blow to its reputation, see

230   Molly Ball, "There's Nothing Better Than a Scared, Rich Candidate," *Atlantic*, October 2016, 56–63.

28   *"then* you can tell me we don't need political consultants anymore": Ball, "Nothing Better," 61.

28   when I read their first books: Stanley Greenberg, *Politics and Poverty: Modernization and Response in Five Poor Neighborhoods* (New York: John Wiley and Sons, 1974), and Douglas Schoen, *Enoch Powell and the Powellites* (New York: St. Martin's Press, 1977).

29   These ideas went on to shape campaigns: The importance of those ideas comes through clearly in each of their memoirs: Douglas Schoen, *The Power of the Vote: Electing Presidents, Overthrowing Dictators, and Promoting Democracy Around the World* (New York: William Morrow, 2007), and Stanley Greenberg, *Dispatches from the War Room: In the Trenches with Five Extraordinary Leaders* (New York: St. Martin's Press, 2009).

31   "Ponderous" was the term his ex-friend: Dick Morris, *Behind the Oval Office: Getting Reelected Against All Odds* (Los Angeles: Renaissance Books, 1999), 24.

CHAPTER ONE

34   "is that voters are not fools": V. O. Key Jr., *The Responsible Electorate* (Cambridge: Harvard University Press, 1966), 7. On Key's biography, see William Harvard, "V. O. Key, Jr.: A Brief Profile," *South Atlantic Urban Studies* 3 (1979), 279–288.

36   "I was very much in a racial culture": "Stanley Greenberg oral history interview," January 27, 2005, Miller Center, available at www.millercenter.org.

36   "I didn't know any Republicans": "Stanley Greenberg oral history," January 27, 2005.

37   revolutions also required cultural change and deft political strategizing: An enormous body of scholarship has grown up around Gramsci. For the basics, see Roger Simon, *Gramsci's Political Thought: An Introduction*, 2nd ed. (London: Lawrence and Wishart, 2015). In this vast literature, Stuart Hall's writings are in a class by themselves, and make for a fascinating contrast with Greenberg. See, for example, Stuart Hall, *The Hard Road to Renewal: Thatcherism and the Crisis of the Left* (London: Verso, 1988). And for an insightful discussion of a topic with special relevance for Greenberg, see Dylan Riley, "Hegemony, Democracy, and Passive Revolution in Gramsci's *Prison Notebooks*," *California Italian Studies* 2 (2011).

37   a giant in the field of urban politics with safely Democratic loyalties: Wilson deserves more attention from historians, but for the key points in his biography see

John DiIulio Jr., "James Q. Wilson," *PS: Political Science and Politics* 45, no. 3 (2012), 559–561.

38   between "radical political man" and "liberal political man": Greenberg, *Politics and Poverty*, 2–3.

38   "We coded and counted the responses of the poor": Greenberg, *Politics and Poverty*, ix.

39   "where the poor hate the rich and labor challenges capital": Greenberg, *Politics and Poverty*, 178.

39   racial identity was often the quickest route toward a political awakening: Greenberg, *Politics and Poverty*, 132.

39   "limited range of political opportunities reflected in the reality of American politics": Greenberg, *Politics and Poverty*, 229.

40   Kennedy's, by contrast, was a throwback to the New Deal: Stanley Greenberg, Gary Orren, John Mollenkopf, and Arthur Solomon, "Voting Prediction Model: Kennedy and McCarthy in Indiana," May 14, 1968, RFK Presidential Campaign, National Headquarters Files, Media Division, Box 2, Primary Surveys, Papers of Robert F. Kennedy, John F. Kennedy Presidential Library.

40   "the choice between Eugene McCarthy and Robert Kennedy revealed your political heart": Stanley Greenberg, *Dispatches from the War Room*, 17.

42   "was the true currency of political power": Douglas Schoen, *The Power of the Vote: Electing Presidents, Overthrowing Dictators, and Promoting Democracy Around the World* (New York: HarperCollins, 2007), 4.

42   "To this day, I'm somewhat unclear on what exactly we were supposed to be doing": Schoen, *The Power of the Vote*, 10.

42   "was the way politics really worked": Schoen, *The Power of the Vote*, 11.

43   that normally took six weeks: Richard Reeves, "Splitting the Jewish Vote," *New York Magazine*, June 18, 1973, 57–63.

43   "how you get your fair piece of the pie": Schoen, *The Power of the Vote*, 28–29.

44   "you should not trust what they say until you figure out what their self-interest is": Douglas Schoen, *Power: The Fifty Truths, the Definitive Insider's Guide* (Regan Arts: New York, 2023).

45   "What the hell does Lindsay care about me": Steve Fraser, *The Limousine Liberal: How an Incendiary Image United the Right and Fractured America* (New York: Basic Books, 2016), 11–22.

45   "a forty-seven-year-old housewife from the outskirts of Dayton, Ohio": Richard Scammon and Ben Wattenberg, *The Real*

232 *Majority* (New York: Coward-McCann, 1970), 70–71.

46 **the heart of what had been FDR's majority:** "Vote for Democratic Party by Income Group, United States," World Political Cleavages and Inequality Database, available at https://wpid.world.

47 **"does *not* mean they are antiyoung, antipoor, or antiblack":** Scammon and Wattenberg, *The Real Majority,* 58.

47 **one of the most famous, and polarizing, figures in politics with a single speech:** Simon Heffer, *Like the Roman: The Life of Enoch Powell* (London: Weidenfeld and Nicholson, 1998), and Paul Corthorn, *Enoch Powell: Politics and Ideas in Modern Britain* (Oxford University Press, 2019).

47 **"the black man will have the whip hand over the white man":** Quoted in Heffer, *Like the Roman,* 451.

48 **"like the Roman, I seem to see 'the River Tiber foaming with much blood'":** Quoted in Heffer, *Like the Roman,* 454.

48 **"Back Britain, not Black Britain":** Heffer, *Like the Roman,* 462.

48 **"would involve Schoen and me working out new ways to run the findings":** R. W. Johnson, "Stick to the Latin," *London Review of Books,* January 1997, available at www.lrb.co.uk.

49 **Powell's supporters followed his lead when he endorsed Labour in 1974:** Douglas Schoen, *Enoch Powell and the Powellites* (New York: St. Martin's Press, 1977), 276

49 **boosting their performance with the bottom half of the electorate by 7 points:** "Vote for Conservative Party by Income Group, United Kingdom," World Political Cleavages and Inequality Database, available at https://wpid .world.

50 **Dwight Eisenhower's reelection in 1956:** "Structure of the Vote by Union Membership, United States, 1956," World Political Cleavages and Inequality Database, available at https://wpid .world.

50 **regularly voted for the Communist Party:** R. W. Johnson, *The Long March of the French Left* (New York: St. Martin's Press, 1981), 141-142.

50 **even more economically stratified than in the US or France:** Ronald Inglehart and Pippa Norris, "Trump and the Populist Authoritarian Parties: The Silent Revolution in Reverse," *Perspectives on Politics* 15.2 (2017), 448, fig. 6.

52 **"Marxian political economy":** Greenberg, *Race and State in Capitalist Development: Comparative Perspectives* (New Haven: Yale University Press, 1980), x.

52 **"but even the racists within their world":** Greenberg, *Dispatches*, 18.

52 **"were not without social democratic impulses":** Stanley Greenberg, *The Two Americas: Our Current Political Deadlock and How to Break It* (New York: St. Martin's Press, 2004), xi.

54 **"No wonder they killed him":** Stanley Greenberg, *Report on Democratic Defection* (Washington, DC: The Analysis Group, 1985), 13–14.

54 **"We're losing money and they're importing all these people from Vietnam, Mexico":** Greenberg, *Democratic Defection*, 8–9.

54 **"They're going to run the country":** Greenberg, *Democratic Defection*, 10.

55 **"that drew on their lives, their history, their needs, interests":** "Stanley Greenberg oral history," January 27, 2005.

56 **"the demons of the 1960s":** Stanley Greenberg, "Popularizing Progressive Politics," in *The New Majority: Toward a Popular Progressive Politics*, ed. Stanley Greenberg and Theda Skocpol (New Haven: Yale University Press, 1997), 288.

56 **"I found the conclusion inflammatory":** Eleanor Clift and Tom Brazaitis, *War Without Bloodshed: The Art of Politics* (New York: Simon & Schuster, 1997), 27.

56 **"Democrats for the Leisure Class":** Baer, *Reinventing Democrats*, 74.

56 **"a quasi-Reaganite formation":** Arthur Schlesinger Jr., "For Democrats, Me-Too Reaganism Will Spell Disaster," *New York Times*, July 6, 1986, 13.

57 **"If you want to know what working people think, you can't turn to these organizations":** Quoted in Philip Gould, *The Unfinished Revolution: How New Labour Changed British Politics Forever* (London: Abacus, 2011), 327.

57 **"a new class politics":** Stanley Greenberg, "From Crisis to Working Majority," *American Prospect*, December 5, 1991, available at www.prospect.org.

57 **"A party that can speak expansively of broad, cross-class issues":** Greenberg, "From Crisis to Working Majority."

58 **an attempt to complete Robert Kennedy's unfinished work:** Greenberg, *Dispatches from the War Room*, 104, 20.

58 **an assault on "conservative hegemony":** Greenberg, *Dispatches from the War Room*, 21.

59 **"the nation's most sought-after campaign strategist":** "A Prince Maker Strikes Again," *Time*,

234 November 21, 1977, available at www.time.com.

60 **"the smoother operator of these partners":** Robert Kaiser, "In Politics, the Pollsters Lead," *Washington Post*, May 18, 1980, available at www.washingtonpost.com.

61 **"we were increasingly struck by the similarities between campaigns and corporate marketing":** Schoen, *The Power of the Vote*, 195.

61 **had become the dominant force in American politics:** Mark Penn and Douglas Schoen, "Reagan's Revolution Ended?" *New York Times*, November 9, 1986, E23.

62 **"often sounds more Republican than his Republican opponent":** Dennis Farney, "Indiana Race for Governor Finds GOP Stumped by Democrat with a Fresh Face, Legendary Name," *Wall Street Journal*, October 24, 1988, A14.

62 **Schoen predicted—correctly, as it turned out:** Penn and Schoen Associates, "Report to the Louisiana Coalition on Voter Opinion in Louisiana," July 17, 1990, Collected Materials, 1943–1992, Box 30, Louisiana Coalition Against Racism and Nazism Records, Amistad Research Center, Tulane University (with thanks to Daniel Schlozman for bringing this document to my attention, and my inbox).

CHAPTER TWO

65 **who could spin out folksy sayings on the campaign trail:** Joe Klein, *The Natural: The Misunderstood Presidency of Bill Clinton* (New York: Doubleday, 2002), 11.

65 **"The change we must make isn't liberal or conservative":** William J. Clinton, "Remarks Announcing Candidacy for the Democratic Presidential Nomination," October 3, 1991, available at www.presidency.ucsb.edu.

68 **he sharpened his political skills with a punishing electoral calendar:** On Clinton's pre-presidential years, see David Maraniss, *First in His Class: A Biography of Bill Clinton* (New York: Touchstone, 1995).

69 **Clinton defined himself as a populist:** Stephen A. Smith, ed., *Preface to the Presidency: Selected Speeches of Bill Clinton, 1974–1992* (Fayetteville,: University of Arkansas Press, 1996), 111.

69 **"Bush has never used the bully pulpit to attack the wealthy for screwing the workers":** Greenberg, *Dispatches*, 32.

70 **"honor the values and promote the interests":** Smith, *Preface to the Presidency*, 21.

70 **"I am pro-choice, strongly":** Smith, *Preface to the Presidency*, 218.

70 **he wanted to please them:** Peter Goldman et al, *Quest for the Presidency 1992* (College Station, : Texas A&M University Press, 1994), 187.

70 **"some appreciation for the conflicting pressures on the candidate":** Greenberg, *Dispatches*, 37.

70 **"The little motherfucker had balls":** Goldman et al., *Quest*, 249.

71 **"the best friend Wall Street ever had":** Paul Richter, "Tsongas Refuses to Vary His Economic Message," *Los Angeles Times*, March 6, 1992, available at www .latimes.com.

71 **Brown cited libertarian hero Milton Friedman in his defense:** Steven Greenhouse, "The 1992 Campaign: Fairness and a Flat Tax," *New York Times*, March 26, 1992, A1.

71 **Black voters delivered crushing majorities for Clinton:** Steve Kornacki, "1992: Bill Clinton Builds a Winning Coalition, Jackson Is Diminished," NBC News, July 29, 2019, available at www .nbcnews.com.

71 **slump was especially pronounced with African Americans:** Ross Baker, "Sorting Out and Suiting Up: The Presidential Nominations," in *The Election of 1992: Reports and Interpretations*, Gerald Pomper et al.,

eds. (Chatham, NJ: Chatham House Publishers, 1993), 61–62.

72 **"politically possible to bring poor blacks and blue-collar white voters together":** "Bill Clinton, in Black and White," *New York Times*, March 11, 1992, A22.

72 **"were a test of my life's work":** Greenberg, *Dispatches*, 40.

73 **best performance for a third party since Teddy Roosevelt's 1912 campaign:** *Congressional Quarterly's Guide*, 797.

73 **made up the base of his coalition:** Baer, *Reinventing Democrats*, 205.

73 **greater numbers than whites with a college degree:** Nate Cohn, "How Educational Differences Are Widening America's Political Rift," *New York Times*, September 8, 2021, available at www.nytimes.com.

73 **his narrow defeat marked an improvement:** For Greenberg's postmortem on Macomb, see Stanley Greenberg, *Middle Class Dreams: The Politics and Power of the New American Majority*, rev. ed. (New Haven: Yale University Press, 1996), 52–53.

73 **rebuilding the New Deal coalition would be even harder:** Zacher, "Polarization of the Rich," 4.

74 **president's approval rating fell from a high:** "Presidential Approval Ratings—Bill Clinton,"

236   Gallup, available at www.news
.gallup.com.

74 **"The administration's
silence on populist themes"**:
Greenberg, *Dispatches*, 91.

75 **"blocked Democrats from
creating a real majority"**:
Greenberg, *Dispatches*, 94.

75 **"was not sent to Washington
to put gays in the military"**:
Greenberg, *Dispatches*, 89.

76 **including hardline
conservatives like Jesse Helms:**
Greenberg, *Dispatches*, 52.

76 **because they conducted early
polling for Perot in 1992:** On their
work for Perot, see Richard Morin,
"Electorate Seems Less Angry
Now," *Washington Post*, October 4,
1992, available at www
.washingtonpost.com.

76 **"The perception across
America was that Clinton was a
liberal"**: Schoen, *Power of the Vote*,
214.

76 **"neuro-personality poll"**:
James Bennett, "The Guru of Small
Things," *New York Times Magazine*,
June 18, 2000, 548.

76 **they zeroed in on two key
demographics:** Schoen, *Power of
the Vote*, 232–233.

78 **"the middle class sides with
the rich"**: Alison Mitchell, "Stung
by Defeats in '94, Clinton

Regrouped and Co-opted G.O.P.
Strategies," *New York Times*,
November 7, 1996, B5.

78 **"It's not about economics"**:
Schoen, *Power of the Vote*, 236.

78 **turnout crashed to the lowest
level since the 1920s:** "National
General Election VEP Turnout
Rates, 1789–Present," US Elections
Project, available at www
.electproject.org.

78 **"political forces that have
battled to an inconclusive and
ugly draw"**: Theda Skocpol and
Stanley Greenberg, "A Politics for
Our Time," in *The New Majority:
Toward a Popular Progressive
Politics*, 4.

78 **"Downscale voters are *not* the
center of the electoral universe"**:
Mark Penn, "Mark Penn Responds:
Controversy, Why Did Clinton
Win?" *American Prospect,* December
19, 2001, available at www.prospect
.org.

79 **"We do not have the natural
majority coalition in American
politics"**: Schoen, *The Power of the
Vote,* 349.

79 **"was trending to the Right"**:
Schoen, *The Power of the Vote*, 225

79 **but the limits were real:**
"Taxes," "Crime," and
"Immigration," Gallup, available at
www.gallup.com; Lydia Saad, "U.S.
Political Ideology Steady;
Conservatives, Moderates Tie,"

Gallup, January 17, 2022, available at
www.gallup.com; "Americans Only
a Little Better Off, but Much Less
Anxious," Pew Research Center,
May 23, 1997, available at www
.pewresearch.org.

**79 "Wishing for a mass
conversion is not a political
strategy":** Schoen, *The Power of the
Vote*, 351.

80 "Penn is the high priest":
Peter Baker, "Polling's High Priest
Maintains Low Profile," *Washington
Post*, November 5, 1996, A9.

80 "Schlumbo": Bennett, "Guru
of Small Things," 546.

**80 "are listening to America
through the same small, secretive
shop":** Bennett, "Guru of Small
Things," 546.

**81 he got in touch with Stan
Greenberg:** Robert Shrum, *No
Excuses: Concessions of a Serial
Campaigner* (New York: Simon &
Schuster, 2007), 310. Greenberg
turned down the offer at first, but
changed his mind when approached
later in the campaign.

**82 "while grasping at the monied
contributions of the well-to-do":**
Skocpol and Greenberg, "A Politics
for Our Time," 4.

**82 moved ahead of Bush for the
first time in the race:** The slogan
was short-lived. Although
Greenberg pushed the campaign in
a more populist direction, he

thought "the people versus the
powerful" was too harsh, and he
persuaded the rest of the campaign
to make the same point using softer
(but also less vivid) language. See
Shrum, *No Concessions*, 341.

**82 "I'm very confident he would
be president-elect today":** John
Harris, "Policy and Politics by the
Numbers," *Washington Post*,
December 31, 2000, A1.

**83 white voters without a college
degree supported the president in
greater numbers:** Cohn,
"Educational Differences."

**83 those same voters were
drifting away from Democrats:**
"Vote for Democratic Party by
Income Group, United States,"
World Political Cleavages and
Inequality Database, available at
https://wpid.world.

**83 winning nearly a third of the
counties that had voted
Republican:** Sean Trende, *The Lost
Majority: Why the Future of
Government Is Up for Grabs—And
Who Will Take It* (New York: St.
Martin's Group, 2012), 58.

**83 the highest-earning
5 percent of the electorate:** Zacher,
"Polarization of the Rich," 5.

**84 "When evil needs public
relations":** *The Rachel Maddow
Show*, August 2, 2012, NBC News,
available at www.nbcnews.com.

238   84   **became a fixture in the DC social circuit:** Susan Baer, "When Marriage and Politics Conflict," *Washingtonian,* August 1, 2006, available at www.washingtonian. com; Anne Kornblut, "Clinton's Powerpointer," *Washington Post,* April 30, 2007.

84   **a larger story about the reinvention of the Democratic Party:** Mark Penn with E. Kinney Zalesne, *Microtrends: The Small Forces Behind Tomorrow's Big Changes* (New York: Grand Central Publishing, 2007).

85   **was the poorest of the bunch:** David Kocieniewski, "On Politics: $400 Million Man a Socialist? Don't Tell That to a Socialist," *New York Times,* September 17, 2000, NJ14.

85   **Penn thrived in the new arrangement:** Ben Smith, "Penn Minus Schoen," *Politico,* March 17, 2007, available at www.politico. com.

85   **claiming that he wanted to spend more time writing:** Schoen followed through on the promise. His first book after the split, a memoir, appeared in 2007. He authored or co-authored a dozen more over the next decade alone, none of them nearly as good as his study of Enoch Powell.

86   **"profoundly anxious and pessimistic about their economic futures":** Schoen, *Power of the Vote,* 363, 348.

86   **"if you are one of those companies holding a lot of subprime loans, watch out":** Penn with Zalesne, *Microtrends,* 226, 228.

86   **"a historic—and profoundly worrying—shift":** Schoen, *Power of the Vote,* 348.

86   **"respect for the seriousness of life and politics":** Penn with Zalesne, *Microtrends,* 135, 131.

86   **contrasting their emerging coalition among working- and middle-class voters:** Mark Penn, "Weekly Strategic Review on Hillary Clinton for President Committee," March 19, 2007, available at www.theatlantic.com.

87   **"but you are the Bobby":** Penn, "Weekly Strategic Review."

87   **"the natural party of young people":** Greenberg, *Dispatches,* 106.

88   **a tactful way of promising to make union troubles disappear:** Mark Schmitt, "Penn, Inc.," *American Prospect,* March 22, 2007, available at www.prospect.org.

89   **"Fake Democratic Pollsters Have Stupid Idea":** Alex Pareene, "Fake Democratic Pollsters Have Stupid Idea," November 21, 2011, available at www.salon.com.

89   **first time voting Republican:**
Douglas Schoen, *The Politics of Life:
My Road to the Middle of a Hostile
and Adversarial World* (New York:
Regan Arts, 2024), 222.

90   **would have been headache
enough for the Obama team:**
Andrew Malcolm, "The Ties That
Bind," *Los Angeles Times,* June 7,
2010, available at www.latimes
.com.

90   **Goni was forced out of office
and driven into exile:** Christina
Talcott, "Political Strategy
Heads South," *Washington Post,*
March 31, 2006, available at www
.washingtonpost.com.

90   **Breaking with years of
narrow victories:** For a
sympathetic discussion of this
experience, see Santiago Anria,
*When Movements Become Parties:
The Bolivian MAS in Comparative
Perspective* (Cambridge: Cambridge
University Press, 2018).

91   **"Obama Doesn't Need
Right-Leaning Whites Anymore":**
Ronald Brownstein, "With New
Support Base, Obama Doesn't Need
Right-Leaning Whites Anymore,"
National Journal, February 1, 2013,
available at https://web.archive.
org/web/20130204041222/http://
www.nationaljournal.com
/thenextamerica/politics/with
-new-support-base-obama
-doesn-t-need-right-leaning
-whites-anymore-20130201.

91   **months in advance with
uncanny accuracy:** Sasha
Issenberg, "How Obama's Team
Used Big Data to Rally Voters," *MIT
Technology Review,* December 19,
2012, available at www
.technologyreview.com.

92   **barely 10 percent of
Democrats called themselves
conservatives:** Lydia Saad,
"Democrats' Identification as
Liberal Now 54%, a New High,"
Gallup, January 12, 2023, available
at www.gallup.com.

93   **"genuine grassroots
movement":** Scott Rasmussen and
Doug Schoen, *Mad as Hell: How the
Tea Party Movement Is
Fundamentally Remaking Our
Two-Party System* (New York:
HarperCollins, 2010), 5.

93   **"mistake the anger of
populists for ignorance":**
Rasmussen and Schoen, *Mad as
Hell,* 29.

94   **received a barrage of emails
urging (and urging, and urging):**
Stanley Greenberg, "How She Lost,"
American Prospect, September 21,
2017, available at www.prospect
.org.

94   **"In 2008, Hillary had
working class voters":** "Campaign
2016: Future of the Democratic
Party," C-Span, July 28, 2016,
available at www.c-span.org.

240   94   **a purely anti-Trump message was "not enough":** Greenberg, "How She Lost."

95   **overseeing low-drama campaigns and wrangling big egos:** Andy Kroll and Patrick Caldwell, "Robby Mook Just Took the Hardest Job in Politics—Saving the Clintons from Themselves," *Mother Jones,* April 9, 2015, available at www.motherjones.com.

95   **key battleground states like Michigan and Wisconsin were safely in their column:** John Wagner, "Clinton's Data-Driven Campaign Relied Heavily on an Algorithm Named Ada. What Didn't She See?" *Washington Post*, November 9, 2016, available at www.washingtonpost.com.

96   **"when Democratic leaders stopped seeing the working class":** Stanley Greenberg, "Democrats, Speak to Working-Class Discontent," *American Prospect,* February 14, 2022, available at www.prospect.org.

96   **"You can't run a party based on New York":** "Doug Schoen Breaks Down the Clinton Collapse," Fox News, February 4, 2017, available at www.foxnews.com.

97   **"feel that there is some point in the whole game":** Schoen, *Powell,* 233.

97   **"Voters think they live in a democracy":** Greenberg, *Dispatches,* 326.

97   **when Trump flipped Macomb County back into the Republican column:** "2016 Michigan Election Results," Michigan Department of State, available at https://mielections.us.

CHAPTER THREE

99   **"and more a collective trauma":** Gould, *Unfinished Revolution,* 147.

99   **"Stan is anxious to meet you here in Little Rock":** Gould, *Unfinished Revolution,* 158.

100   **Labour was less than a century old:** Andrew Thorpe, *A History of the British Labour Party,* rev. ed. (London: Bloomsbury, 2017), 36–58.

100   **94 percent of the country identified as white:** The 1991 census was the first to produce data on the country's racial demographics, on which see K. Sillitoe and P. H. White, "Ethnic Group and the British Census: The Search for a Question," *Journal of the Royal Statistical Society* 155, no. 1 (1992), 141–163. For the United States, see "Population by Race and Hispanic or Latino Origin for the United States: 1990 and 2000," United States Census Bureau, April 2, 2001, available at www.census.gov.

100   **modified versions of attacks that Gould had just seen take down Labour:** E. J. Dionne Jr., "Bush Said to Import British Tactics," *Washington Post*, October 8, 1992, available at www.washingtonpost.com.

101   **Blair laid out his case:** Tony Blair, "Let Us Face the Future: The 1945 Anniversary Lecture," *Fabian Pamphlet* 571 (1995).

102   **Labour had *never* held two full, consecutive terms:** Richard Cracknell, Elise Uberoi, and Matthew Burton, *UK Election Statistics: 1918–2023, A Long Century of Elections* (London: House of Commons Library, 2023), 16.

102   **"is that 1945 was the exception and not the rule":** Blair, "Let Us Face the Future," 3.

102   **where two-thirds of workers did not belong to a trade union:** "Trade Union Membership, UK 1995–2021: Statistical Bulletin," Department for Business, Energy, and Industrial Strategy, May 25, 2002, available at https://assets.publishing.service.gov.uk.

103   **"making sure every stone is put in its rightful place":** Blair, "Let Us Face the Future," 5.

103   **but he didn't feel the cause in his bones:** On Blair's early life, see Anthony Seldon with Chris Ballinger, Daniel Collings, and Peter Snowden, *Blair*, 2nd ed. (London: The Free Press, 2004), 3–199.

104   **"is a far more intellectual exercise than people ever think":** Tony Blair, "Foreword" to *The Unfinished Revolution: How New Labour Changed British Politics Forever*, by Philip Gould (London: Abacus, 2011), xv.

104   **"is a new political consensus of the left-of-centre":** Blair, "Let Us Face the Future," 4.

104   **"a normal person's view of politics":** Tony Blair, *A Journey: My Political Life* (New York: Alfred A. Knopf, 2010), 70.

104   **and he wanted almost everyone to be part of it:** Blair, "Let Us Face the Future," 13.

105   **"tolerant, fair, enterprising, inclusive":** Blair, "Let Us Face the Future," 12.

105   **but the reference to building "one nation":** Although the concept is often associated with the nineteenth-century statesman Benjamin Disraeli, the term "one-nation conservatism" was coined in 1924 by Tory prime minister Stanley Baldwin, on which see Emily Jones, "Impressions of Disraeli: Mythmaking and the History of One Nation Conservatism, 1881–1940," *Revue Française de Civilisation Britannique* XXVIII, no. 1 (2023), available at

242   https://journals.openedition.org
/rfcb.

105   "If socialism is not [to] be
merely an abstract moralism":
Blair, "Let Us Face the Future," 13.

106   "became a kind of defining
text for me": Gould, *Unfinished
Revolution*, 167.

106   "an elitist and suburban
party with contempt for working
Americans": Greenberg, *Dispatches
from the War Room*, 182.

106   "New Labour was always
about challenging the
assumptions of elitism": Gould,
Unfinished Revolution, 418.

107   "almost above everything":
Gould, *Unfinished Revolution*, 167.

107   "either we trust the people
or we don't": Gould, *Unfinished
Revolution*, 468.

107   "however powerless,
however marginalised": Gould,
Unfinished Revolution, 467.

107   like evidence of wildly
misplaced life priorities: Gould,
Unfinished Revolution, 416.

107   "Voters," he said, "need
relentless reassurance":
Greenberg, *Dispatches*, 191.

108   "things that matter to
people in their lives": Gould,
Unfinished Revolution, 253.

108   "are in the hands of the
many, not the few": Lucy Ward,
"Fabians Split on Blairite
Makeover," *The Guardian*,
August 20, 1999, available at www
.theguardian.com.

108   "were far more likely to be
tough than soft": Blair, *Journey*, 57.

109   "The Conservatives work
for the privileged few": Greenberg,
Dispatches, 192–193.

109   "I didn't like division or
discord": Blair, *Journey*, 28.

109   "I just don't believe the
problem with Britain is the few at
the top": Greenberg, *Dispatches*,
232.

109   "I never heard a real voter
longing for unity and deploring
division": Greenberg, *Dispatches*,
203.

110   "they are not addressing a
problem that people think needs
solving": Greenberg, *Dispatches*,
194.

110   "in which all of the people,
not just a few, can share": Ewen
Macaskill, "Blair's Promise—
Everyone Can Be a Winner," *The
Guardian*, October 2, 1996, available
at www.theguardian.com.

110   "Not just" was the key
flourish: Greenberg liked the
formulation so much that he
borrowed it when he came onto Al
Gore's 2000 campaign. "Let's make

sure that our prosperity enriches not just the few, but all working families," Gore declared in his acceptance speech at the Democratic National Convention, just a few weeks after hiring Greenberg.

111   **"The pledges worked better than anything else I have ever tested":** Gould, *Unfinished Revolution*, 265.

111   **"I spent most of the rest of the day in a state of shock":** Gould, *Unfinished Revolution*, 382.

111   **was assuming a "classless quality":** Greenberg, *Dispatches*, 191.

111   **described a "class collapse" in their polls:** Greenberg, *Dispatches*, 208.

111   **"that was more important than maximizing his vote":** Greenberg, *Dispatches*, 208.

112   **in greater numbers than at any point since the 1970s:** "Vote for Labour Party by Income Group, United Kingdom," World Political Cleavages and Inequality Database, available at https://wpid.world.

112   **Labour won college-educated voters for the first time in its history:** "Vote for Labour Party by Education Level, United Kingdom," World Political Cleavages and Inequality Database, available at https://wpid.world.

113   **a 7-point drop from the 1992 campaign:** Cracknell et al, *UK Election Statistics*, 29. For more, see Harold Clarke, David Sanders, Marianne Stewart, and Paul Whiteley, "Britain (Not) at the Polls, 2001," *PS: Political Science and Politics* 36, no. 1 (2003), 59–64, and Geoffrey Evans and James Tilley, *The New Politics of Class: The Political Exclusion of the British Working Class* (Oxford: Oxford University Press, 2017), 170-190.

113   **weren't the only people trying to find their place:** For Greenberg's reservations, see *Dispatches*, 218–219.

113   **"For the first time," Gould remembered, "I felt exalted":** Gould, *Unfinished Revolution*, 384.

113   **shrugged off the historical baggage and resurrected the phrase:** Tony Blair, "The Third Way: New Politics for the New Century," *Fabian Pamphlet* 588 (1995).

114   **"so we can occupy the territory":** Quoted in Lily Geismer, "How the Third Way Made Neoliberal Politics Seem Inevitable," *The Nation*, December 13, 2022, available at www.thenation.com.

114   **that Labour was delivering on its pledge to modernize Britain:** On New Labour's mixed

244   domestic record in Blair's first term, see Seldon, *Blair*, 423–439.

115   launched a consulting firm in London: John Rentoul, "Labour Conference: PM's Poll Winners Put Their Skills Up for Hire," *Independent*, October 3, 1997, available at www.independent .co.uk.

115   "modernization without concrete gains for the middle class loses meaning for voters": Greenberg, *Dispatches*, 219.

115   "a whole raft of often confusing and abstract third way messages": "Full Text: Philip Gould's Leaked Memo," *The Guardian*, July 19, 2000, available at www.theguardian.com.

116   "we are not believed to have delivered": "Leaked Memo," available at www.theguardian.com.

116   "battle for real things": Greenberg, *Dispatches*, 226.

116   with a list of watchwords for the looming campaign: "Leaked Memo," available at www .theguardian.com.

116   "It's just that I was choosing not to take it": Greenberg, *Dispatches*, 232.

116   "human potential, economically and as citizens": Greenberg, *Dispatches*, 237.

117   the lowest in almost a century: Cracknell et al, *UK Election Statistics*, 29, Clarke et al., "Britain (Not) at the Polls," 60–61; Greenberg, *Dispatches*, 258.

117   support for Blair in the bottom half of the income distribution: "Vote for Labour Party by Income Group, United Kingdom," World Political Cleavages and Inequality Database, available at https://wpid.world.

117   "'Being in touch' with opinion was no longer the lodestar": Gould, *Unfinished Revolution*, 417.

118   "between his own thoughts and what the groups seemed to say": Blair, *Journey*, 298.

118   he accepted a diminished place in the race: Greenberg, *Dispatches*, 261.

118   a "polling war" between the dueling American strategists: Gould, *Unfinished Revolution*, 485.

119   it was still hovering around historic lows: Cracknell et al., *UK Election Statistics*, 16, 29.

119   left the public uncertain about the real Tony Blair: Greenberg, *Dispatches*, 265.

120   "but failed to substitute a new political choice": Greenberg, *Dispatches*, 268.

120 "whether Labour represented the working or middle class": Evans and Tilley, *The New Politics of Class,* 61.

120 "gives the opportunity for the Conservatives to reinvent themselves": Quoted in Seldon, *Blair,* 430.

120 Euro-skepticism blended with hostility to immigration, crime, and welfare abuse: Gould, *Unfinished Revolution,* 430.

120 "Labour's achievements were just swept away by what was effectively racism": Gould, *Unfinished Revolution,* 474.

120 "was not a process over which the electorate felt they had sufficient control or influence": Gould, *Unfinished Revolution,* 433.

121 "The one thing that could lose me the next election is immigration": Nicholas Watt and Patrick Wintour, "How Immigration Came to Haunt Labour: The Inside Story," *The Guardian,* March 24, 2015, available at www.theguardian.com.

122 The essential struggle of the new era: Patrick Wintour, "'Cross-dressing' on Political Policy Is Here to Stay, Says PM," *The Guardian,* July 31, 2006, available at www .theguardian.com.

122 "the most disconnected and rootless speech ever made by a Labour leader": Steve Richards,

Whatever It Takes: The Real Story of Gordon Brown and New Labour (London: Fourth Estate, 2010), 235.

123 his advisers told themselves: Richards, *Whatever It Takes,* 434.

123 No party had enough seats to form a parliamentary majority: Cracknell et al, *UK Election Statistics,* 29.

123 Greenberg's firm was back on Labour's team: Patrick Wintour, "Labour Conference: What Is the Inspiration Behind Ed Miliband's Speech?" *The Guardian,* September 27, 2011, available at www.theguardian.com.

124 support for gay marriage and action on climate change: Jim Messina, "What My British Win Taught Me About 2016," *Politico,* May 17, 2015, available at www .politico.com.

125 "the candidate who provided the clearest economic vision looking ahead prevailed": Messina, "British Win."

125 that might break up the United Kingdom: Patrick Wintour, "David Cameron warns of Labour-SNP 'Coalition of Chaos,'" *The Guardian,* April 17, 2015, available at www.theguardian.com.

126 "America is a genuinely exceptional nation that embraces its multiculturalism": Stan Greenberg, "Right-Wing Wins

246   Come at Too High a Price," *Politico*,
May 17, 2015.

**127   "You can be successful and
care," he insisted:** Blair, *Journey*, 10.

**127   not even a herculean
capacity for self-destruction
could endanger his place at the
top:** For a full accounting of those
impulses at work, see Tom Bower,
Boris Johnson: The Gambler (London:
Ebury Publishing, 2020).

**127   "an alienation of the people
from the power they should hold":**
Boris Johnson, "There Is Only One
Way to Get the Change We
Want—Vote to Leave the EU,"
Telegraph, March 16, 2016, available
at www.telegraph.co.uk.

**127   "I'm never coming back to
wherever this is."** Heather Stewart,
"Labour Europe Minister
Apologises After Calling Voter a
'Horrible Racist,'" *The Guardian*,
May 19, 2016, available at www
.theguardian.com. On how this
divide expressed itself in the Brexit
referendum, see Evans and Tilley,
The New Politics of Class, 201–207.

**128   allowing him to transcend
the conventional left-right
divide:** Blair, *Journey*, 70.

**128   "The party system does not
map to how normal people think":**
Andrew Sullivan, "Transcript:
Dominic Cummings on Boris,
Brexit, Immigration," *Weekly Dish*,

April 7, 2022, available at https://
andrewsullivan.substack.com.

**128   "which completely
bamboozled the media":** Sullivan,
"Dominic Cummings."

**128   in a referendum with higher
turnout than any election since
1992:** Cracknell et al., *UK Election
Statistics*, 98.

**129   Corbyn joined the House of
Commons after the same 1983
Thatcher landslide:** On Corbyn's
unlikely rise, see Alex Nunns, *The
Candidate: Jeremy Corbyn's
Improbable Path to Power* (New York:
Or Books, 2018).

**129   "a slightly quaint
irrelevance":** Quoted in Sam
Knight, "The Astonishing Rise of
Jeremy Corbyn," *New Yorker*,
May 16, 2016, available at www
.newyorker.com.

**129   beating even Blair's total in
1994:** Rowena Mason, "Labour
Leadership: Jeremy Corbyn Elected
with Huge Mandate," *The Guardian*,
September 12, 2015, available at
www.theguardian.com.

**130   "Together, we'll take on the
privileged, and put the people in
power":** "Full Text: Jeremy
Corbyn's Speech," *Spectator*,
September 24, 2019, available at
www.spectator.co.uk.

**130   the real story was Labour's
collapse:** Cracknell et al., *UK
Election Statistics*, 16.

130   **with fewer seats than at any time since 1935:** A transformation analyzed in David Cutts, Matthew Goodwin, Oliver Heath, and Paula Surridge, "Brexit, the 2019 General Election, and the Realignment of British Politics," *Political Quarterly* 91, no. 1 (2020), 7–23.

131   **were drifting apart:** For data on 2019, see "How Britain Voted in the 2019 Election," Ipsos, December 20, 2019, available at www.ipsos.com. On the divide within the British elite, see Piketty, "Brahmin Left Versus Merchant Right," 128–130.

131   **"to lose your advantage in the very working-class communities which the Labour movement was founded to represent":** Cutts et al., "Realignment," 17.

131   **one of the party's most high-profile strategists—Stan Greenberg:** Kate Devlin, "Blair and Clinton Strategist Stan Greenberg Switches to Help Lib Dems Get Elected," *The Times,* July 19, 2019, available at www.thetimes.co.uk.

132   **the sweetest victory in the election:** Mike Corder and Jill Lawless, "Boris Johnson Goes North to Celebrate Crushing Election Win," Associated Press, December 14, 2019, available at www.apnews.com.

133   **making him the wealthiest resident of 10 Downing Street in**

British history: Rupert Neat, "Does Rishi Sunak's £730m Fortune Make Him Too Rich to Be PM?" *The Guardian*, October 22, 2022, available at www.theguardian.com.

134   **when Corbyn was barred from running as a Labour candidate:** Jim Pickard and George Parker, "Keir Starmer's Ruthless Remaking of the Labour Party," *Financial Times*, June 7, 2023, available at www.ft.com.

134   **"what's the point of a Labour government?":** Rachel Sylvester, "Starmer Is All Strategists and No Strategy," *The Times,* June 26, 2023, available at www.thetimes.co.uk.

134   **"turned it into a glorified protest movement with cult trimmings":** Kylie MacLellan and Joanna Taylor, "Blair Tells Labour: Change or You Will Disappear," Reuters, December 18, 2019, available at www.reuters.com.

134   **After he was knighted in 2022:** Jon Stone, "Public Overwhelmingly Against Tony Blair Knighthood, Poll Finds," *Independent,* January 4, 2022, available at www.independent. co.uk.

134   **written by Murdoch's former wife Wendi Deng:** Mark Seal, "Seduced and Abandoned," *Vanity Fair*, February 19, 2014, available at www.vanityfair.com.

134 **at a conference in the Bahamas hosted by soon-to-be-discredited crypto kingpin Sam Bankman Fried:** Nina Bambysheva, "Royal Flush: Inside Crypto's Most Exclusive Gathering," *Forbes*, May 3, 2002, available at www.forbes.com.

135 **a long way from the political revolution that Blair promised:** Blair, "Let Us Face the Future," 4.

CHAPTER FOUR

136 **declared a state of emergency in the first week of its existence:** Shira Robinson, *Citizen Strangers: Palestinians and the Birth of Israel's Liberal Settler State* (Stanford: Stanford University Press, 2013), 35–36.

136 **no single party has ever won an outright majority:** On Israeli politics over the long run, see Dahlia Scheindlin, *The Crooked Timber of Democracy in Israel: Promise Unfulfilled* (Boston: De Gruyter, 2023). For class divides within the left and right, see Yonatan Berman, "Inequality, Identity, and the Long-Run Evolution of Political Cleavages in Israel, 1949–2019," in *Political Cleavages and Social Inequalities: A Study of Fifty Democracies, 1948–2020*, 568–586.

137 **Labor's first defeat was followed by decades of trench warfare with the leading rightwing party, Likud:** Although the names for the chief parties in

the left and right coalitions have changed over the years, for simplicity's sake I use the names that both factions ultimately settled on—Labor for the left, Likud for the right—throughout the chapter.

137 **"Pasokification," after the breakdown of Greece's once formidable PASOK party:** Jacob Cox, "PASOKification: Fall of the European Center Left or a Transformation of the System," *Governance* 6 (2019), available at https://digitalscholarship.unlv.edu/governance-unlv/.

137 **the number of seats held by Labor in the Knesset since 1969:** "Israeli Elections," Israel Democracy Institute, available at https://en.idi.org.il/israeli-elections-and-parties/.

138 **so did the gap between the rich and the poor:** Momi Dahan, "Income Inequality in Israel: A Distinctive Evolution" (CESifo Working Paper No. 6542, 2017).

138 **they would prefer a more socialist approach to the economy than a capitalist one:** "Election Study 2022," Israel National Election Studies, available at https://socsci4.tau.ac.il/.

138 **connected issues of security for Israel and the future of the Palestinian occupation:** Roi Zur and Ryan Bakker, "The Israeli Parties' Positions in Comparative

Perspective," *Party Politics* (2023), 1–12.

139　was a voluble critic of the American constitution: Scheindlin, *Crooked Timber*, 45.

140　economy was in trouble, with inflation rates rising above 100 percent: "Inflation, Consumer Prices (Annual %)—Israel," World Bank, available at www.data. worldbank.org; James Harding, *Alpha Dogs: The Americans Who Turned Political Spin into a Global Business* (New York: Farrar, Straus and Giroux, 2007), 85–89.

140　"We are 100 percent Zionists": Pfeffer, "Strange Death," 14.

140　one of the chief reasons that Israel did not have a universal health insurance: On the relationship between the Labor Party and the Histadrut, see Michael Shalev, *Labour and the Political Economy in Israel* (Oxford: Oxford University Press, 1992).

141　set firm limits to the public conversation: Scheindlin, *Crooked Timber*, 59–61.

141　"was an alien idea to socialists": Pfeffer, "Strange Death," 25.

141　"There is no coexistence with cancer, and Arabs are a metastasizing cancer!": Scheindlin, *Crooked Timber*, 104, 121.

141　"a classically Hitlerist type": Tom Segev, *A State at Any Cost: The Life of David Ben-Gurion*, trans. Haim Watzman (New York: Farrar, Straus and Giroux, 2019), 648.

142　they were part of a "war to the death": Benyamin Neuberger, "Democratic and Anti-Democratic Roots of the Israeli Political System," *Israel Studies Review*, 34.2 (2019), 68.

142　"sometimes seemed as large as the distance between New Yorkers and Mississippians": Schoen, *Power of the Vote*, 70.

143　later saying it was one of the toughest in his career: Schoen, *Power of the Vote*, 76.

143　hurling tomatoes at Peres while chanting "Begin, King of Israel": William Claiborne, "Begin Finds New Political Base Among Israel's Sephardic Jews," *Washington Post*, June 29, 1981, available at www.washingtonpost.com.

143　"traitor, traitor, traitor": David Shipler, "Israelis Worry Over What Some View as a Tendency to 'Growth of Fascism,'" *New York Times*, June 25, 1981, available at www.nytimes.com.

143　"pave the way toward fascism in public life": Shipler, "Israelis Worry."

144　then resumed barnstorming through Mizrahi neighborhoods: Shipler, "Israelis Worry."

250   144   "a mystification of the whole Palestinian problem, where it can't be dealt with rationally": Shipler, "Israelis Worry."

144   "there is always a democratic way to elect a fascist government": Shipler, "Israelis Worry."

144   Likud eked out a win by the slimmest of margins: "Israeli Elections," available at https://en.idi.org.il/israeli-elections-and-parties/.

145   "but none of them want Cousin Mordechai to be unemployed": Daniel Elazar, "The Israeli Knesset Elections, 1992: A First Analysis," Jerusalem Center for Public Affairs, 1992, available at www.jcpa.org.

145   decisive steps to crush the soaring inflation rate: "Inflation, Consumer Prices (Annual %)—Israel," World Bank, available at www.data.worldbank.org.

146   the *Histadrut* never regained its earlier standing: Lev Luis Grinberg and Gershon Shafir, "Economic Liberalization and the Breakup of the Histadrut's Domain," in *The New Israel: Peacemaking and Liberalization*, eds. Gershon Shafir and Yoav Peled (Boulder: Westview Press, 2000), 103–128.

146   "Today it's measured by how close you are to Yasser Arafat": Pfeffer, "Strange Death," 8.

147   "We must choose between protracted war with the Arab world": Scheindlin, *Crooked Timber*, 138.

147   an additional 15 percent favored deportation: Scheindlin, *Crooked Timber*, 122.

147   "I think he is the right medicine": William Claiborne, "Kahane Gains a Following in Israel," *Washington Post*, August 25, 1985, available at www.washingtonpost.com.

147   It was a popular opinion in his demographic: Claiborne, "Kahane Gains a Following."

148   opening a gap that persists down to the present: Berman, "Political Cleavages in Israel," 575–584.

148   "modern-day Rasputin": Lee Hockstader, "A Campaign Spin in Tel Aviv," *Washington Post*, April 7, 1999, available at www.washingtonpost.com.

148   Yahad only won three seats in the election: "Israeli Elections," available at https://en.idi.org.il/israeli-elections-and-parties/.

149   received qualified backing from two mostly Arab parties: Scheindlin, *Crooked Timber*, 139–140.

149   **Israel's occupation was gaining strength on the ground**: Shira Robinson, "Supremacy Unleashed," in *The Routledge Handbook of Citizenship in the Middle East and North Africa,* eds. Roel Meijer, James Sater, and Zahra Babar (London: Routledge Press, 2021), 313–314.

149   **had just finished their first poll for Labor:** Schoen, *Power of the Vote*, 82.

150   **"I can't lose to somebody like that":** Schoen, *Power of the Vote*, 83.

150   **"I'll never compromise on security":** "TV Ads Target Undecideds as Israeli Vote Nears," *Tampa Bay Times*, May 12, 1996, available at www.tampabay.com; Schoen, *Power of the Vote*, 87.

150   **Peres broke down and wept:** Schoen, *Power of the Vote*, 89.

151   **"but I know what is needed by the people of Israel":** Greenberg, *Dispatches*, 308.

151   **It was his campaign ever:** On Barak's military career and its influence on his approach to politics, see Connie Bruck, "The Commando," *New Yorker*, April 17, 2000, 81–95.

151   **"he had an extraordinarily instinctive understanding of how to sell diet products":** Schoen, *Power of the Vote*, 84.

152   **"one direct way: toward peace":** Greenberg, *Dispatches*, 276.

152   **"I don't feel like a politician, even now":** Greenberg, *Dispatches*, 274.

152   **about a million people in a country of five million:** "The Population of Israel, 1990–2009," UN Statistics Division, October 20, 2010, available at https://unstats.un.org.

153   **"you had better improve fast":** Harding, *Alpha Dogs*, 102–104; Greenberg, *Dispatches*, 287–289.

153   **were broken into (twice) by burglars:** Greenberg, *Dispatches*, 278.

154   **"Israelis longed for Israel to be normal":** Greenberg, *Dispatches*, 305.

154   **"he wants us to lose":** Greenberg, *Dispatches*, 289.

155   **where incomes were flatlining and unemployment had spiked:** "Evolution of Average Income, Israel, 1950–2022," World Inequality Database, available at https://wid.world; "Unemployment, Total (% of Total Labor Force) (Modeled ILO Estimate)—Israel," World Bank, available at https://data.worldbank.org.

155   **"Labor leaders just couldn't get themselves to take the**

252   economy seriously": Greenberg, *Dispatches*, 292.

155   "treated like half-people": Greenberg, *Dispatches*, 293.

155   "government that works for all, not just the extremist groups": Greenberg, *Dispatches*, 285.

156   "an aspiration for a government that would address normal problems": Greenberg, *Dispatches*, 285.

156   to give the public a sense of what they were voting for: Inspired by Barak's success, Bob Shrum brought the same emphasis on his candidate's military biography to John Kerry's 2004 presidential bid, where Shrum was a senior adviser. (Greenberg was also part of Kerry's team, though he only joined the campaign in the final weeks of the race.)

157   he did not want to be bound by a single perspective on the race: Schoen, *Power of the Vote*, 90–92.

157   that opened during the realignment of the 1970s: "Vote for Left-Wing, Center, and Arab Parties by Race/Ethnicity/Sociocultural Group, Israel," World Political Cleavages and Inequality Database, available at https://wpid .world.

157   narrowing the gap between Mizrahi and Ashkenazi "Vote for Left-Wing, Center, and Arab Parties by Race / Ethnicity / Sociocultural Group, Israel," World Political Cleavages and Inequality Database, available at https://wpid.world. For a judicious assessment of the campaign, see Gideon Doron, "Barak, One—One Israel, Zero, or, How Labor Won the Prime Ministerial Race and Lost the Knesset Elections," in *The Elections in Israel 1999*, eds. Asher Arian and Michal Shamir (Albany: State University of New York Press, 2002), 179-194.

158   One Israel's share of the popular vote: "Israeli Elections," available at https://en.idi.org.il /israeli-elections-and-parties/.

158   "You can't form a government with Shas": Greenberg, *Dispatches*, 307.

159   "The public has completely lost confidence in the current government": Greenberg, *Dispatches*, 332.

159   could have ended his political career: Greenberg, *Dispatches*, 341.

159   "you are going to lose the election": Greenberg, *Dispatches*, 343.

160   remained persistently below the overall average: Scheindlin, *Crooked Timber*, 154.

160   rose by an astonishing 45 points: "Vote for Right-Wing and Ultra-Orthodox Parties by

Subjective Social Class, Israel," World Political Cleavages and Inequality Database, available at https://wpid.world.

161   **"Barak finished off the peace narrative":** Pfeffer, "Strange Death," 6.

161   **whose findings showed broad support for a centrist coalition:** Schoen, *Power of the Vote*, 98–99.

162   **"the hidden issue of the campaign":** Schoen, *Power of the Vote*, 101.

162   **political culture that was speeding to the right:** Tamar Hermann, Or Anabi, Yaron Kaplan, and Inna Orly Sapozhnikova, "20th Edition of the Israeli Democracy Index," Israel Democracy Institute, January 15, 2023, available at https://en.idi.org.il.

163   **opposed having the government start negotiations with the Palestinians:** Clyde Haberman, "Israel's Likud Passes Torch, Naming Netanyahu Leader," *New York Times*, March 26, 1993, A2.

164   **coalition brought together a rightwing party headed by Netanyahu's former chief of staff:** Aaron Boxerman, "History Made as Arab Israeli Ra'am Party Joins Bennett-Lapid Coalition," *Times of Israel*, June 3, 2021, available at www.timesofisrael.com.

164   **referred to Kach founder Rabbi Meir Kahane as a "saint":** Ruth Margalit, "Itamar Ben-Gvir, Israel's Minister of Chaos," *New Yorker*, February 27, 2023, available at www.newyorker.com.

164   **pushed for an overhaul of the judiciary:** Carrie Keller-Lynn, "Israel's Judicial Overhaul: What Is the Coalition Planning and Where Does It Stand?" *Times of Israel*, March 4, 2023, available at www.timesofisrael.com/.

165   **"And, of course, who's going to be the victim?":** Margalit, "Ben-Gvir."

165   **they returned to a single chant: "democracy!":** Josef Federman, "Netanyahu Launches Contentious Overhaul as Thousands Protest," Associated Press, February 13, 2023, available at www.apnews.com.

167   **"The sense of being so lonely, so weird, so misunderstood":** Sally Abed, Yael Berda, Eli Cook, and Joshua Leifer, "A Historic Junction," *Dissent* (Winter 2024), available at www.dissentmagazine.org.

167   **it was becoming more and more common to see applied to Israel:** See, for example, Joseph Krauss, "Amnesty Joins Rights Groups in Accusing Israel of Apartheid," Associated Press, February 1, 2022, available at https://apnews.com.

254   CHAPTER FIVE

169   **"in the name of peace, democracy, and freedom for all":** "Mandela's Speech," *Washington Post*, February 12, 1990, available at www.washingtonpost.com.

170   **about 70 percent Black and 20 percent white:** Amory Gethin, "Extreme Inequality, Elite Transformation, and the Changing Structure of Political Cleavage in South Africa, 1994–2019," in *Political Cleavages and Social Inequalities: A Study of Fifty Democracies, 1948–2020,* eds., Amory Gethin, Clara Martínez-Toledano, and Thomas Piketty, 518.

170   **believe the country is going in the wrong direction:** "South Africa's Unemployment Nightmare," Ipsos South Africa, May 8, 2023, available at www.ipsos.com.

170   **some of the highest levels of economic inequality in the world:** On which see Victor Sulla, Precious Zikhali, and Pablo Facundo Cuevas, *Inequality in Southern Africa: An Assessment of the Southern African Customs Union* (Washington, DC: World Bank Group, 2022), available at http://documents.worldbank .org/.

170   **during the worst days of the Great Depression:** Kopano Gumbi and Anait Miridzhanian, "South African Labour Market Recovery Stalls Months Before Election,"

Reuters, February 20, 2024, available at www.reuters.com.

170   **has publicly admitted that the country risks becoming a failed state:** Lucy Pawle, "South Africa Could Become Failed State, Says ANC's Fikile Mbalula," BBC, May 23, 2023, available at www.bbc .com.

171   **"I've gone from a shack to a shack":** Peter Goodman, "End of Apartheid in South Africa? Not in Economic Terms," *New York Times*, October 24, 2017, available at www .nytimes.com.

171   **one of the most racially and economically polarized electorates in the world:** Gethin, "Extreme Inequality," 516–526.

171   **"Radical economic transformation":** Amogelang Mbatha and Michael Cohen, "South Africa Radical Economic Transformation: Zuma vs. Ramaphosa," *Bloomberg*, May 1, 2017, available at www.bloomberg .com.

171   **almost no overlap between the two:** Which is not to say that the countries were strangers to each other. On connections between the two during the apartheid era, see Sasha Polakow-Suransky, *The Unspoken Alliance: Israel's Secret Relationship with Apartheid South Africa* (New York: Pantheon, 2010). For a comparative analysis of their recent histories, see Andy Clamo,

Neoliberal Apartheid: Palestine/ Israel and South Africa After 1994 (Chicago: University of Chicago Press, 2017).

172 **a research program on South Africa funded by the Ford Foundation:** "Stanley Greenberg oral history," January 27, 2005.

172 **"fundamental to everything I have done as an adult":** Greenberg, *Dispatches*, 110.

172 **"not as a political party . . . but as a Parliament of the African people":** Nelson Mandela, *Nelson Mandela: The Struggle Is My Life*, 3rd ed. (Noida, India: Popular Prakashan, 1990), 175.

173 **an overwhelmingly Christian country where social conservatism runs deep:** For a brief summary of the ANC's long history, see Anthony Butler, *The Idea of the ANC* (Athens: Ohio University Press, 2012).

173 **Mandela was a member of the South African Communist Party:** Tom Lodge, *Red Road to Freedom: A History of the South African Communist Party 1921–2021* (Rochester, NY: James Currey, 2022), 323–324.

173 **"the people shall govern!":** "The Freedom Charter," African National Congress, June 26, 1955, available at www.anc.org.za.

174 **Political violence surged:** Carienne Du Plessis and Martin Plaut, *Understanding South Africa* (London: Hurst and Company, 2019), 45.

174 **"a massive transfer of resources":** Nelson Mandela, "Address by Nelson Mandela at the World Economic Forum Annual Conference," January 31, 1991, available at www.mandela.gov.za.

174 **"ensure business confidence":** "Nelson Mandela's 1992 Davos Address," World Economic Forum, December 6, 2013, available at www.weforum.org.

175 **"Do you want to fly in the face of this reality?":** Patti Waldmeir, *Anatomy of a Miracle: The End of Apartheid and the Birth of the New South Africa* (New Brunswick: Rutgers University Press, 1997), 241.

176 **"We would like to work with these people":** Greenberg, *Dispatches*, 116.

176 *Newsweek* **hadn't mentioned:** "Six Men and a Donkey," *Newsweek*, October 31, 1992, available at www.newsweek.com.

176 **"I was here in a country on a precipice":** Greenberg, *Dispatches*, 151.

177 **"I assumed that all the returning ANC white exiles were**

256 **communists"**: Greenberg, *Dispatches*, 113.

177 **"check-the-box meeting with unions that lack the energy to organize anybody"**: Greenberg, *Dispatches*, 116.

177 **gave the group an imposing presence within the campaign**: On the roots of COSATU's influence, Mpfariseni Budeli, "Trade Unionism and Politics in Africa: The South African Experience," *Comparative and International Law Journal of Southern Africa* 45, no. 3 (2012), 454–481.

177 **"was in danger of losing the country's major urban areas"**: Greenberg, *Dispatches*, 121.

178 **"'Africans are going to seize power after years of powerlessness'"**: Greenberg, *Dispatches*, 127.

178 **"Apartheid," Greenberg insisted, "is a trap"**: Greenberg, *Dispatches*, 129.

179 **"not theoretical or abstract things"**: Greenberg, *Dispatches*, 129.

179 **"gave them permission to hope for something better"**: Greenberg, *Dispatches*, 128.

180 **"must be measured by the quality of life of ordinary people"**: "ANC Manifesto, 1994," African National Congress, March 15, 1994, available at www.anc1912.org.za.

181 **"read more like appeals to the world by prisoners behind enemy lines"**: Greenberg, *Dispatches*, 154.

181 **"just ahead of the campaign's internal goal"**: Gethin, "Extreme Inequality," 512.

181 **turnout was stratospheric**: "Structure of the Vote by Race / Ethnicity / Sociocultural Group, South Africa, 1994," World Political Cleavages and Inequality Database, available at https://wpid.world; "Appendix Figures and Tables: Figure D1—Electoral Turnout in South Africa, 1994–2019," World Political Cleavages and Inequality Database," available at https://wpid .world.

181 **"Nowhere else do people read the material world so accurately, and in such a nuanced way"**: Greenberg, *Dispatches*, 171.

182 **"so they could learn some of their wisdom"**: Greenberg, *Dispatches*, 134.

182 **"The time to build is upon us"**: Nelson Mandela, "Inaugural Speech," May 10, 1994, available at www.africa.upenn.edu.

183 **was a remarkable ascent for Mbeki**: For an admiring but not uncritical assessment, see Adekeye Adebajo, *Thabo Mbeki* (Athens: Ohio University Press), 2017.

183 **a retreat from the ANC's promises in 1994**: Daryl Glaser

summarizes the contrasting perspectives on this tenure in "Mbeki and His Legacy: A Critical Introduction," in *Mbeki and After: Reflections on the Legacy of Thabo Mbeki* (Johannesburg: Wits University Press, 2010), 3–40.

183 **the economy grew at an anemic rate:** "GDP growth (annual %)—South Africa," World Bank, available at https://data.worldbank.org/.

184 **its approval ratings among coloureds and South Asians had collapsed:** Greenberg, *Dispatches*, 171.

184 **"The best thing is for me not to vote at all":** Greenberg, *Dispatches*, 166–167.

185 **a voice for whites who opposed apartheid but worked inside the system to end it:** On the DP and its successor, the Democratic Alliance, see Roger Southall, *Whites and Democracy in South Africa* (Rochester, NY: Boydell and Brewer, 2022), 43–60 and 156–179.

185 **Doug Schoen's name came to the DP through R. W. Johnson:** A story that Johnson told in *Foreign Native: An African Journey* (Johannesburg: Jonathan Ball, 2020), 203–204.

185 **the slogan he recommended for the campaign: "Fight Back":** Schoen, *Power*, 184–185.

186 **"little Stan Greenberg":** Melissa Levin, "Little Stan Greenberg Is Dead," *Africa Is a Country*, August 5, 2013, available at https://africasacountry.com.

186 **"Don't Fight Black":** Lynne Duke, "In South Africa Race, Race Is Still the Issue," *Washington Post*, May 23, 1999, available at www.washingtonpost.com.

186 **a plurality of whites believed the DP cared about people like them:** Duke, "Race Is Still the Issue."

186 **"a racially polarized and dispiriting election":** Greenberg, *Dispatches*, 167.

186 **"in the perception of a government that does little about poverty and starvation":** Greenberg, *Dispatches*, 168.

187 **the only demographic with the numbers to make a majority:** "Structure of the Vote by Race / Ethnicity / Sociocultural Group, South Africa, 1999," World Political Cleavages and Inequality Database, available at https://wpid.world; "Figure D1—Electoral Turnout," World Political Cleavages and Inequality Database, available at https://wpid.world.

187 **roared ahead on Mbeki's watch:** Even Schoen's mentor R. W. Johnson, whose overall assessment of the ANC is brutal, has a comparatively generous view of this

258

period, on which see R. W. Johnson, *South Africa's Brave New World: The Beloved Country Since the End of Apartheid* (New York: Overlook Press, 2009), 412–473.

188 **driving racial polarization to historic lows:** "Vote for African National Congress by Race / Ethnicity / Sociocultural Group, South Africa," World Political Cleavages and Inequality Database, available at https://wpid.world.

189 **shaved nine years off the average lifespan:** Pride Chigwedere, Sofia Gruskin, George R. Seage, Tun-Hou Lee, and M. Essex, "Estimating the Lost Benefits of Antiretroviral Drug Use in South Africa," *Journal of Acquired Immune Deficiency Syndrome* 49, no. 4 (December 2008), 410–415; "Life Expectancy at Birth, Total (Years)—South Africa," World Bank, available at www.data .worldbank.org.

189 **had less trust in parliament, police, and the courts than under apartheid:** Christine Tamir and Abby Budiman, "In South Africa, Racial Divisions and Pessimism About Democracy Loom Over Elections," Pew Research Center, May 3, 2019, available at www .pewresearch.org.

189 **almost three dozen striking mineworkers in the town of Marikana:** Nick Davies, "Marikana Massacre," *The Guardian*, May 19,

2015, available at www.theguardian .com.

189 **targeting migrants from Zimbabwe:** "South Africa: Events of 2008," Human Rights Watch, 2009, available at www.hrw.org.

190 **blaming them for taking jobs, raising crime rates:** Tamir and Budiman, "Racial Divisions and Pessimism."

190 **endorsing both prayer in schools and land expropriation:** Johnson, *Brave New World*, 640.

190 **the ANC would hold power "until Jesus comes":** Matome Letsoalo, "Zuma Promises Not to Crucify Jesus 'This Time,'" News 24, December 29, 2014, available at www.news24.com.

190 **acquitted of rape in a 2006 trial:** Michael Wines, "A Highly Charged Rape Trial Tests South Africa's Ideals," *New York Times*, April 10, 2006, available at www .nytimes.com.

190 **While Zuma railed against "white monopoly capital":** Renee Bonorchis, Paul Burkhardt, and Loni Prinsloo, "South Africa Moves to Tackle Corruption as Zuma Loses Influence," *Bloomberg*, January 17, 2018, available at www .bloomberg.com.

191 **two-thirds of South Africans were unhappy with the state of their democracy:** Tamir and

Budiman, "Racial Divisions and Pessimism."

191 **wasn't ready to abandon the party en masse:** "Appendix Figures and Tables: Figure D1—Abstention by Population Group," World Political Cleavages and Inequality Database," available at https://wpid .world.

192 **"a broken man presiding over a broken society":** Thulani Gqirana, "Maimane: Zuma Laughed While South Africans Cried," *Mail and Guardian*, February 18, 2015, available at https://mg.co.za.

192 **"My Little Stan Greenberg heart broke":** Greenberg, "Little Stan Greenberg."

193 **"tried to turn the DA 'woke'":** Paddy Harper and Lizeka Tandwa, "The USA, Maimane and the DA: How Mmusi Maimane's Plan to Change the DA Fell Apart," *Mail and Guardian*, February 19, 2023, available at https://mg.co.za.

193 **the first time it lost ground in a general election:** For more on the causes of the DA's underwhelming performance, see Southall, *Whites and Democracy in South Africa*, 168–173.

193 **"Fight Back South Africa":** Michael Kimberly, "FF Plus Attributes Gains to Its Fight-Back Slogan," *Herald Live*, May 10, 2019, available at www.heraldlive.co.za.

194 **a platform that combined ethno-nationalism with tributes to Marx and Lenin:** Erin Conway-Smith, "How Far Can Populism Go in South Africa?" *Foreign Affairs*, May 7, 2019, available at www .foreignaffairs.com.

194 **where the DA and NP votes are merged together:** Gethin, "Extreme Inequality," 512.

195 **"The whites will all leave but the Blacks will all die":** Andrew Kenny, "The Travails of the New South Africa," *Quadrant Online*, December 1, 2009, available at www.quadrant.org.au.

195 **"Maybe the old people are still buying it, but we're not":** Lynsey Chutel, "Mandela Goes from Hero to Scapegoat as South Africa Struggles," *New York Times*, July 18, 2023, available at www .nytimes.com.

196 **they were 25 percentage points less likely to do so:** Gethin, "Extreme Inequality," 524.

196 **the ANC was a line of defense against an even worse outcome:** On the material benefits of ANC government for the poor, see Evan Liberman, *Until We Have Won Our Liberty South Africa After Apartheid* (Princeton: Princeton University Press, 2022), 169–205.

196 **"We want money and we want jobs":** Norimitsu Onishi, "First Black Leader of South

260   Africa's Opposition Seeks to Unseat the A.N.C.," *New York Times*, July 24, 2015, available at www.nytimes.com.

196   **blackouts climbed to record highs:** Azarrah Karrim, "July Unrest," News 24, *News 24*, July 8, 2022, available at www.news24.com; Alexandra Wexler, "South Africa Seeks State Power Chief After CEO Says He Was Poisoned," *Wall Street Journal*, January 21, 2023, available at www.wsj.com.

197   **he said that he had stopped following the news:** Interview with author, May 19, 2023.

CONCLUSION

199   **where his share of the two-party vote was lower than any Republican:** "What Happened in 2022 National Crosstabs," Catalist, available at https://www.dropbox.com/s/reogtn1057fzwp5/Catalist_What_Happened_2022_Public_National_Crosstabs_2023_05_18.xlsx?dl=0.

199   **12 points better than its performance with non-college graduates:** "What Happened in 2022."

200   **and emphasize their most popular positions:** See, for example, Eriz Levitz, "David Shor on Why Trump Was Good for the GOP and How Dems Can Win in 2022," *New York*, March 3, 2021, available at www.nymag.com.

201   **both sides charged the other with manipulating the data:** For a summary of the debate, see Ezra Klein, "David Shor Is Telling Democrats What They Don't Want to Hear," *New York Times*, October 8, 2021, available at www.nytimes.com.

201   **"How is it possible that Republicans are representing the majority of people who struggle?":** Bryan Metzger, "This 40-Year Veteran Lawmaker Shows Top Democrats One Eye-Popping Chart Revealing Her Party's Problem Winning Over the Working Class," *Business Insider*, March 27, 2023, available at www.businessinsider.com.

203   **almost half of the country described itself as independent:** The total peaked at 49 percent in March 2023 before falling to 40 percent by the end of the year, a total that by historical standards is still quite high. See "Party Affiliation," Gallup, available at https://news.gallup.com.

203   **said that just thinking about politics was exhausting:** "Americans' Dismal Views of the Nation's Politics," Pew Research Center, September 19, 2023, available at www.pewresearch.org.

203   **"But they're not":** Lainey Newman and Theda Skocpol, *Rust Belt Union Blues: Why Working-Class Voters Are Turning Away from the Democratic Party* (New York:

Columbia University Press, 2023), 202.

206 **after spending almost $1 billion on the campaign:** Shane Goldmacher, "Michael Bloomberg Spent More Than $900 Million on His Failed Presidential Run," *New York Times*, March 20, 2020, available at www.nytimes.com.

206 **he was not going to be welcome in mainstream Democratic circles anytime soon:** Daniel Strauss, "Mark Penn on No Labels: 'No Role, Real or Imagined,'" *New Republic*, July 12, 2023, available at www.tnr.com.

207 **business-friendly moderation would have a champion in the party:** For a critical (and quite funny) portrait of Gottheimer, see Grim, *The Squad*, 59–71.

207 **"sounded more like a 'race war' than a conventional campaign":** Stanley Greenberg, "To Save America, Look at America as It Is," *American Prospect*, January 20, 2021, available at www.prospect.org.

207 **"had a 'come-to-Jesus' meeting with the principal managers of the economy":** Greenberg, *Dispatches*, 419.

209 **"there are forces at play not always visible and direct":** Greenberg, *Dispatches*, 419.

210 **a neoliberal pivot (which never arrived):** For an argument that Bidenomics marked a decisive break with neoliberalism, see Felicia Wong, Suzanne Kahn, Mike Konczal, and Matt Hughes, "Sea Change: How a New Economics Went Mainstream," Roosevelt Institute, November 16, 2023, available at https://rooseveltinstitute.org. Doug Henwood provides a more skeptical appraisal in "Bidenomics Puts Business, Not Workers, First," *Jacobin*, December 24, 2023, available at www.jacobin.com.

212 **"make more sh*t in America":** John Fetterman, "Make More Sh*t in America," YouTube, September 22, 2022, available at www.youtube.com.

212 **platforms that prioritized kitchen table issues:** "Trump's Kryptonite: How Progressives Can Win Back the Working Class," Center for Working Class Politics, June 13, 2023, available at https://www.workingclasspolitics.org.

213 **(still) viewed Republicans as the party of business:** Mike Lux, "A Strategy for Factory Towns: Executive Summary," American Family Voices, February 22, 2023, available at www.americanfamilyvoices.org.

FURTHER READING
219 **Joseph Buttigieg:** Father, as you probably know, of Pete.

Columbia Global Reports is a nonprofit publishing imprint from Columbia University that commissions authors to produce works of original thinking and on-site reporting from all over the world, on a wide range of topics. Our books are short—novella-length, and readable in a few hours—but ambitious. They offer new ways of looking at and understanding the major issues of our time. Most readers are curious and busy. Our books are for them.

If this book changed the way you look at the world, and if you would like to support our mission, consider making a gift to Columbia Global Reports to help us share new ideas and stories.

Visit globalreports.columbia.edu to support our upcoming books, subscribe to our newsletter, and learn more about Columbia Global Reports. Thank you for being part of our community of readers and supporters.